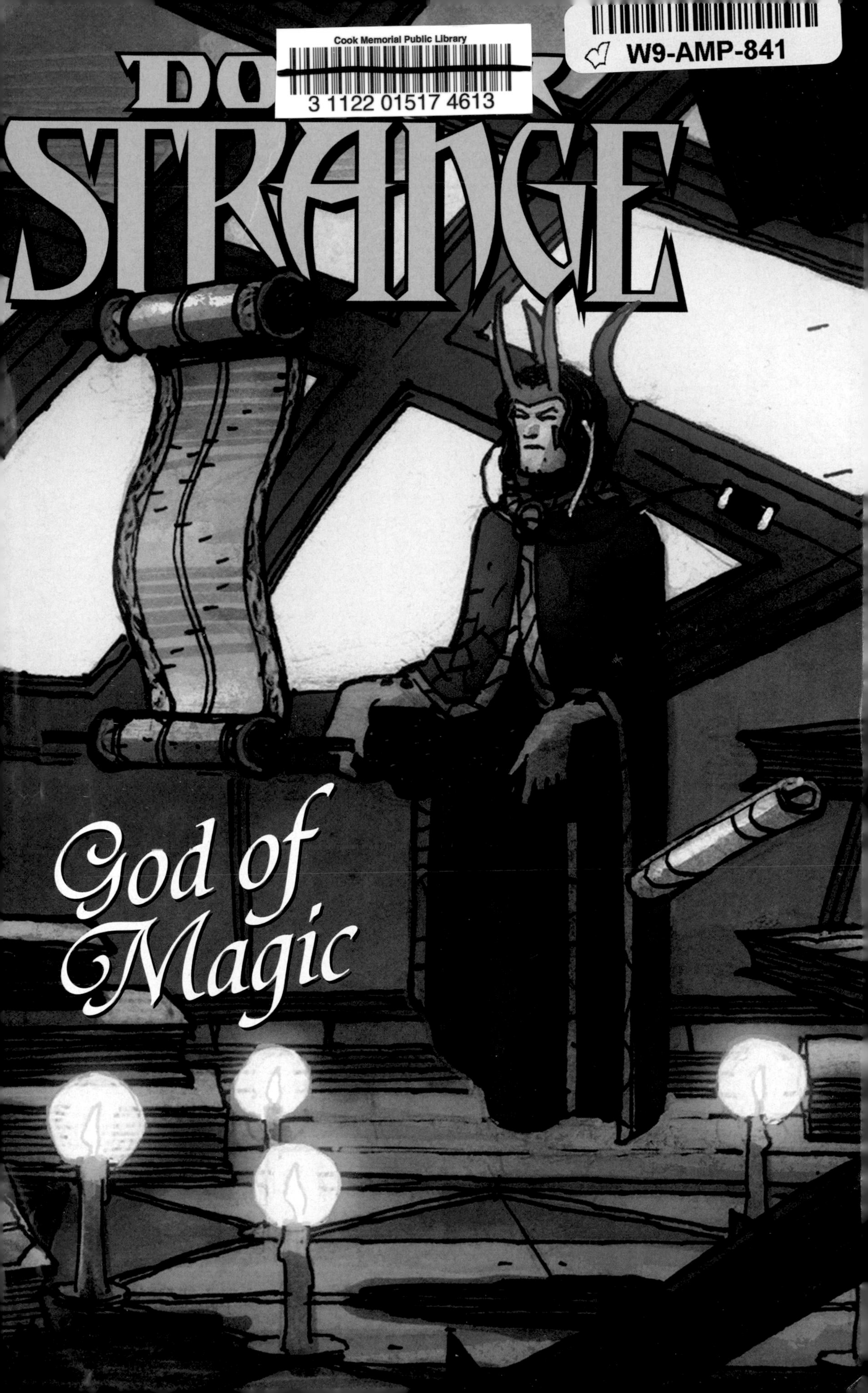
DO
STRANGE
God of Magic

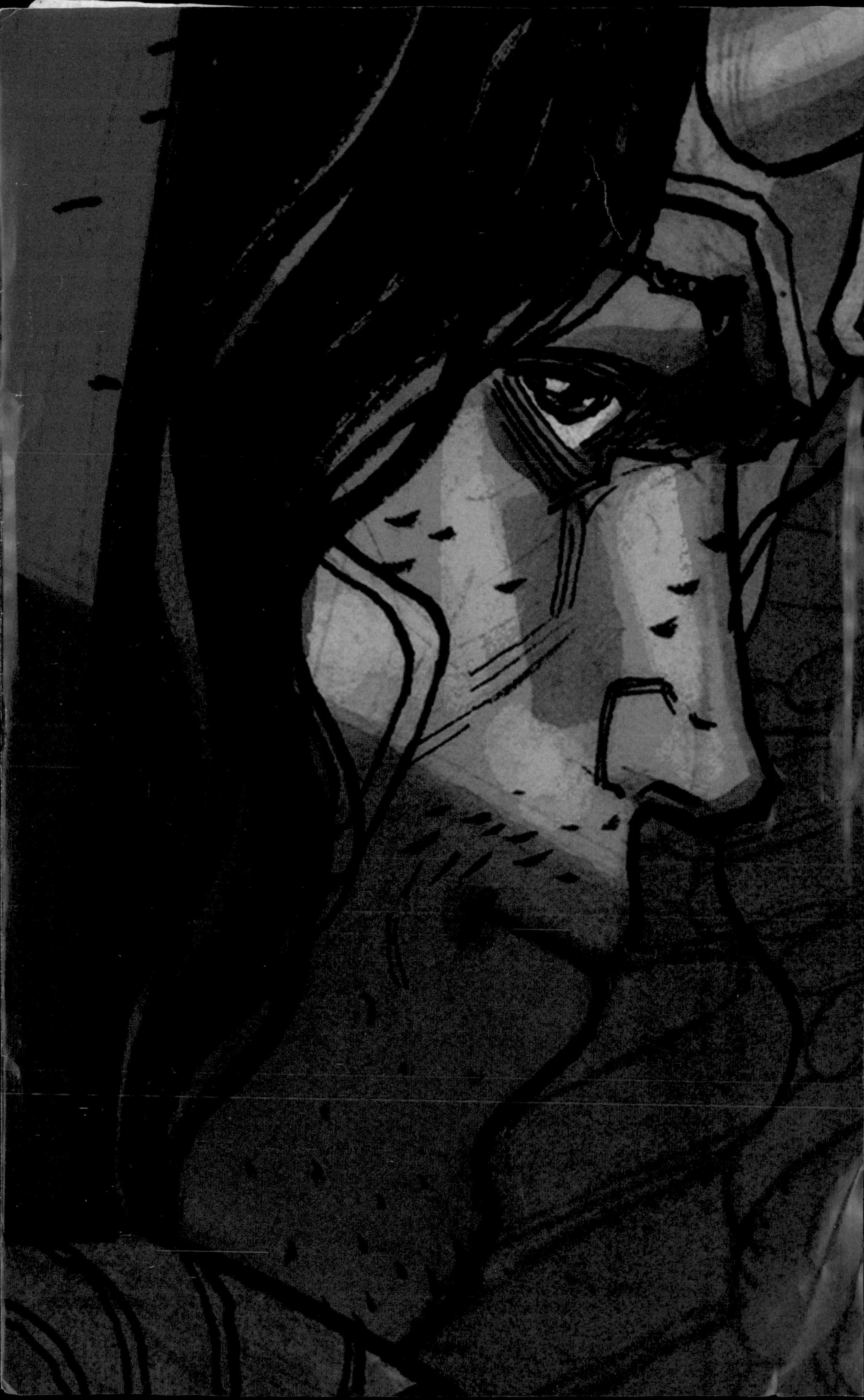

STEPHEN STRANGE WAS A PREEMINENT SURGEON UNTIL A CAR ACCIDENT DAMAGED THE NERVES IN HIS HANDS. HIS EGO DROVE HIM TO SCOUR THE GLOBE FOR A MIRACLE CURE. INSTEAD, HE FOUND A MYSTERIOUS WIZARD CALLED THE ANCIENT ONE WHO TAUGHT HIM MAGIC AND THAT THERE ARE THINGS IN THIS WORLD BIGGER THAN HIMSELF. THESE LESSONS ENABLED STEPHEN TO BECOME THE SORCERER SUPREME, EARTH'S FIRST DEFENSE AGAINST ALL MANNER OF MAGICAL THREATS. HIS PATIENTS CALL HIM...

DOCTOR STRANGE

AFTER DEFEATING AN INVASION BY ANTI-MAGIC ZEALOTS FROM ANOTHER DIMENSION, STEPHEN WAS POISONED ON A QUEST TO COLLECT AN ENCHANTED ARTIFACT--ONE OF THE LAST REMAINING IN OUR REALM. HIS FRIEND, LIBRARIAN ZELMA STANTON, TRANSFERRED THE DEADLY POISON TO HERSELF TO SAVE HIM. TO SAVE HER IN TURN, STEPHEN CONFERRED SOME OF HIS MAGICAL IMMUNITY--OVER HIS ASSISTANT WONG'S OBJECTIONS.

WHEN LAST WE SAW THEM, WONG HAD LEFT THE SANCTUM SANCTORUM, AND STRANGE AND ZELMA, HIS NEW APPRENTICE, WERE LEARNING HOW TO NAVIGATE THE NEW MAGICAL LANDSCAPE.

~ God of Magic ~

WRITER
Donny Cates

ARTIST
Gabriel Hernandez Walta

COLOR ARTIST
Jordie Bellaire

FLASHBACK ARTIST, No. 383
Niko Henrichon

LETTERER
VC's Cory Petit

COVER ART
Mike del Mundo

ASSISTANT EDITOR
Kathleen Wisneski

EDITOR
Nick Lowe

DOCTOR STRANGE CREATED BY STAN LEE & STEVE DITKO

COLLECTION EDITOR: **JENNIFER GRÜNWALD**
ASSISTANT EDITOR: **CAITLIN O'CONNELL**
ASSOCIATE MANAGING EDITOR: **KATERI WOODY**
EDITOR, SPECIAL PROJECTS: **MARK D. BEAZLEY**

VP PRODUCTION & SPECIAL PROJECTS: **JEFF YOUNGQUIST**
SVP PRINT, SALES & MARKETING: **DAVID GABRIEL**
BOOK DESIGNER: **ADAM DEL RE**

EDITOR IN CHIEF: **C.B. CEBULSKI**
CHIEF CREATIVE OFFICER: **JOE QUESADA**
PRESIDENT: **DAN BUCKLEY**
EXECUTIVE PRODUCER: **ALAN FINE**

DOCTOR STRANGE BY DONNY CATES VOL. 1: GOD OF MAGIC. Contains material originally published in magazine form as DOCTOR STRANGE #381-385. First printing 2018. ISBN 978-1-302-91064-8. Published by MARVEL WORLDWIDE, INC., a subsidiary of MARVEL ENTERTAINMENT, LLC. OFFICE OF PUBLICATION: 135 West 50th Street, New York, NY 10020. Copyright © 2018 MARVEL No similarity between any of the names, characters, persons, and/or institutions in this magazine with those of any living or dead person or institution is intended, and any such similarity which may exist is purely coincidental. **Printed in Canada.** DAN BUCKLEY, President, Marvel Entertainment; JOHN NEE, Publisher; JOE QUESADA, Chief Creative Officer; TOM BREVOORT, SVP of Publishing; DAVID BOGART, SVP of Business Affairs & Operations, Publishing & Partnership; DAVID GABRIEL, SVP of Sales & Marketing, Publishing; JEFF YOUNGQUIST, VP of Production & Special Projects; DAN CARR, Executive Director of Publishing Technology; ALEX MORALES, Director of Publishing Operations; DAN EDINGTON, Managing Editor; SUSAN CRESPI, Production Manager; STAN LEE, Chairman Emeritus. For information regarding advertising in Marvel Comics or on Marvel.com, please contact Vit DeBellis, Custom Solutions & Integrated Advertising Manager, at vdebellis@marvel.com. For Marvel subscription inquiries, please call 888-511-5480. **Manufactured between 4/27/2018 and 5/29/2018 by SOLISCO PRINTERS, SCOTT, QC, CANADA.**

10 9 8 7 6 5 4 3 2 1

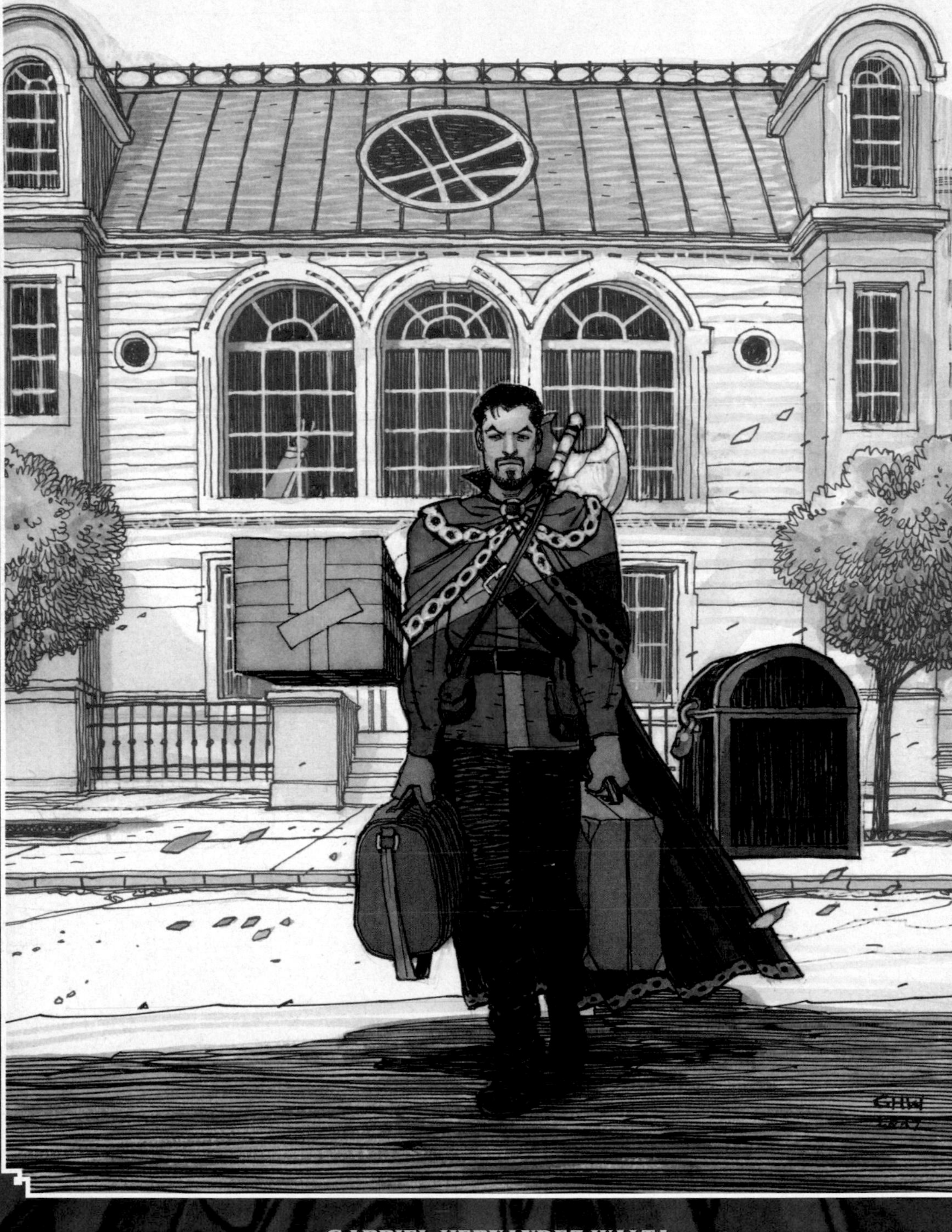
GHW

GABRIEL HERNANDEZ WALTA
381 VARIANT

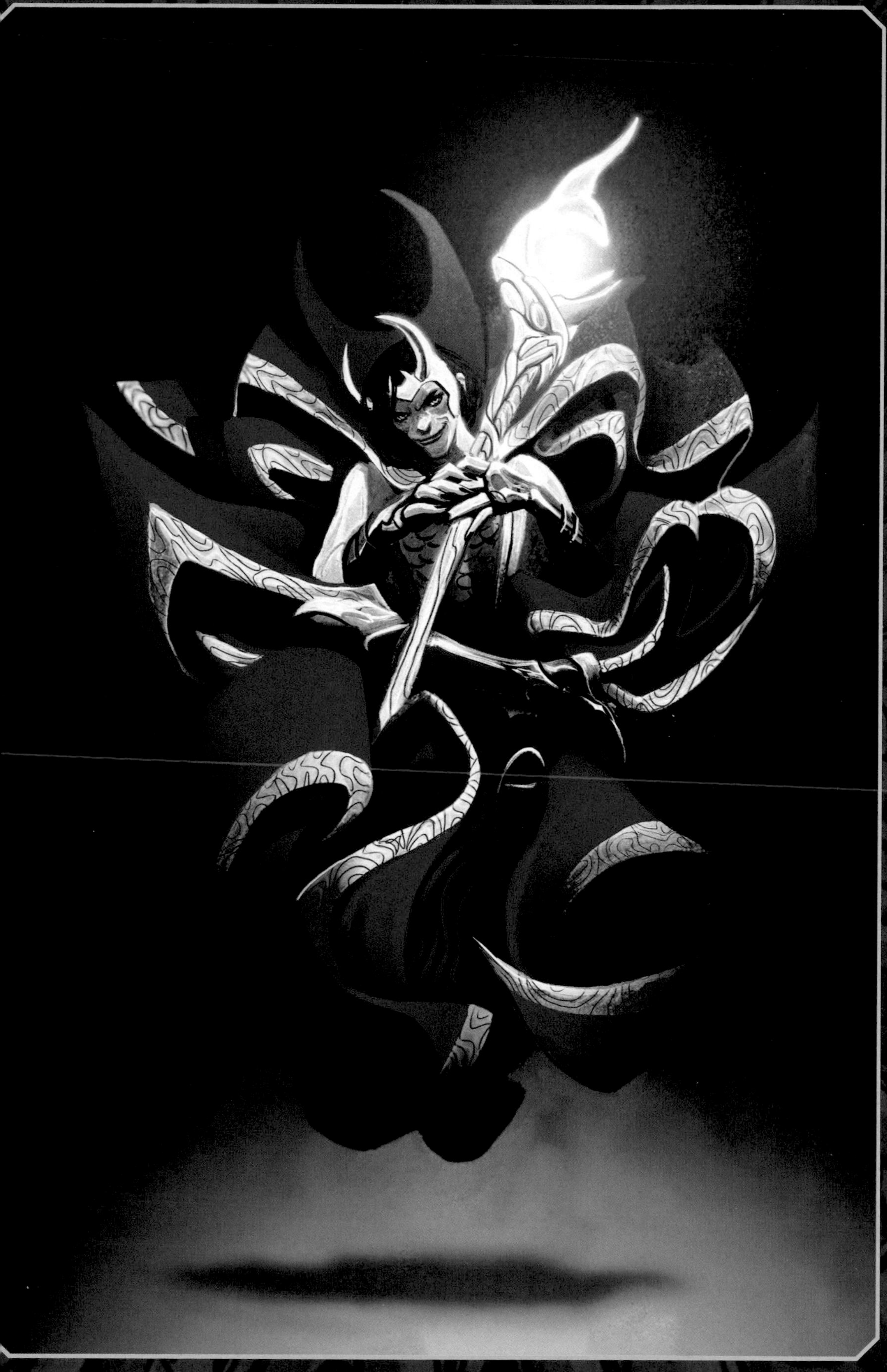

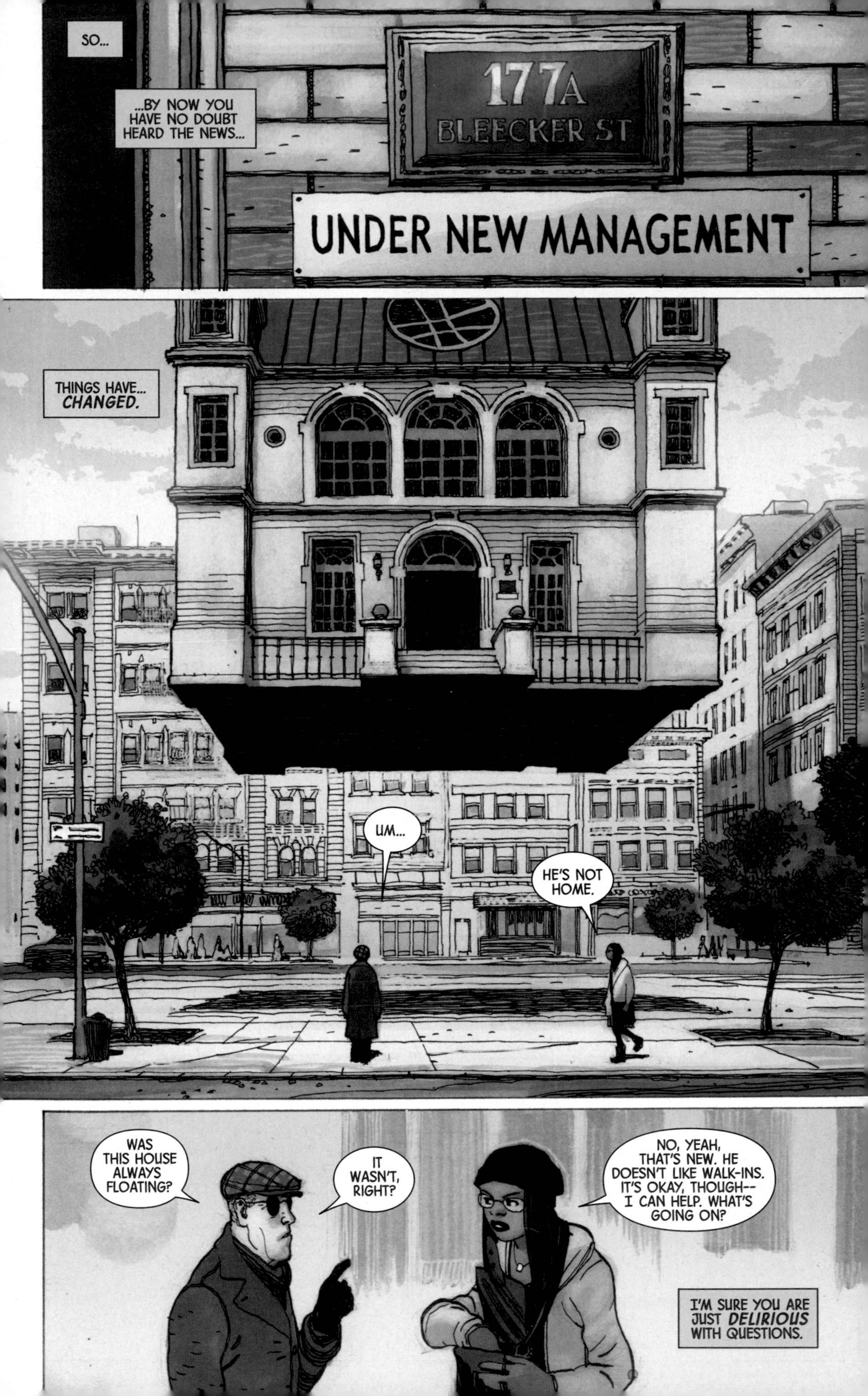
SO...
...BY NOW YOU HAVE NO DOUBT HEARD THE NEWS...
177A BLEECKER ST
UNDER NEW MANAGEMENT
THINGS HAVE... *CHANGED.*
UM...
HE'S NOT HOME.
WAS THIS HOUSE ALWAYS FLOATING?
IT WASN'T, RIGHT?
NO, YEAH, THAT'S NEW. HE DOESN'T LIKE WALK-INS. IT'S OKAY, THOUGH-- I CAN HELP. WHAT'S GOING ON?
I'M SURE YOU ARE JUST *DELIRIOUS* WITH QUESTIONS.

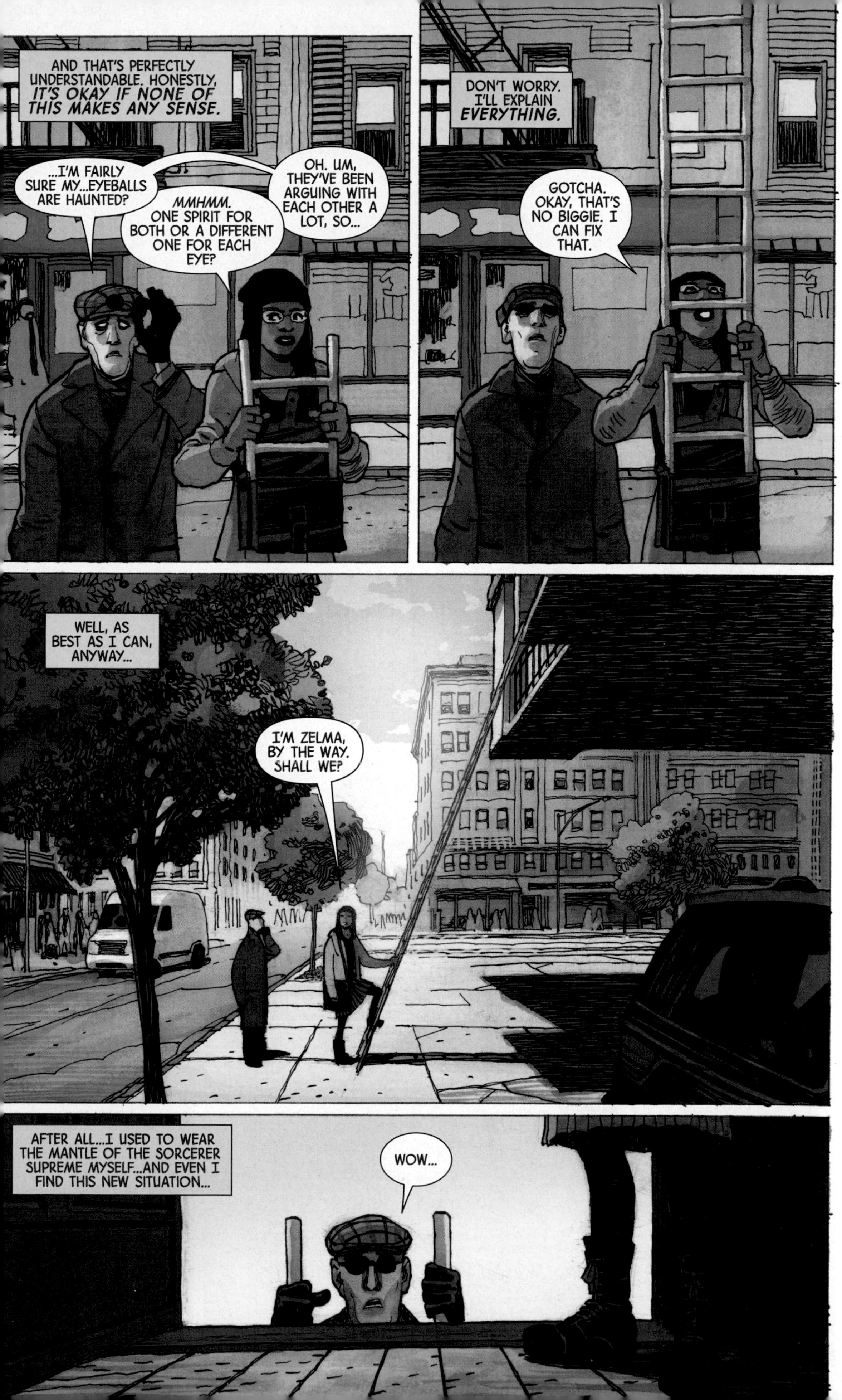
AND THAT'S PERFECTLY UNDERSTANDABLE. HONESTLY, IT'S OKAY IF NONE OF THIS MAKES ANY SENSE.
...I'M FAIRLY SURE MY...EYEBALLS ARE HAUNTED?
MMHMM. ONE SPIRIT FOR BOTH OR A DIFFERENT ONE FOR EACH EYE?
OH. UM, THEY'VE BEEN ARGUING WITH EACH OTHER A LOT, SO...
DON'T WORRY. I'LL EXPLAIN EVERYTHING.
GOTCHA. OKAY, THAT'S NO BIGGIE. I CAN FIX THAT.
WELL, AS BEST AS I CAN, ANYWAY...
I'M ZELMA, BY THE WAY. SHALL WE?
AFTER ALL...I USED TO WEAR THE MANTLE OF THE SORCERER SUPREME MYSELF...AND EVEN I FIND THIS NEW SITUATION...
WOW...

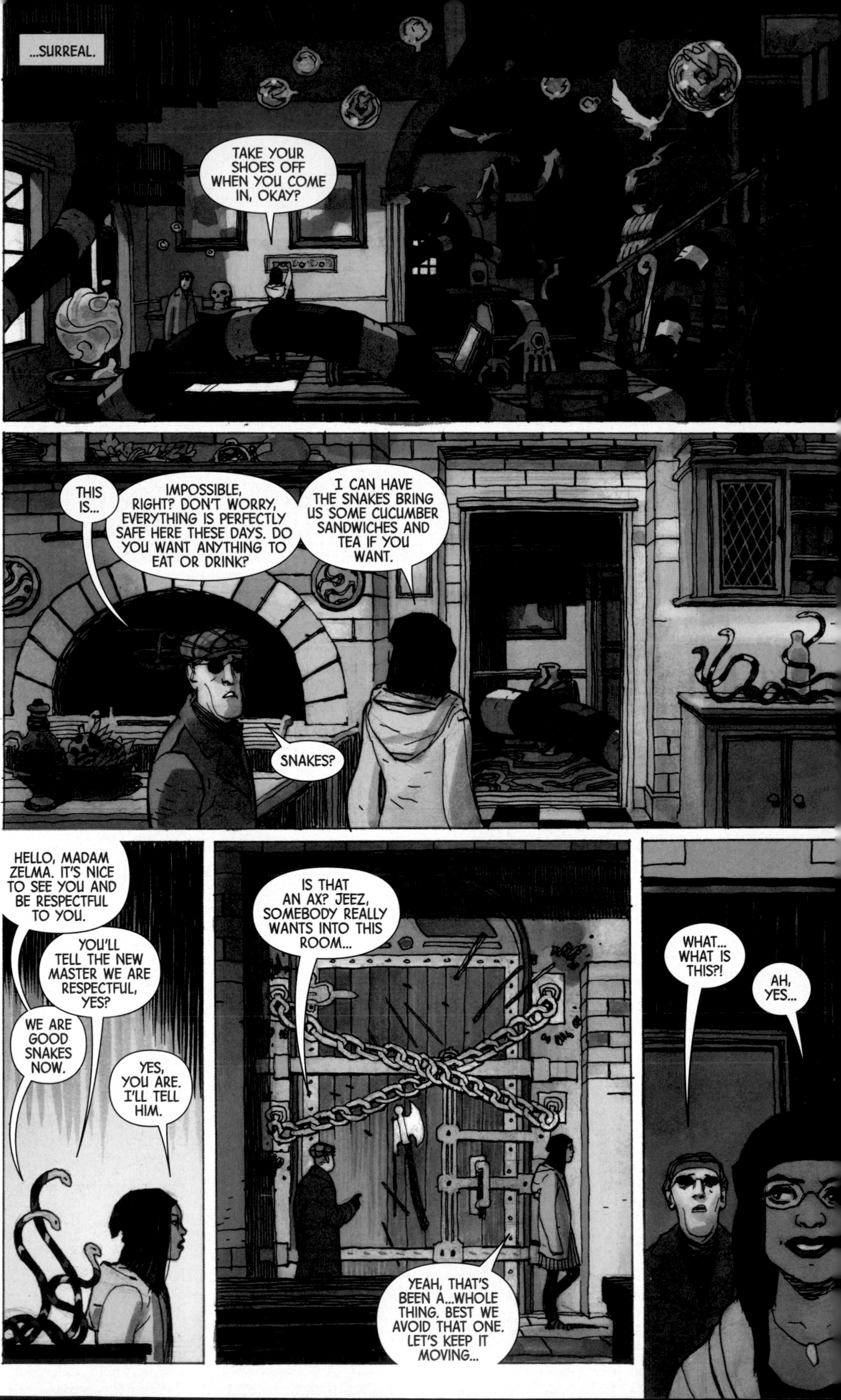
...SURREAL.
TAKE YOUR SHOES OFF WHEN YOU COME IN, OKAY?
THIS IS...
IMPOSSIBLE, RIGHT? DON'T WORRY, EVERYTHING IS PERFECTLY SAFE HERE THESE DAYS. DO YOU WANT ANYTHING TO EAT OR DRINK?
I CAN HAVE THE SNAKES BRING US SOME CUCUMBER SANDWICHES AND TEA IF YOU WANT.
SNAKES?
HELLO, MADAM ZELMA. IT'S NICE TO SEE YOU AND BE RESPECTFUL TO YOU.
YOU'LL TELL THE NEW MASTER WE ARE RESPECTFUL, YES?
WE ARE GOOD SNAKES NOW.
YES, YOU ARE. I'LL TELL HIM.
IS THAT AN AX? JEEZ, SOMEBODY REALLY WANTS INTO THIS ROOM...
YEAH, THAT'S BEEN A...WHOLE THING. BEST WE AVOID THAT ONE. LET'S KEEP IT MOVING...
WHAT... WHAT IS THIS?!
AH, YES...

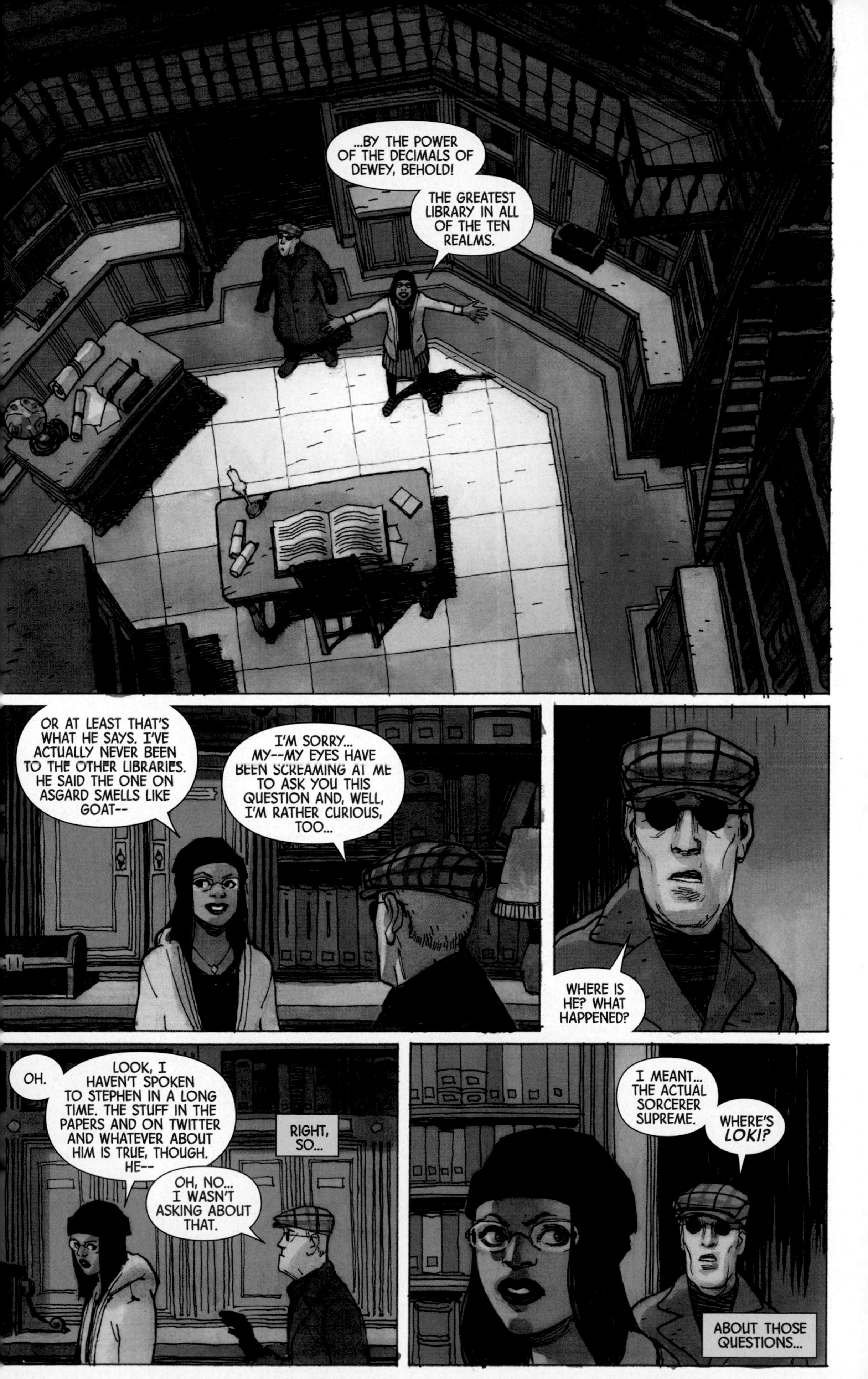
...BY THE POWER OF THE DECIMALS OF DEWEY, BEHOLD!
THE GREATEST LIBRARY IN ALL OF THE TEN REALMS.
OR AT LEAST THAT'S WHAT HE SAYS. I'VE ACTUALLY NEVER BEEN TO THE OTHER LIBRARIES. HE SAID THE ONE ON ASGARD SMELLS LIKE GOAT--
I'M SORRY... MY--MY EYES HAVE BEEN SCREAMING AT ME TO ASK YOU THIS QUESTION AND, WELL, I'M RATHER CURIOUS, TOO...
WHERE IS HE? WHAT HAPPENED?
OH.
LOOK, I HAVEN'T SPOKEN TO STEPHEN IN A LONG TIME. THE STUFF IN THE PAPERS AND ON TWITTER AND WHATEVER ABOUT HIM IS TRUE, THOUGH. HE--
RIGHT, SO...
OH, NO... I WASN'T ASKING ABOUT THAT.
I MEANT... THE ACTUAL SORCERER SUPREME.
WHERE'S LOKI?
ABOUT THOSE QUESTIONS...

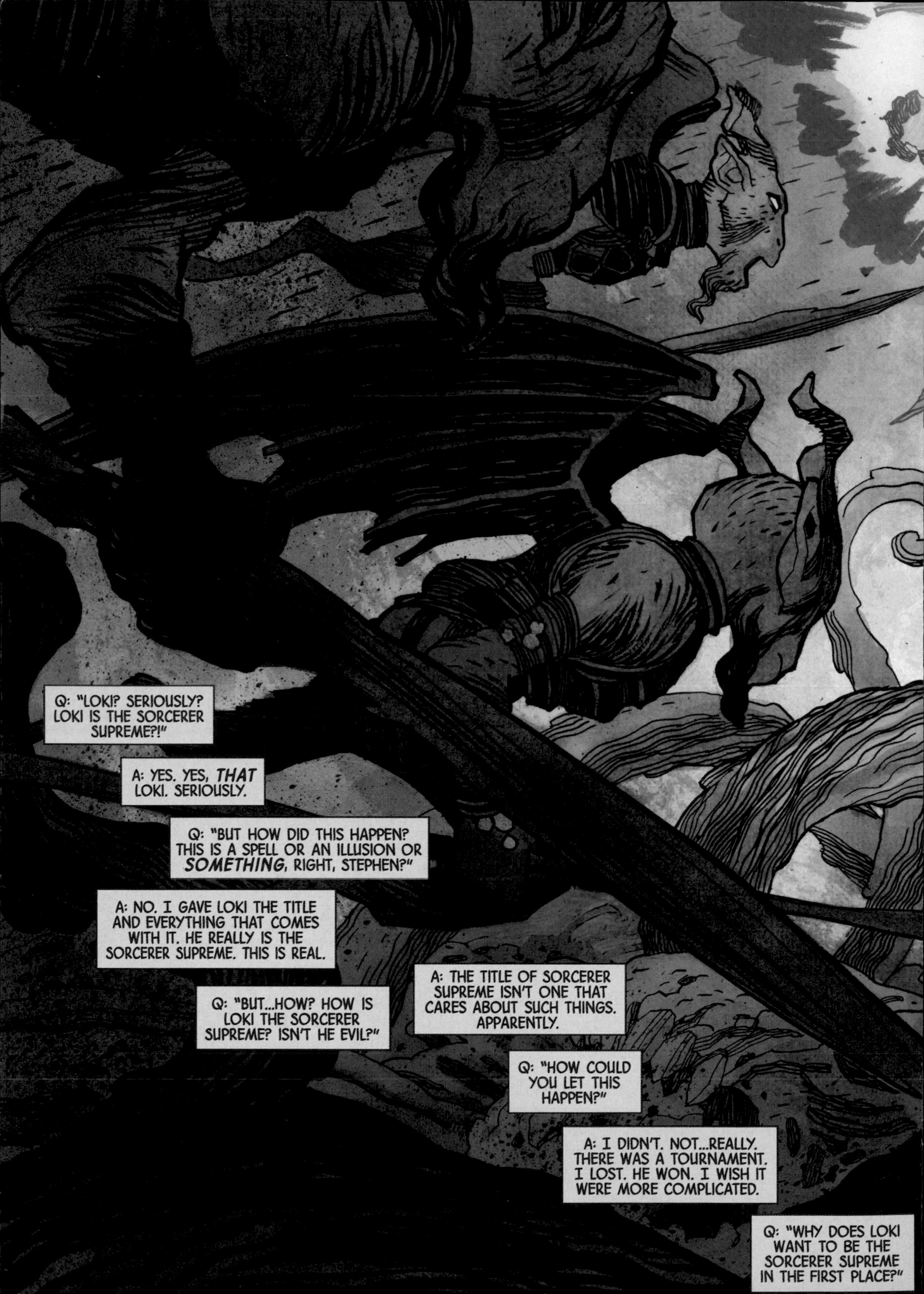
Q: "LOKI? SERIOUSLY? LOKI IS THE SORCERER SUPREME?!"
A: YES. YES, *THAT* LOKI. SERIOUSLY.
Q: "BUT HOW DID THIS HAPPEN? THIS IS A SPELL OR AN ILLUSION OR *SOMETHING*, RIGHT, STEPHEN?"
A: NO. I GAVE LOKI THE TITLE AND EVERYTHING THAT COMES WITH IT. HE REALLY IS THE SORCERER SUPREME. THIS IS REAL.
Q: "BUT...HOW? HOW IS LOKI THE SORCERER SUPREME? ISN'T HE EVIL?"
A: THE TITLE OF SORCERER SUPREME ISN'T ONE THAT CARES ABOUT SUCH THINGS. APPARENTLY.
Q: "HOW COULD YOU LET THIS HAPPEN?"
A: I DIDN'T. NOT...REALLY. THERE WAS A TOURNAMENT. I LOST. HE WON. I WISH IT WERE MORE COMPLICATED.
Q: "WHY DOES LOKI WANT TO BE THE SORCERER SUPREME IN THE FIRST PLACE?"

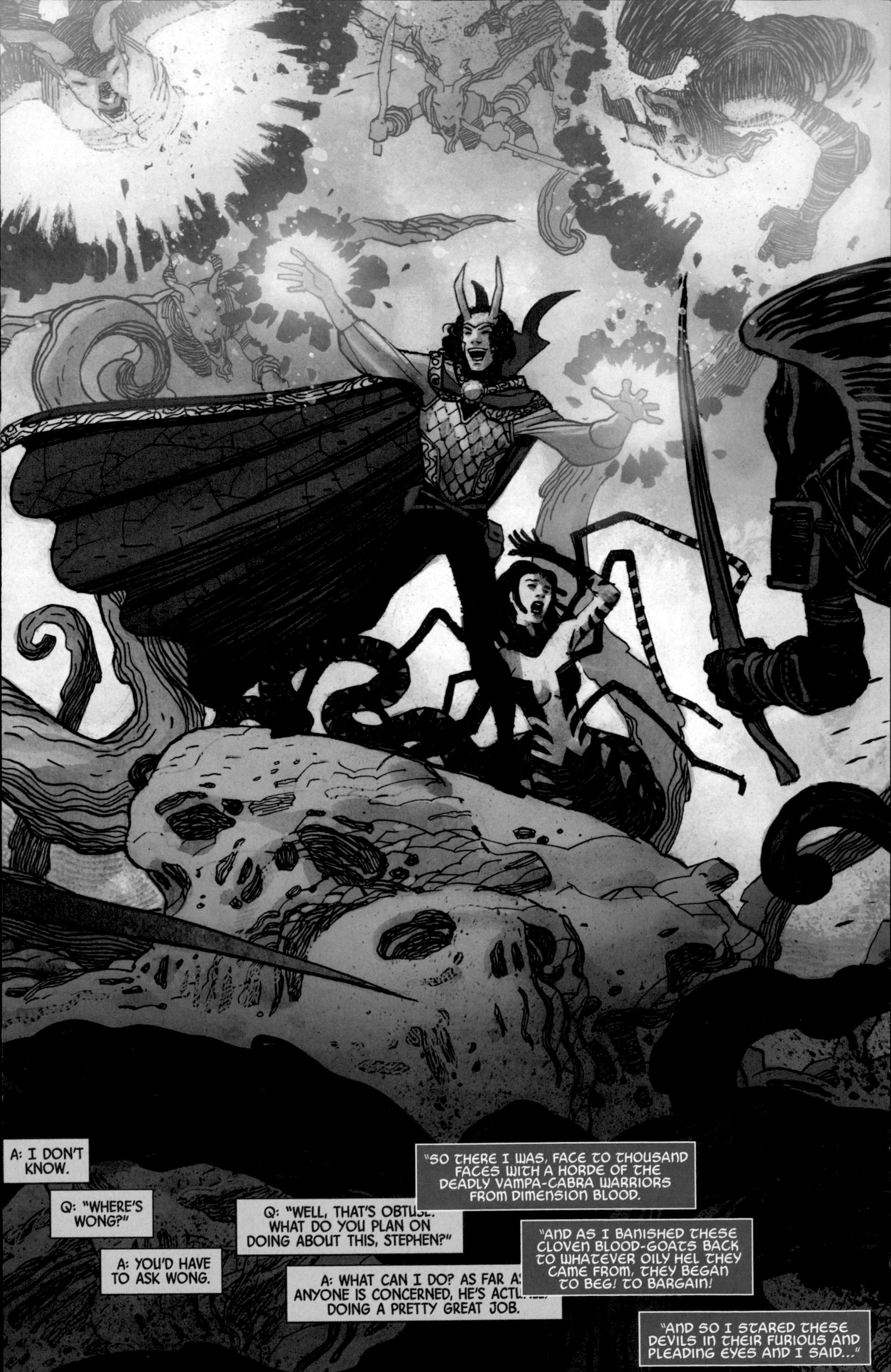

A: I DON'T KNOW.
Q: "WHERE'S WONG?"
A: YOU'D HAVE TO ASK WONG.
Q: "WELL, THAT'S OBTU WHAT DO YOU PLAN ON DOING ABOUT THIS, STEPHEN?"
A: WHAT CAN I DO? AS FAR A ANYONE IS CONCERNED, HE'S ACTU DOING A PRETTY GREAT JOB.
"SO THERE I WAS, FACE TO THOUSAND FACES WITH A HORDE OF THE DEADLY VAMPA-CABRA WARRIORS FROM DIMENSION BLOOD.
"AND AS I BANISHED THESE CLOVEN BLOOD-GOATS BACK TO WHATEVER OILY HEL THEY CAME FROM, THEY BEGAN TO BEG! TO BARGAIN!
"AND SO I STARED THESE DEVILS IN THEIR FURIOUS AND PLEADING EYES AND I SAID..."

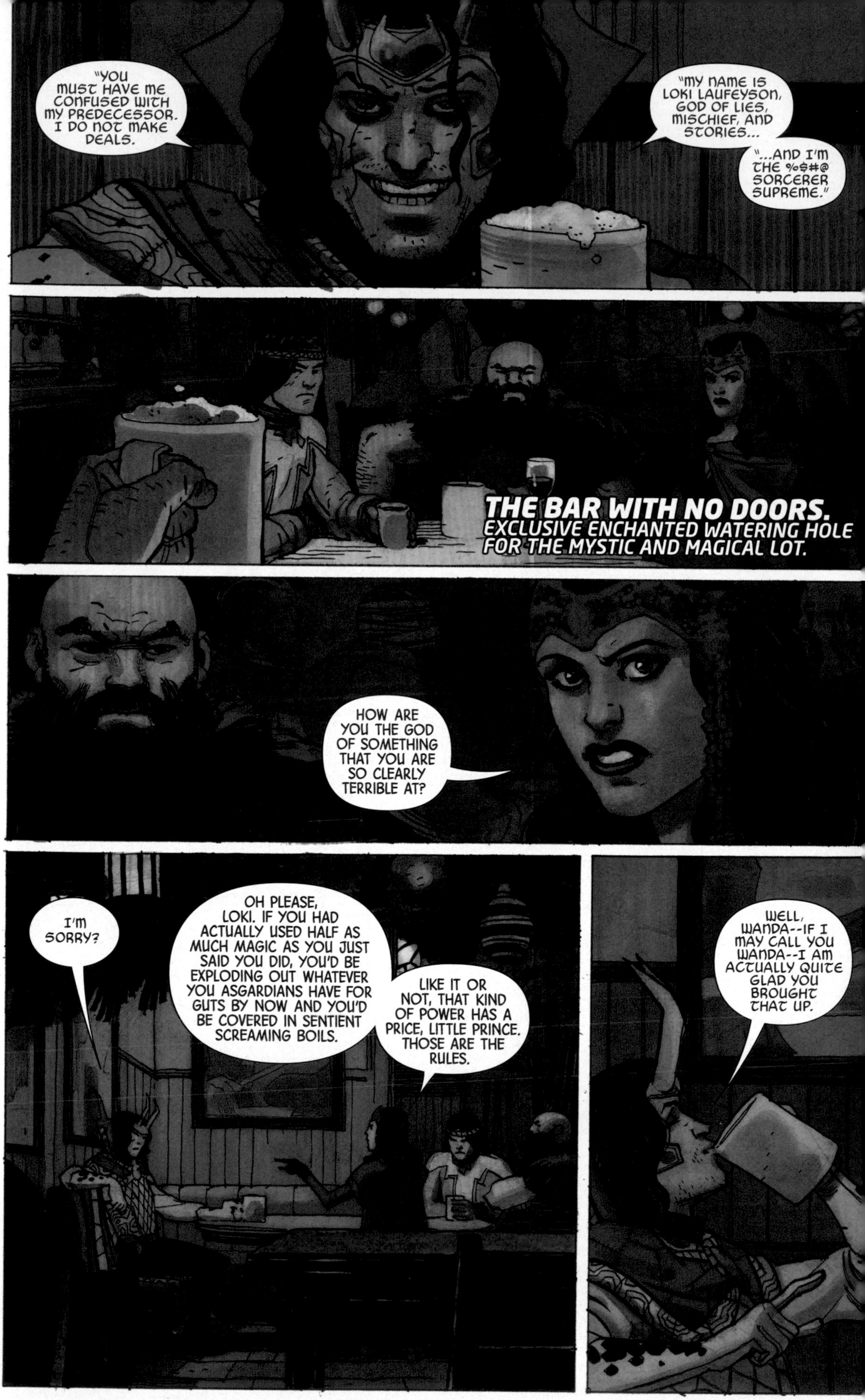
"YOU MUST HAVE ME CONFUSED WITH MY PREDECESSOR. I DO NOT MAKE DEALS.
"MY NAME IS LOKI LAUFEYSON, GOD OF LIES, MISCHIEF, AND STORIES...
"...AND I'M THE %$#@ SORCERER SUPREME."
THE BAR WITH NO DOORS.
EXCLUSIVE ENCHANTED WATERING HOLE FOR THE MYSTIC AND MAGICAL LOT.
HOW ARE YOU THE GOD OF SOMETHING THAT YOU ARE SO CLEARLY TERRIBLE AT?
I'M SORRY?
OH PLEASE, LOKI. IF YOU HAD ACTUALLY USED HALF AS MUCH MAGIC AS YOU JUST SAID YOU DID, YOU'D BE EXPLODING OUT WHATEVER YOU ASGARDIANS HAVE FOR GUTS BY NOW AND YOU'D BE COVERED IN SENTIENT SCREAMING BOILS.
LIKE IT OR NOT, THAT KIND OF POWER HAS A PRICE, LITTLE PRINCE. THOSE ARE THE RULES.
WELL, WANDA--IF I MAY CALL YOU WANDA--I AM ACTUALLY QUITE GLAD YOU BROUGHT THAT UP.

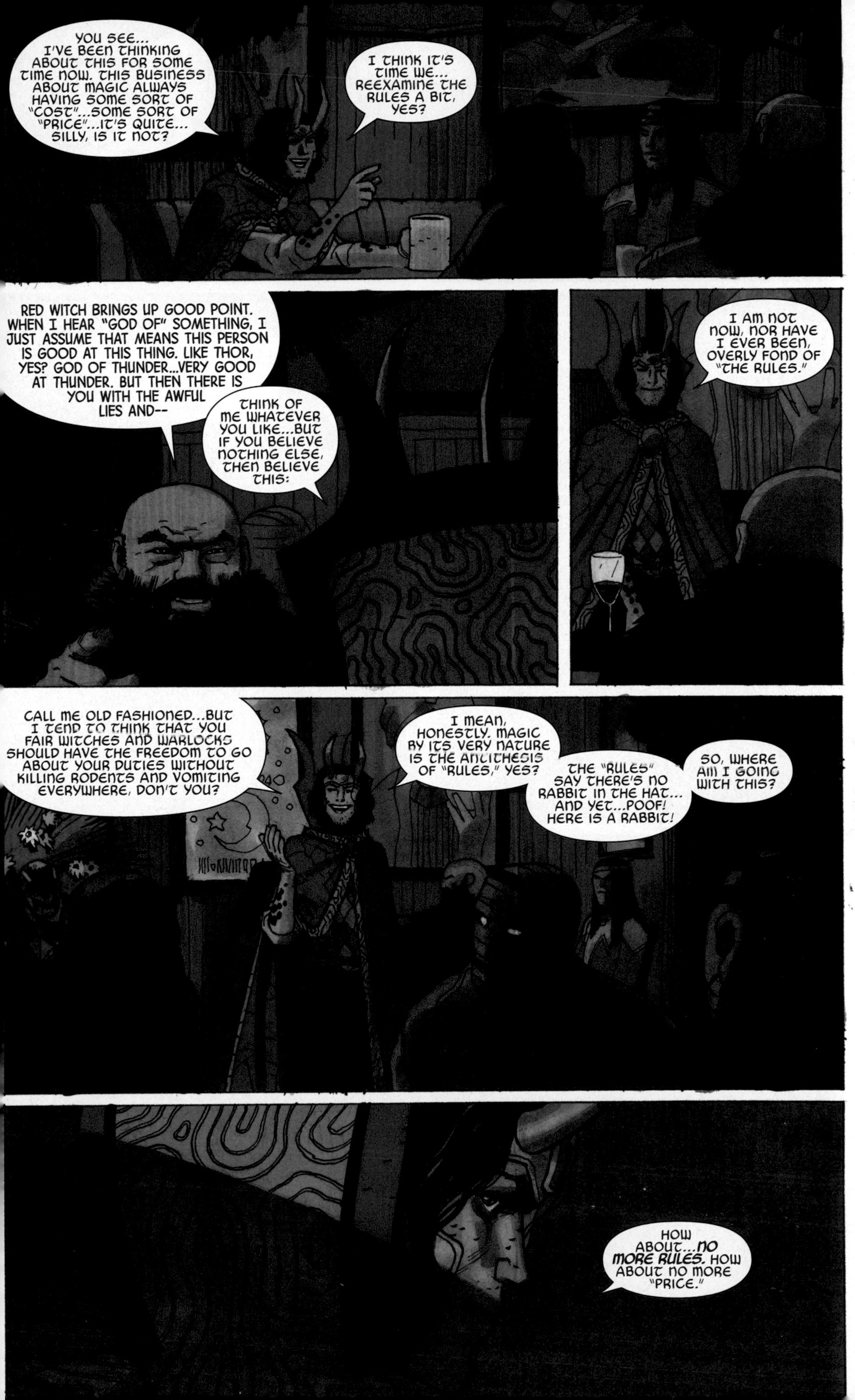
YOU SEE... I'VE BEEN THINKING ABOUT THIS FOR SOME TIME NOW. THIS BUSINESS ABOUT MAGIC ALWAYS HAVING SOME SORT OF "COST"...SOME SORT OF "PRICE"...IT'S QUITE... SILLY, IS IT NOT?
I THINK IT'S TIME WE... REEXAMINE THE RULES A BIT, YES?
RED WITCH BRINGS UP GOOD POINT. WHEN I HEAR "GOD OF" SOMETHING, I JUST ASSUME THAT MEANS THIS PERSON IS GOOD AT THIS THING. LIKE THOR, YES? GOD OF THUNDER...VERY GOOD AT THUNDER. BUT THEN THERE IS YOU WITH THE AWFUL LIES AND--
THINK OF ME WHATEVER YOU LIKE...BUT IF YOU BELIEVE NOTHING ELSE, THEN BELIEVE THIS:
I AM NOT NOW, NOR HAVE I EVER BEEN, OVERLY FOND OF "THE RULES."
CALL ME OLD FASHIONED...BUT I TEND TO THINK THAT YOU FAIR WITCHES AND WARLOCKS SHOULD HAVE THE FREEDOM TO GO ABOUT YOUR DUTIES WITHOUT KILLING RODENTS AND VOMITING EVERYWHERE, DON'T YOU?
I MEAN, HONESTLY. MAGIC BY ITS VERY NATURE IS THE ANTITHESIS OF "RULES," YES?
THE "RULES" SAY THERE'S NO RABBIT IN THE HAT... AND YET...POOF! HERE IS A RABBIT!
SO, WHERE AM I GOING WITH THIS?
HOW ABOUT...**NO MORE RULES.** HOW ABOUT NO MORE "PRICE."

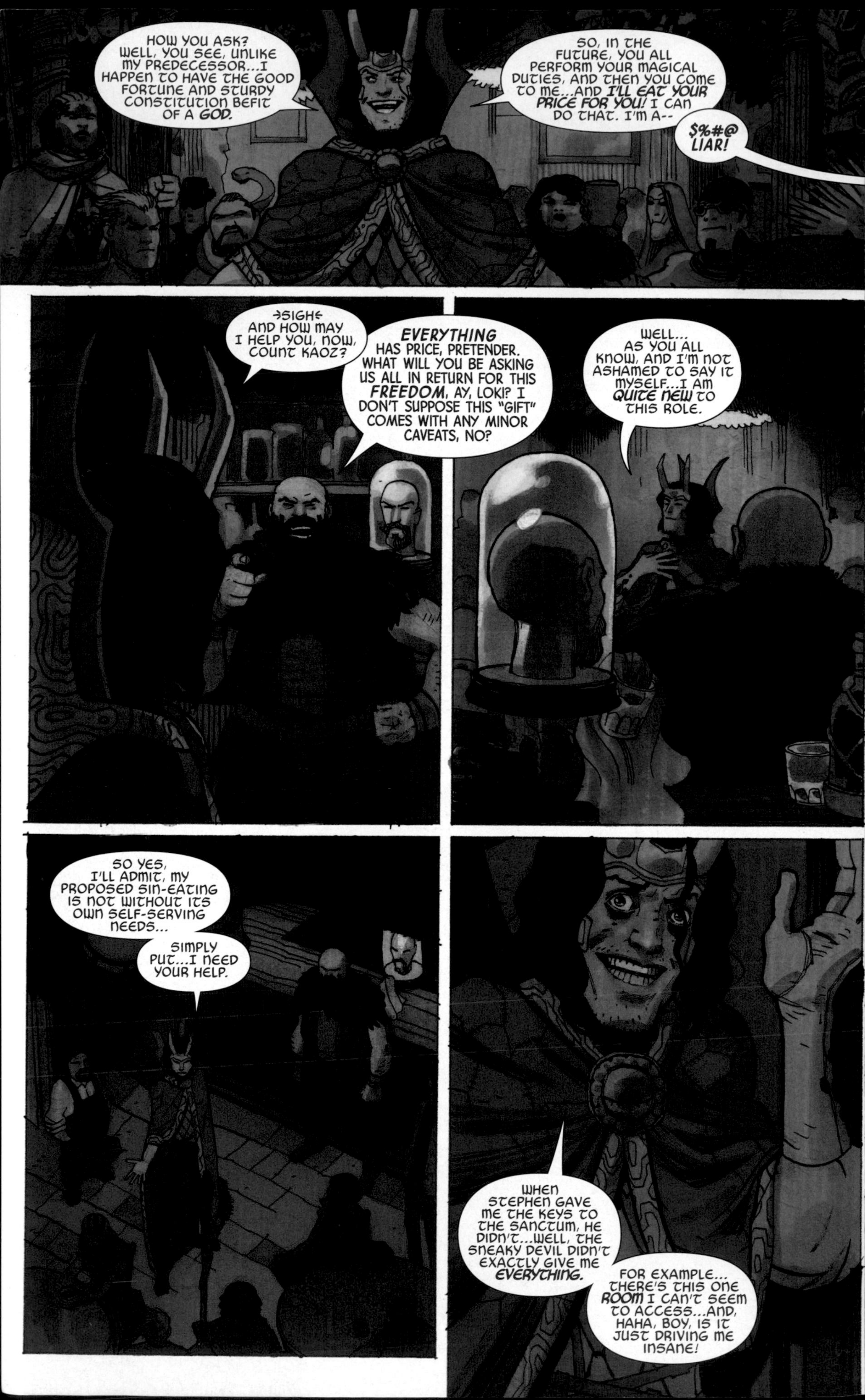
HOW YOU ASK? WELL, YOU SEE, UNLIKE MY PREDECESSOR...I HAPPEN TO HAVE THE GOOD FORTUNE AND STURDY CONSTITUTION BEFIT OF A GOD.
SO, IN THE FUTURE, YOU ALL PERFORM YOUR MAGICAL DUTIES, AND THEN YOU COME TO ME...AND I'LL EAT YOUR PRICE FOR YOU! I CAN DO THAT. I'M A--
$%#@ LIAR!
>SIGH< AND HOW MAY I HELP YOU, NOW, COUNT KAOZ?
EVERYTHING HAS PRICE, PRETENDER. WHAT WILL YOU BE ASKING US ALL IN RETURN FOR THIS FREEDOM, AY, LOKI? I DON'T SUPPOSE THIS "GIFT" COMES WITH ANY MINOR CAVEATS, NO?
WELL... AS YOU ALL KNOW, AND I'M NOT ASHAMED TO SAY IT MYSELF...I AM QUITE NEW TO THIS ROLE.
SO YES, I'LL ADMIT, MY PROPOSED SIN-EATING IS NOT WITHOUT ITS OWN SELF-SERVING NEEDS...
SIMPLY PUT...I NEED YOUR HELP.
WHEN STEPHEN GAVE ME THE KEYS TO THE SANCTUM, HE DIDN'T...WELL, THE SNEAKY DEVIL DIDN'T EXACTLY GIVE ME EVERYTHING.
FOR EXAMPLE... THERE'S THIS ONE ROOM I CAN'T SEEM TO ACCESS...AND, HAHA, BOY, IS IT JUST DRIVING ME INSANE!

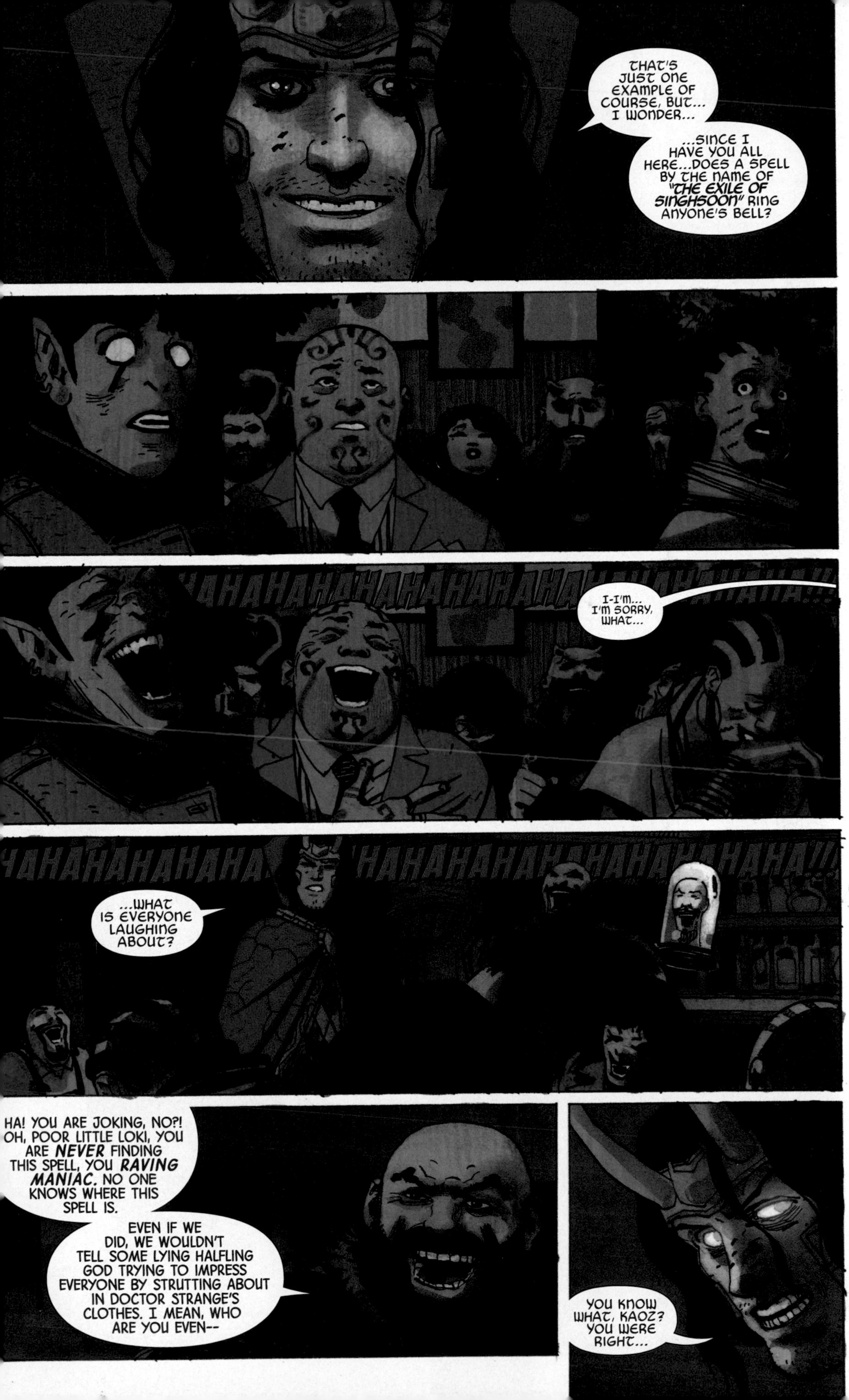
THAT'S JUST ONE EXAMPLE OF COURSE, BUT... I WONDER...
...SINCE I HAVE YOU ALL HERE...DOES A SPELL BY THE NAME OF "THE EXILE OF SINGHSOON" RING ANYONE'S BELL?
HAHAHAHAHAHAHAHAHAHAHAHAHAHAHA!!
I-I'M... I'M SORRY, WHAT...
HAHAHAHAHAHAHAHAHAHAHAHAHAHAHA!!
...WHAT IS EVERYONE LAUGHING ABOUT?
HA! YOU ARE JOKING, NO?! OH, POOR LITTLE LOKI, YOU ARE NEVER FINDING THIS SPELL, YOU RAVING MANIAC. NO ONE KNOWS WHERE THIS SPELL IS.
EVEN IF WE DID, WE WOULDN'T TELL SOME LYING HALFLING GOD TRYING TO IMPRESS EVERYONE BY STRUTTING ABOUT IN DOCTOR STRANGE'S CLOTHES. I MEAN, WHO ARE YOU EVEN--
YOU KNOW WHAT, KAOZ? YOU WERE RIGHT...

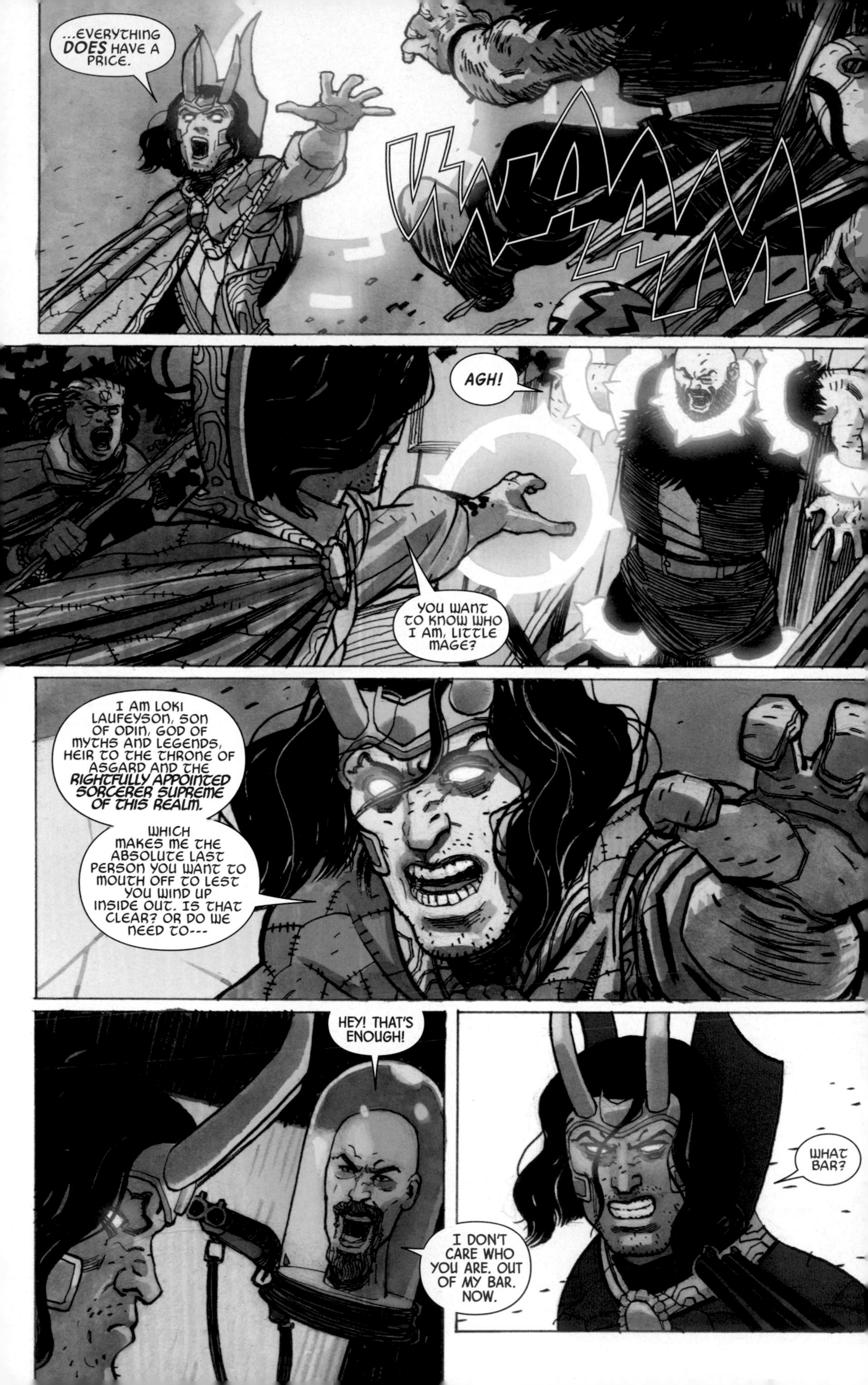
...EVERYTHING DOES HAVE A PRICE.
KWAAAM
AGH!
YOU WANT TO KNOW WHO I AM, LITTLE MAGE?
I AM LOKI LAUFEYSON, SON OF ODIN, GOD OF MYTHS AND LEGENDS, HEIR TO THE THRONE OF ASGARD AND THE RIGHTFULLY APPOINTED SORCERER SUPREME OF THIS REALM.
WHICH MAKES ME THE ABSOLUTE LAST PERSON YOU WANT TO MOUTH OFF TO LEST YOU WIND UP INSIDE OUT. IS THAT CLEAR? OR DO WE NEED TO---
HEY! THAT'S ENOUGH!
I DON'T CARE WHO YOU ARE. OUT OF MY BAR. NOW.
WHAT BAR?

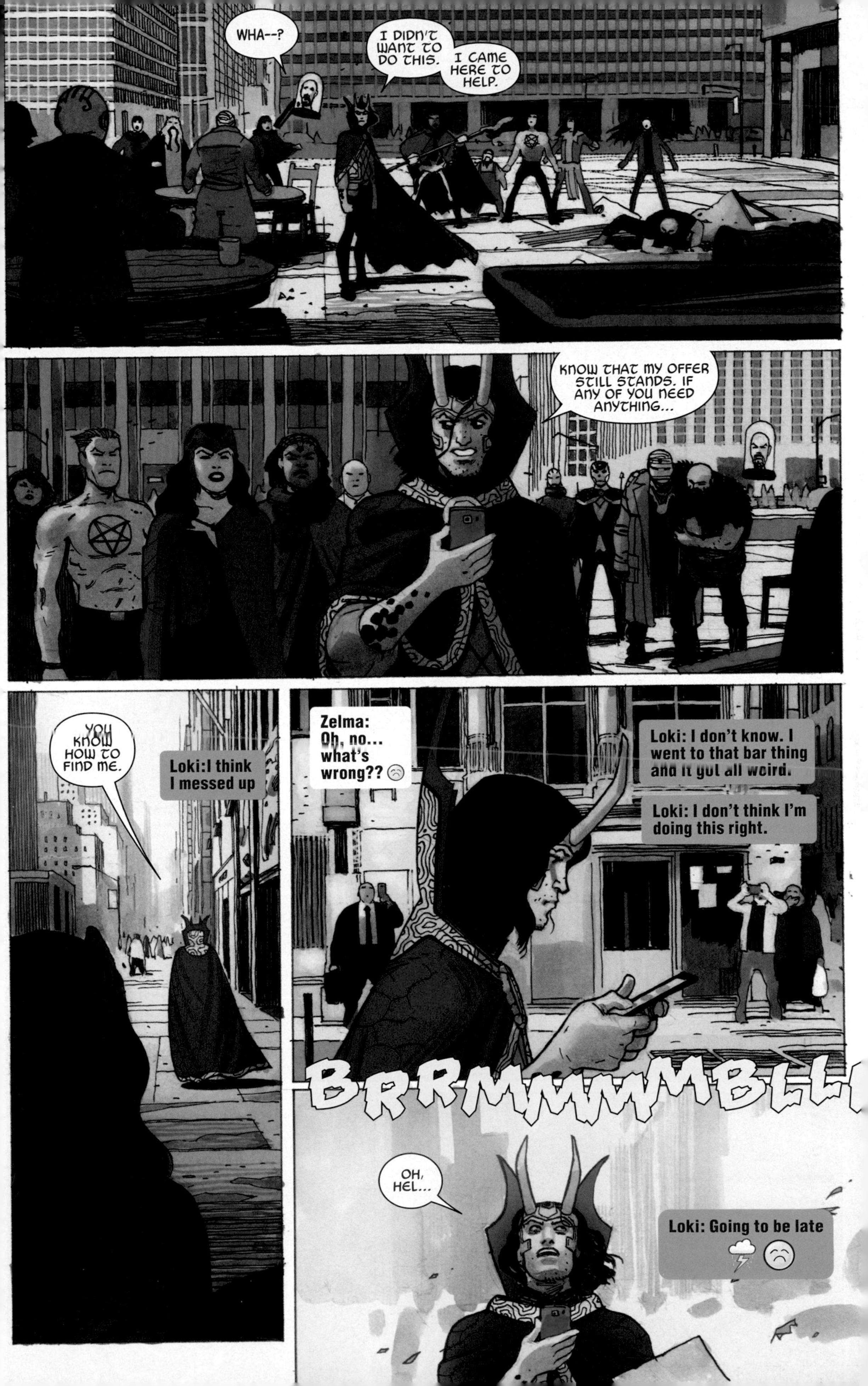

WHA--?
I DIDN'T WANT TO DO THIS.
I CAME HERE TO HELP.
KNOW THAT MY OFFER STILL STANDS. IF ANY OF YOU NEED ANYTHING...
YOU KNOW HOW TO FIND ME.
Loki:I think I messed up
Zelma: Oh, no... what's wrong??
Loki: I don't know. I went to that bar thing and it got all weird.
Loki: I don't think I'm doing this right.
BRRMMMMMBLL
OH, HEL...
Loki: Going to be late

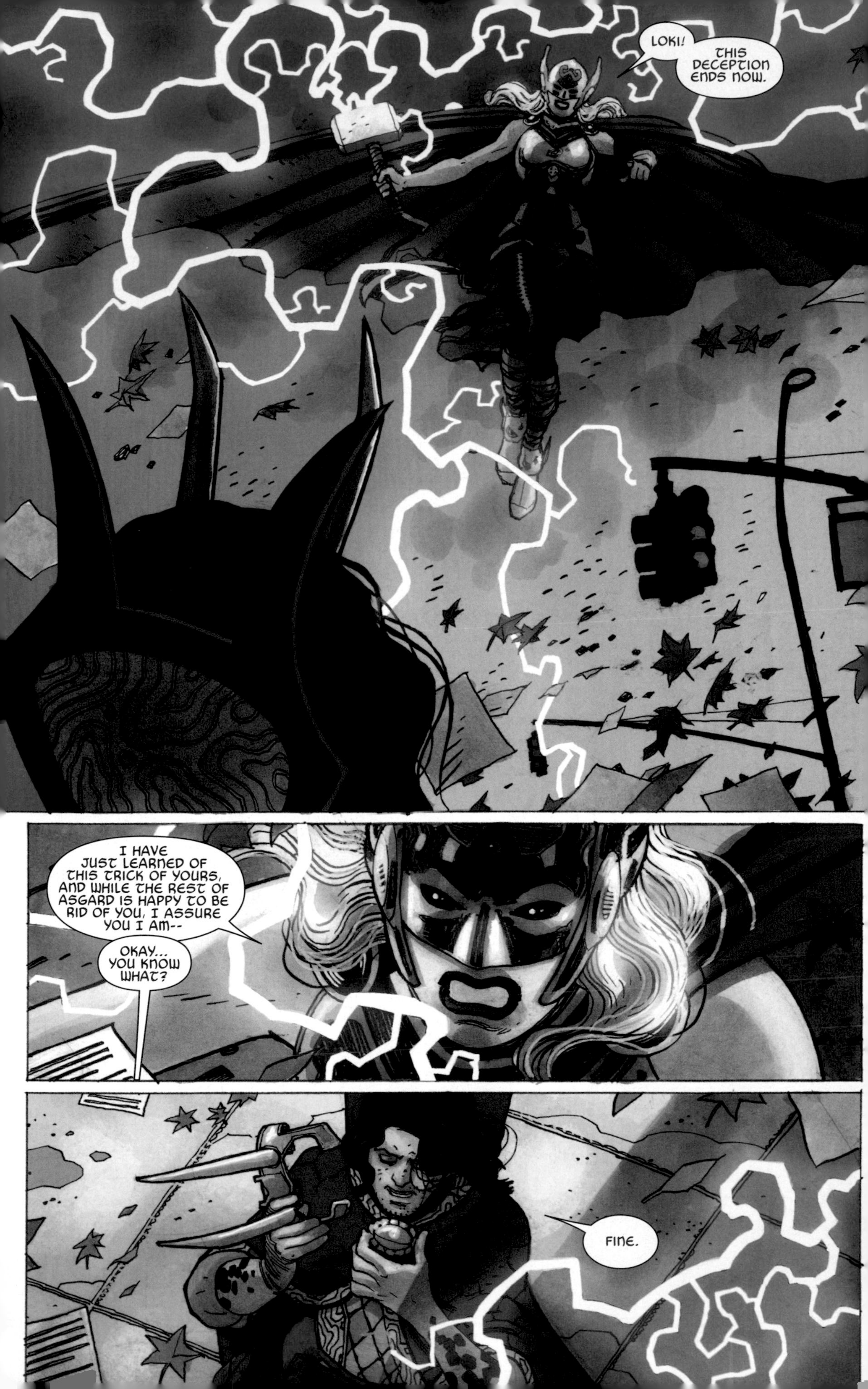
LOKI!
THIS DECEPTION ENDS NOW.
I HAVE JUST LEARNED OF THIS TRICK OF YOURS, AND WHILE THE REST OF ASGARD IS HAPPY TO BE RID OF YOU, I ASSURE YOU I AM--
OKAY... YOU KNOW WHAT?
FINE.

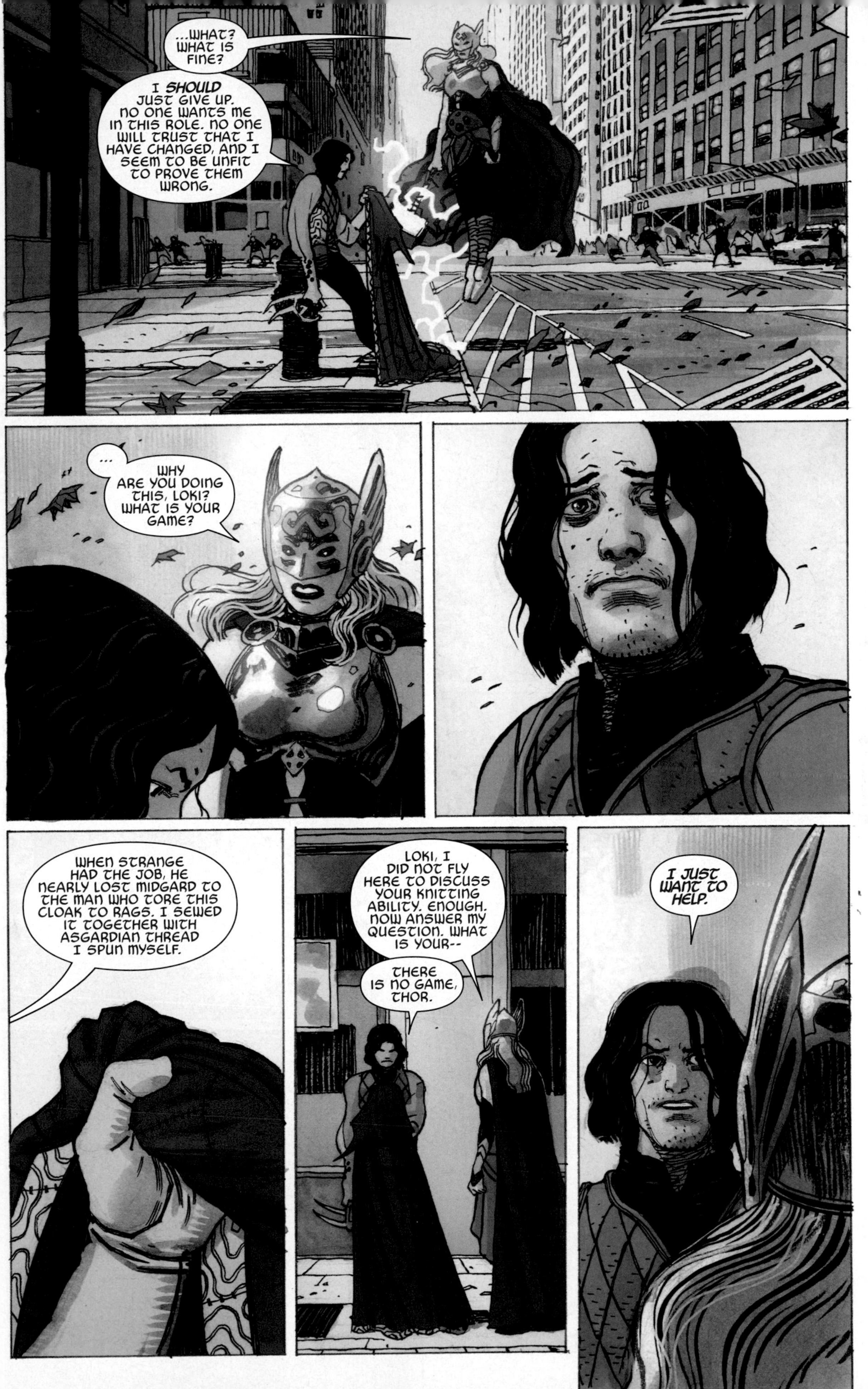

...WHAT? WHAT IS FINE?
I *SHOULD* JUST GIVE UP. NO ONE WANTS ME IN THIS ROLE. NO ONE WILL TRUST THAT I HAVE CHANGED, AND I SEEM TO BE UNFIT TO PROVE THEM WRONG.
...
WHY ARE YOU DOING THIS, LOKI? WHAT IS YOUR GAME?
WHEN STRANGE HAD THE JOB, HE NEARLY LOST MIDGARD TO THE MAN WHO TORE THIS CLOAK TO RAGS. I SEWED IT TOGETHER WITH ASGARDIAN THREAD I SPUN MYSELF.
LOKI, I DID NOT FLY HERE TO DISCUSS YOUR KNITTING ABILITY. ENOUGH. NOW ANSWER MY QUESTION. WHAT IS YOUR--
THERE IS NO GAME, THOR.
I JUST WANT TO HELP.

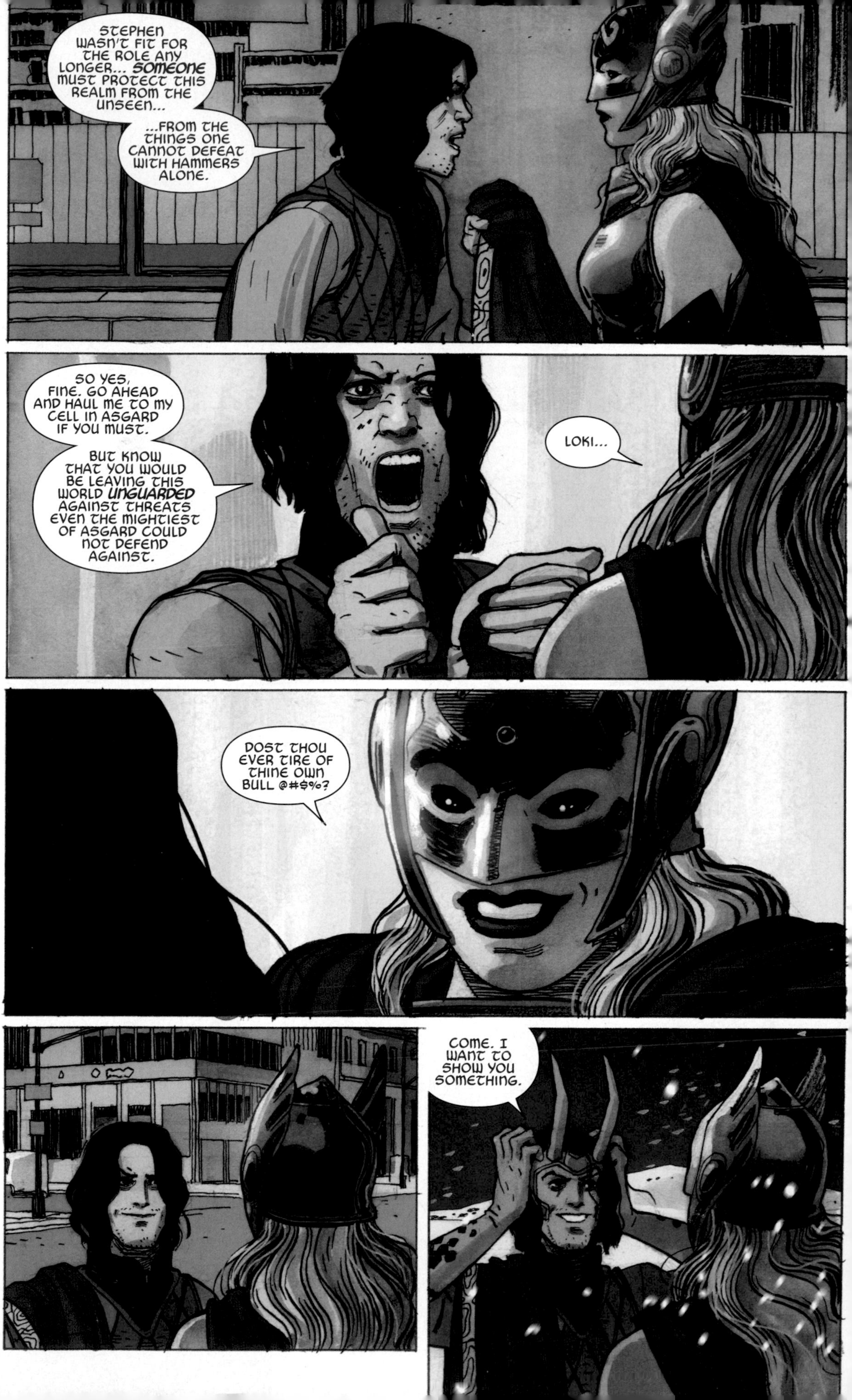
STEPHEN WASN'T FIT FOR THE ROLE ANY LONGER... SOMEONE MUST PROTECT THIS REALM FROM THE UNSEEN...
...FROM THE THINGS ONE CANNOT DEFEAT WITH HAMMERS ALONE.
SO YES, FINE. GO AHEAD AND HAUL ME TO MY CELL IN ASGARD IF YOU MUST.
BUT KNOW THAT YOU WOULD BE LEAVING THIS WORLD UNGUARDED AGAINST THREATS EVEN THE MIGHTIEST OF ASGARD COULD NOT DEFEND AGAINST.
LOKI...
DOST THOU EVER TIRE OF THINE OWN BULL @#$%?
COME. I WANT TO SHOW YOU SOMETHING.

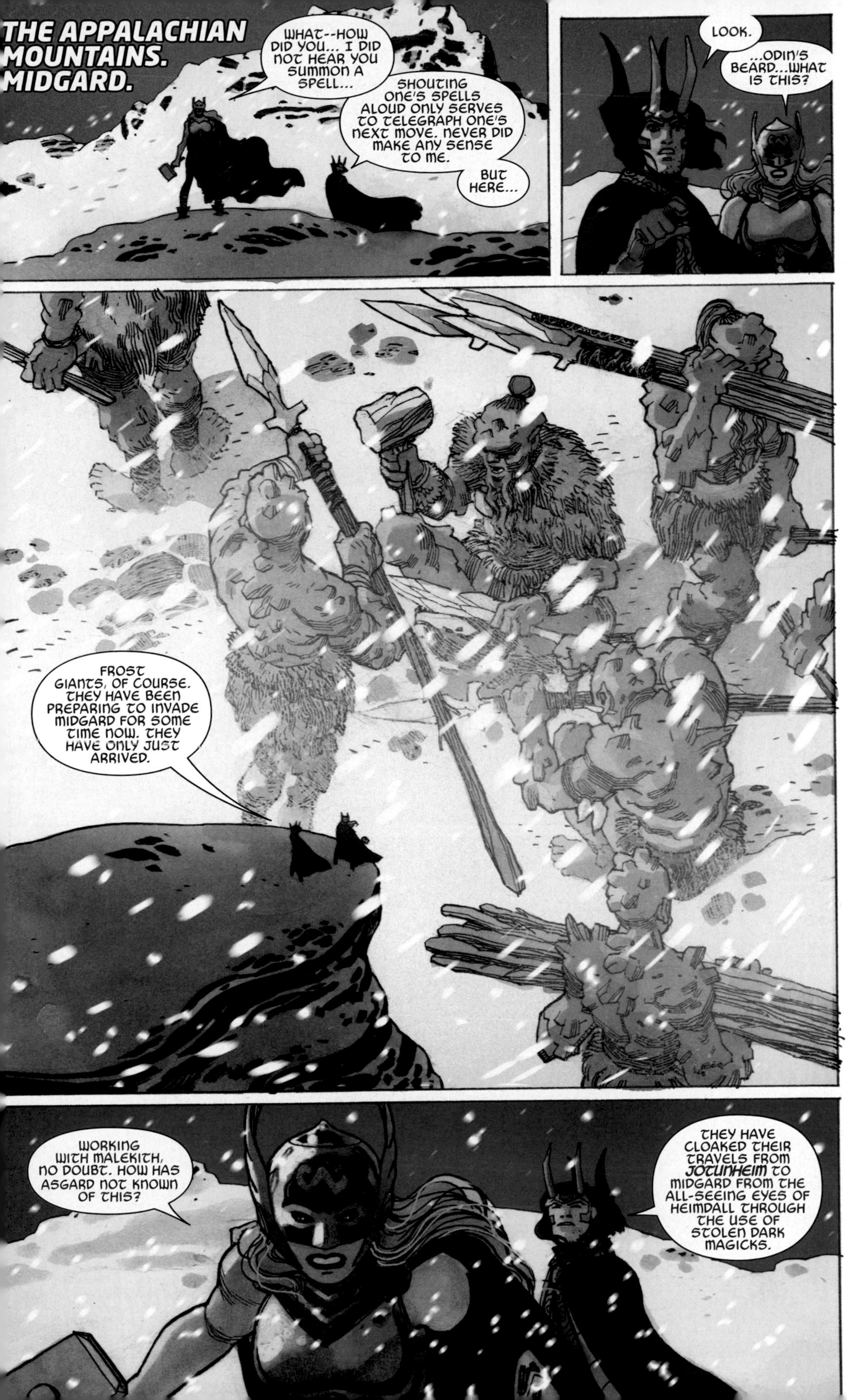
THE APPALACHIAN MOUNTAINS. MIDGARD.
WHAT--HOW DID YOU... I DID NOT HEAR YOU SUMMON A SPELL...
SHOUTING ONE'S SPELLS ALOUD ONLY SERVES TO TELEGRAPH ONE'S NEXT MOVE. NEVER DID MAKE ANY SENSE TO ME.
BUT HERE...
LOOK.
...ODIN'S BEARD...WHAT IS THIS?
FROST GIANTS, OF COURSE. THEY HAVE BEEN PREPARING TO INVADE MIDGARD FOR SOME TIME NOW. THEY HAVE ONLY JUST ARRIVED.
WORKING WITH MALEKITH, NO DOUBT. HOW HAS ASGARD NOT KNOWN OF THIS?
THEY HAVE CLOAKED THEIR TRAVELS FROM JOTUNHEIM TO MIDGARD FROM THE ALL-SEEING EYES OF HEIMDALL THROUGH THE USE OF STOLEN DARK MAGICKS.

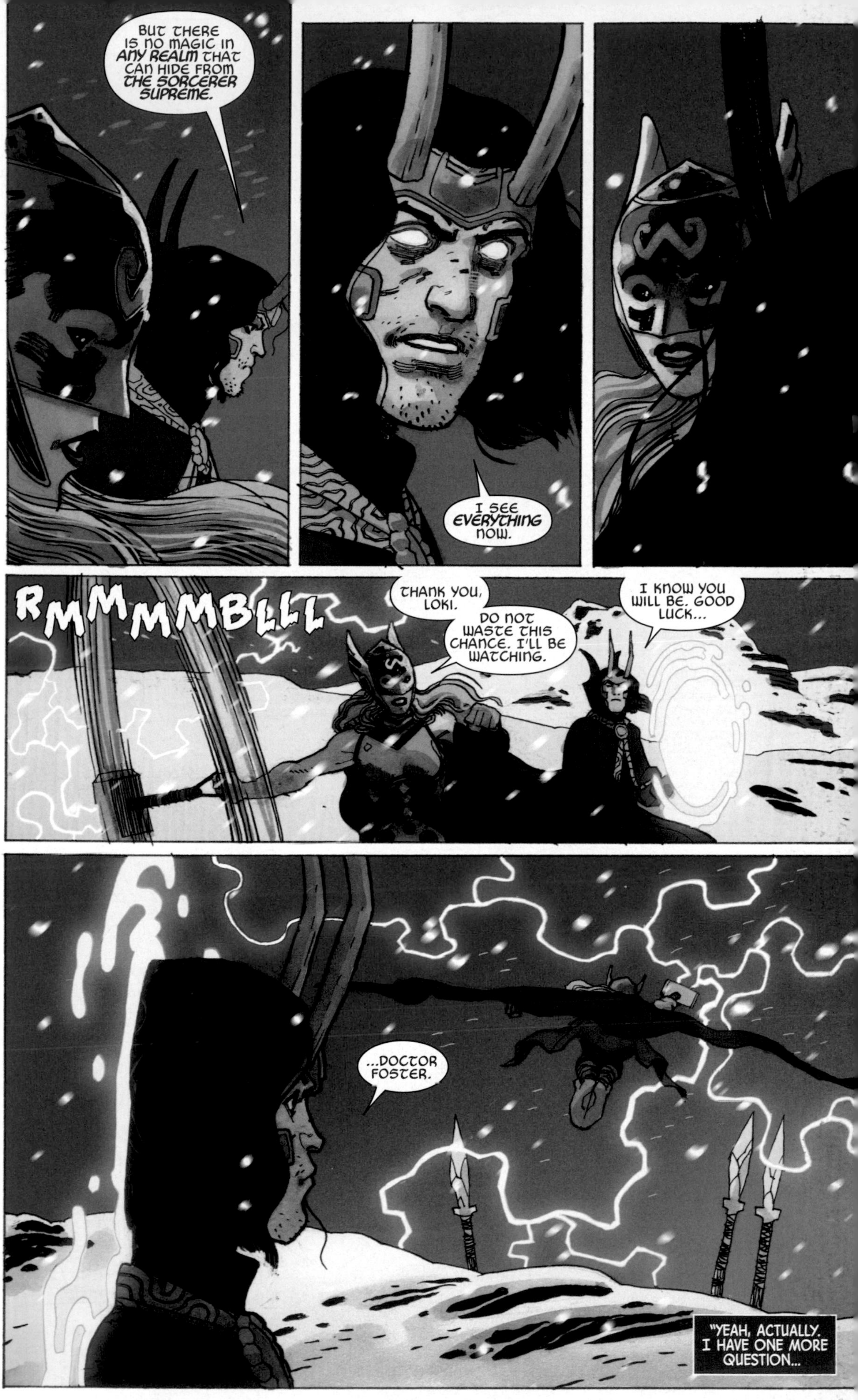
BUT THERE IS NO MAGIC IN ANY REALM THAT CAN HIDE FROM THE SORCERER SUPREME.
I SEE EVERYTHING NOW.
RMMMMMBLLL
THANK YOU, LOKI.
DO NOT WASTE THIS CHANCE. I'LL BE WATCHING.
I KNOW YOU WILL BE. GOOD LUCK...
...DOCTOR FOSTER.
"YEAH, ACTUALLY. I HAVE ONE MORE QUESTION...

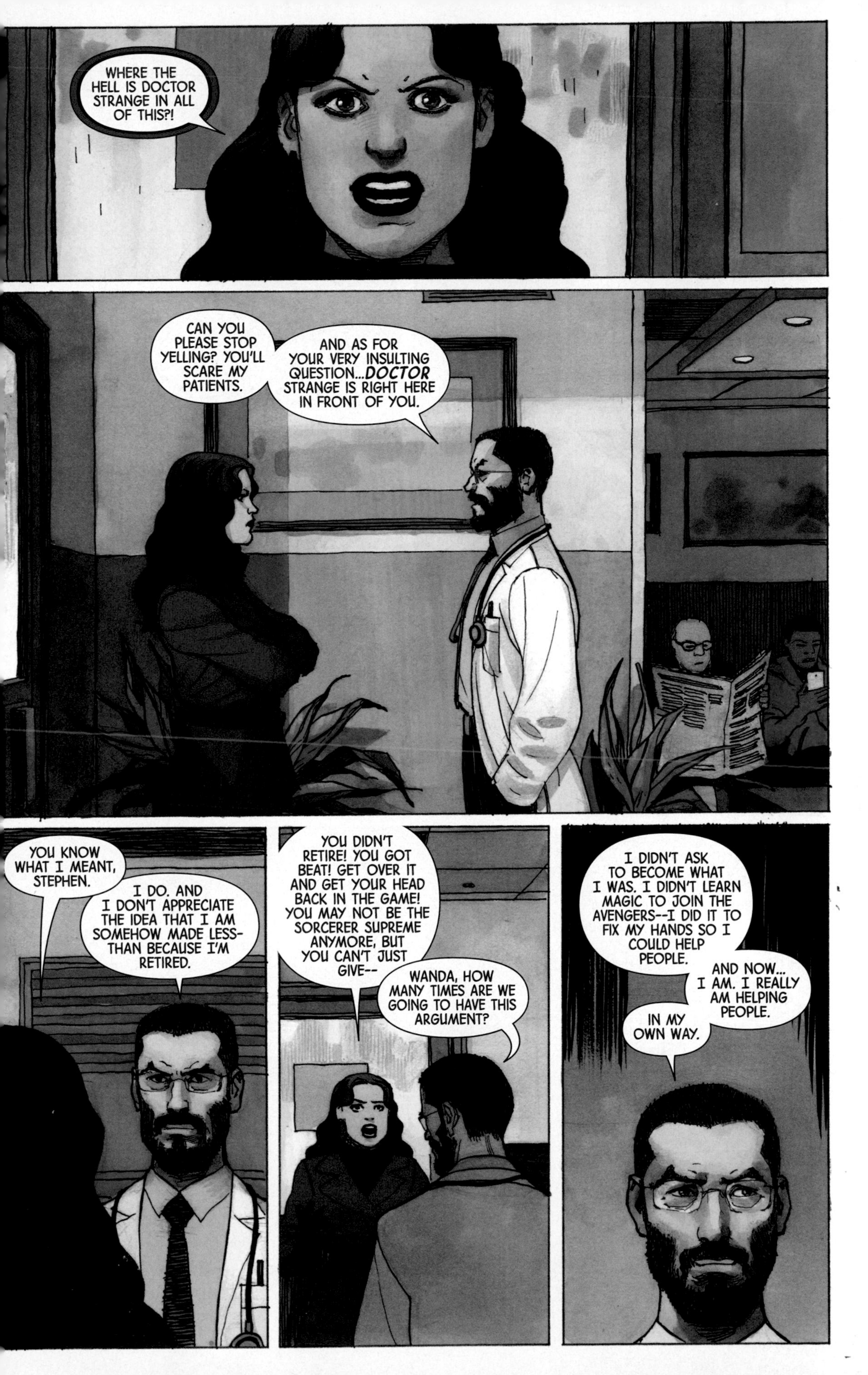
WHERE THE HELL IS DOCTOR STRANGE IN ALL OF THIS?!
CAN YOU PLEASE STOP YELLING? YOU'LL SCARE MY PATIENTS.
AND AS FOR YOUR VERY INSULTING QUESTION...DOCTOR STRANGE IS RIGHT HERE IN FRONT OF YOU.
YOU KNOW WHAT I MEANT, STEPHEN.
I DO. AND I DON'T APPRECIATE THE IDEA THAT I AM SOMEHOW MADE LESS-THAN BECAUSE I'M RETIRED.
YOU DIDN'T RETIRE! YOU GOT BEAT! GET OVER IT AND GET YOUR HEAD BACK IN THE GAME! YOU MAY NOT BE THE SORCERER SUPREME ANYMORE, BUT YOU CAN'T JUST GIVE--
WANDA, HOW MANY TIMES ARE WE GOING TO HAVE THIS ARGUMENT?
I DIDN'T ASK TO BECOME WHAT I WAS. I DIDN'T LEARN MAGIC TO JOIN THE AVENGERS--I DID IT TO FIX MY HANDS SO I COULD HELP PEOPLE.
AND NOW... I AM. I REALLY AM HELPING PEOPLE.
IN MY OWN WAY.

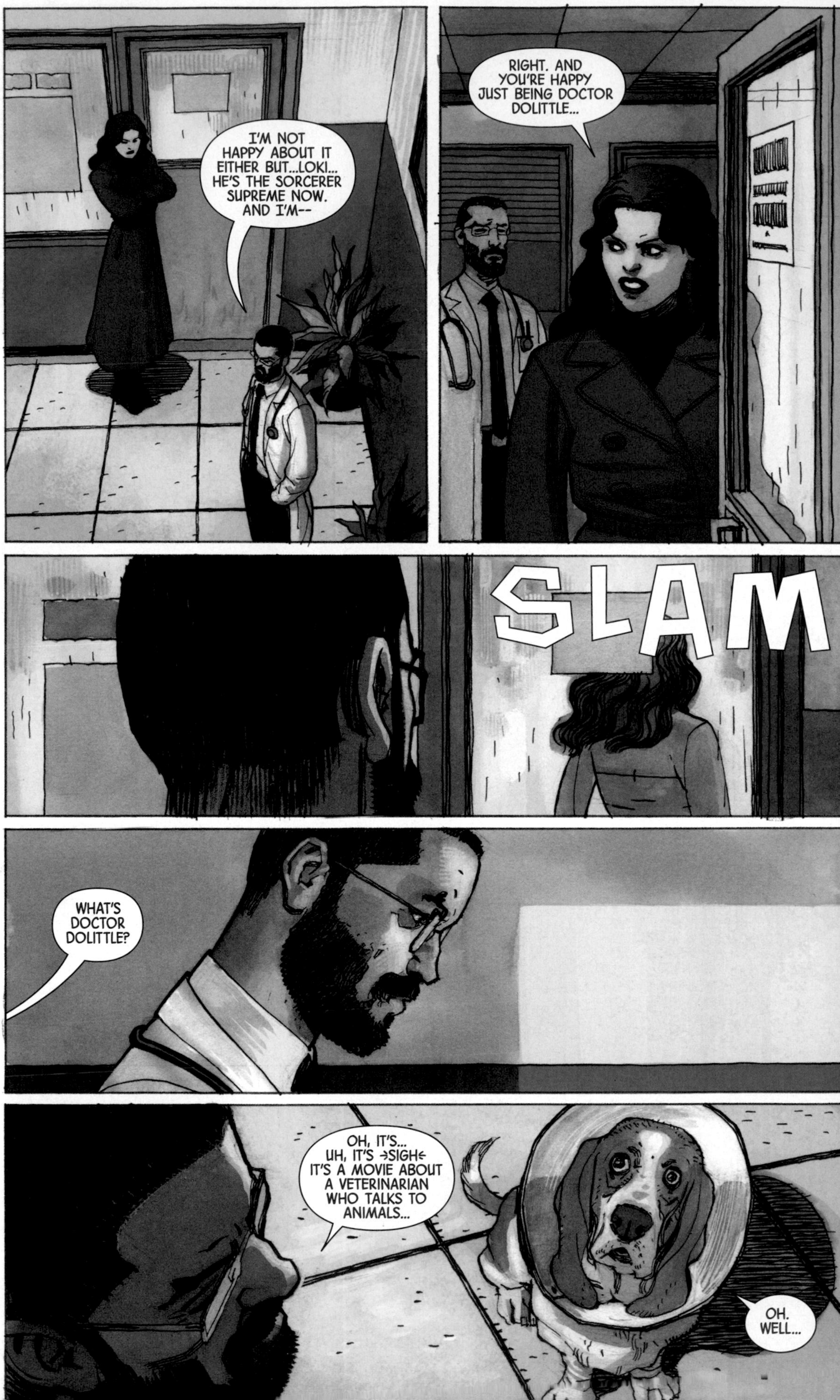
I'M NOT HAPPY ABOUT IT EITHER BUT...LOKI... HE'S THE SORCERER SUPREME NOW. AND I'M--
RIGHT. AND YOU'RE HAPPY JUST BEING DOCTOR DOLITTLE...
SLAM
WHAT'S DOCTOR DOLITTLE?
OH, IT'S... UH, IT'S →SIGH← IT'S A MOVIE ABOUT A VETERINARIAN WHO TALKS TO ANIMALS...
OH. WELL...

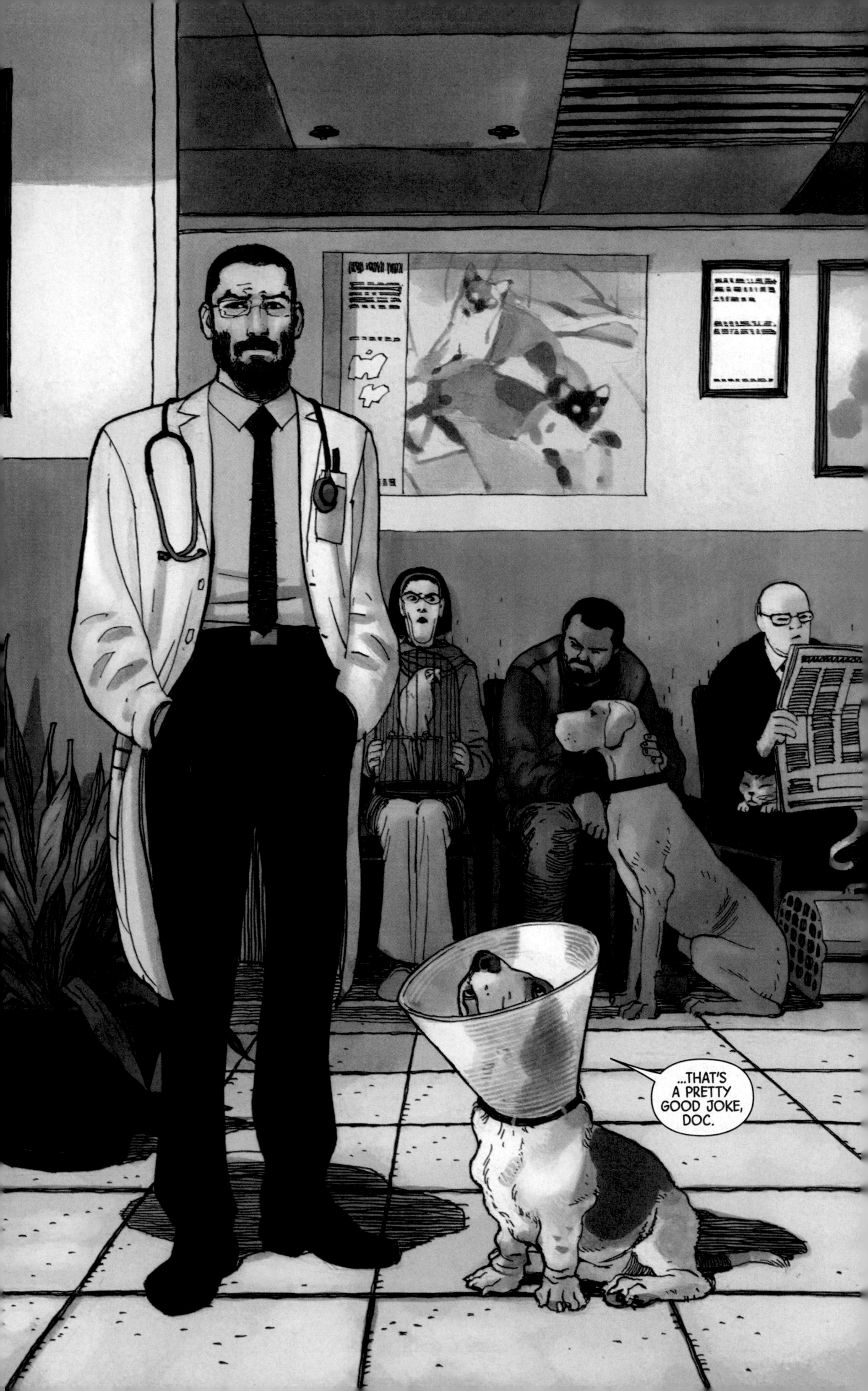
...THAT'S A PRETTY GOOD JOKE, DOC.

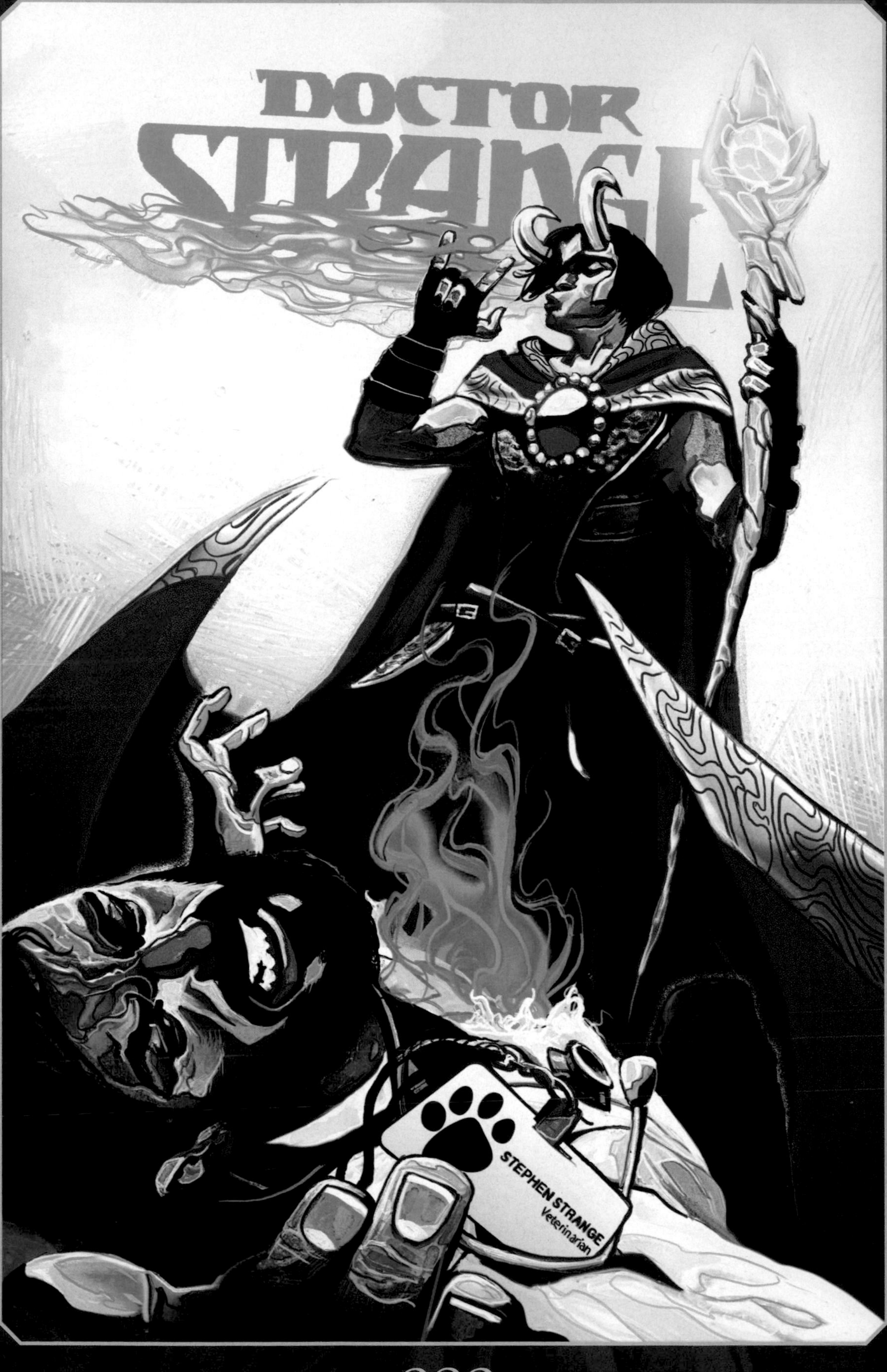
DOCTOR STRANGE
STEPHEN STRANGE
Veterinarian

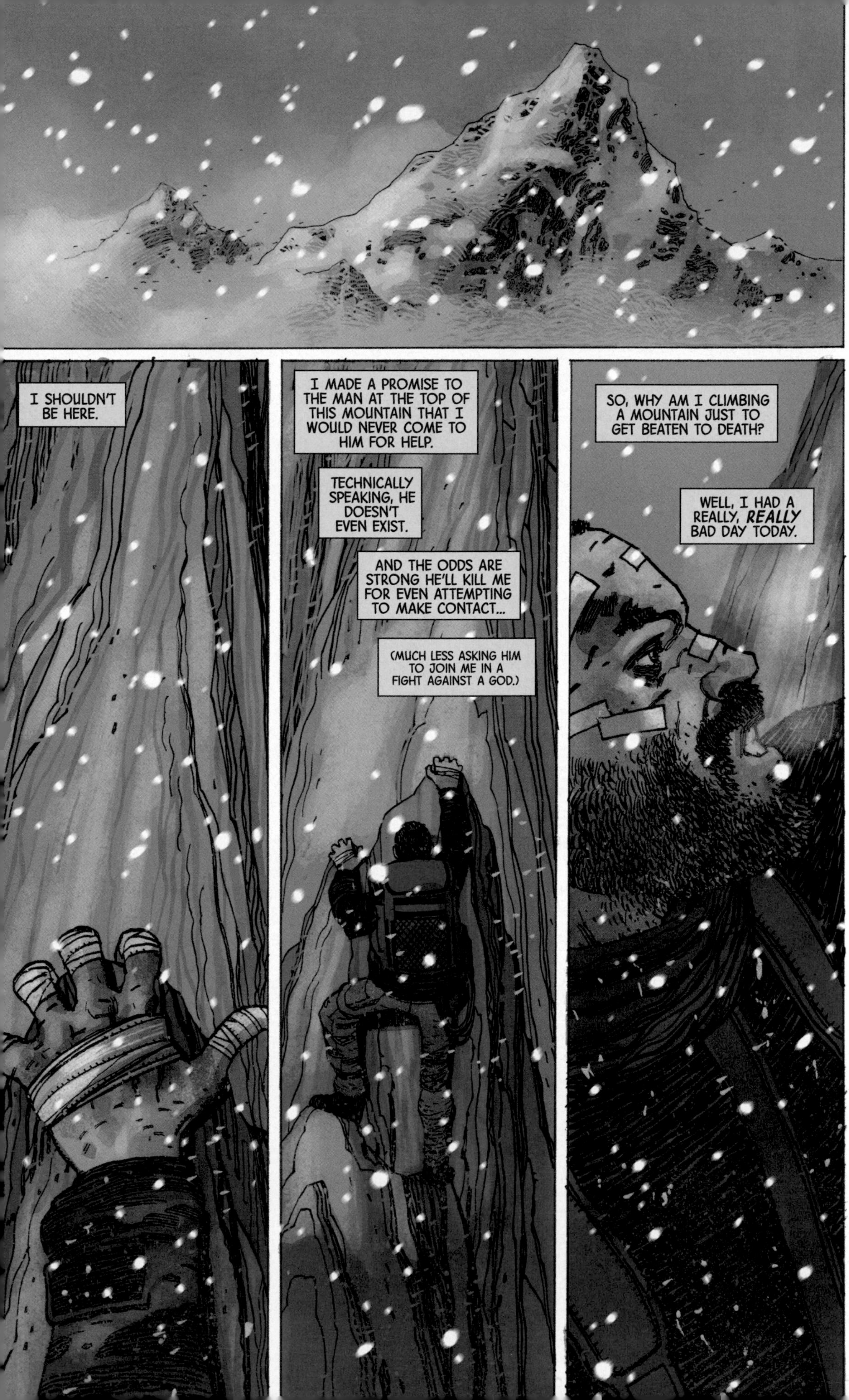
I SHOULDN'T BE HERE.
I MADE A PROMISE TO THE MAN AT THE TOP OF THIS MOUNTAIN THAT I WOULD NEVER COME TO HIM FOR HELP.
TECHNICALLY SPEAKING, HE DOESN'T EVEN EXIST.
AND THE ODDS ARE STRONG HE'LL KILL ME FOR EVEN ATTEMPTING TO MAKE CONTACT...
(MUCH LESS ASKING HIM TO JOIN ME IN A FIGHT AGAINST A GOD.)
SO, WHY AM I CLIMBING A MOUNTAIN JUST TO GET BEATEN TO DEATH?
WELL, I HAD A REALLY, *REALLY* BAD DAY TODAY.

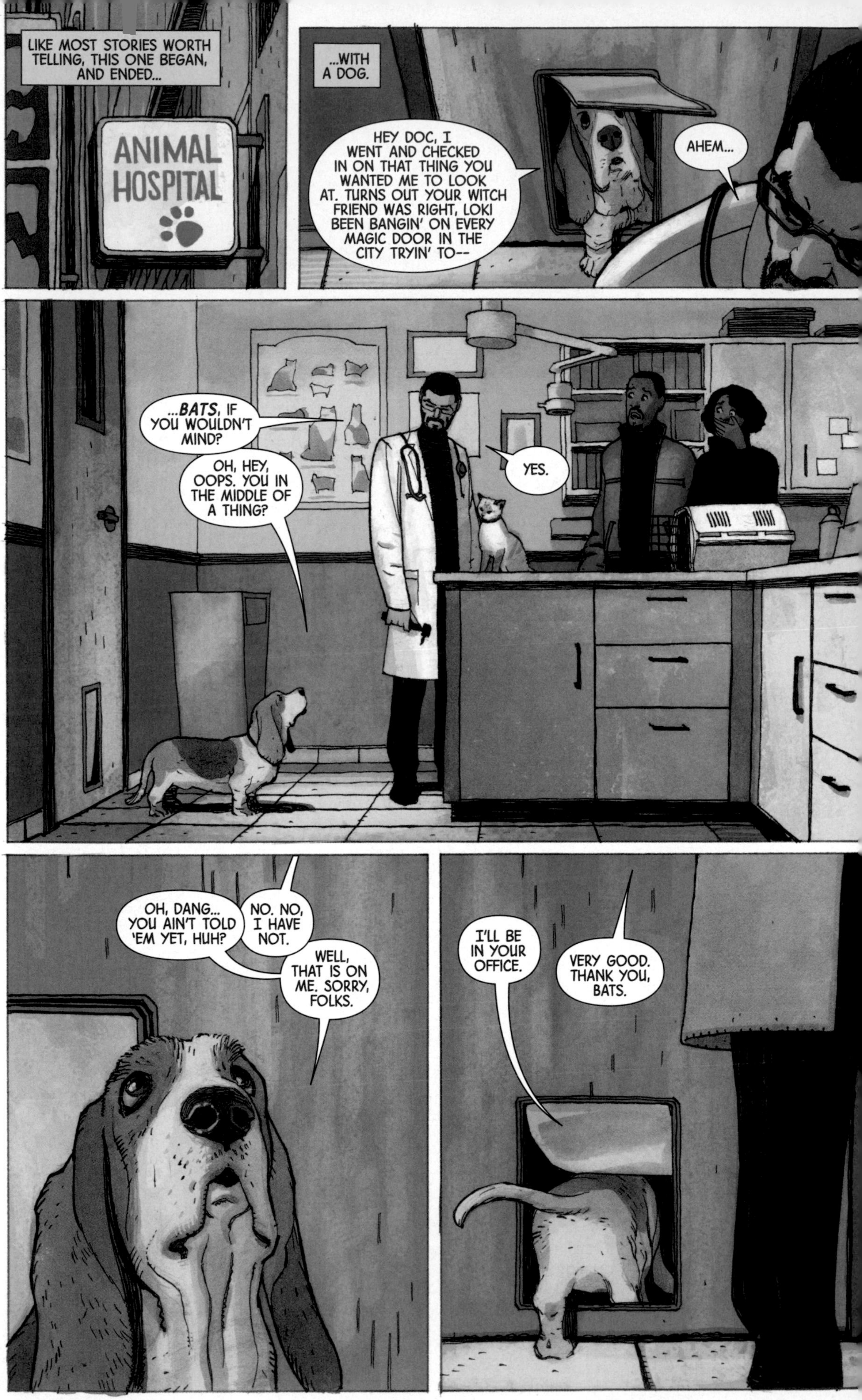
LIKE MOST STORIES WORTH TELLING, THIS ONE BEGAN, AND ENDED...
ANIMAL HOSPITAL
...WITH A DOG.
HEY DOC, I WENT AND CHECKED IN ON THAT THING YOU WANTED ME TO LOOK AT. TURNS OUT YOUR WITCH FRIEND WAS RIGHT, LOKI BEEN BANGIN' ON EVERY MAGIC DOOR IN THE CITY TRYIN' TO--
AHEM...
...BATS, IF YOU WOULDN'T MIND?
OH, HEY, OOPS. YOU IN THE MIDDLE OF A THING?
YES.
OH, DANG... YOU AIN'T TOLD 'EM YET, HUH?
NO. NO, I HAVE NOT.
WELL, THAT IS ON ME. SORRY, FOLKS.
I'LL BE IN YOUR OFFICE.
VERY GOOD. THANK YOU, BATS.

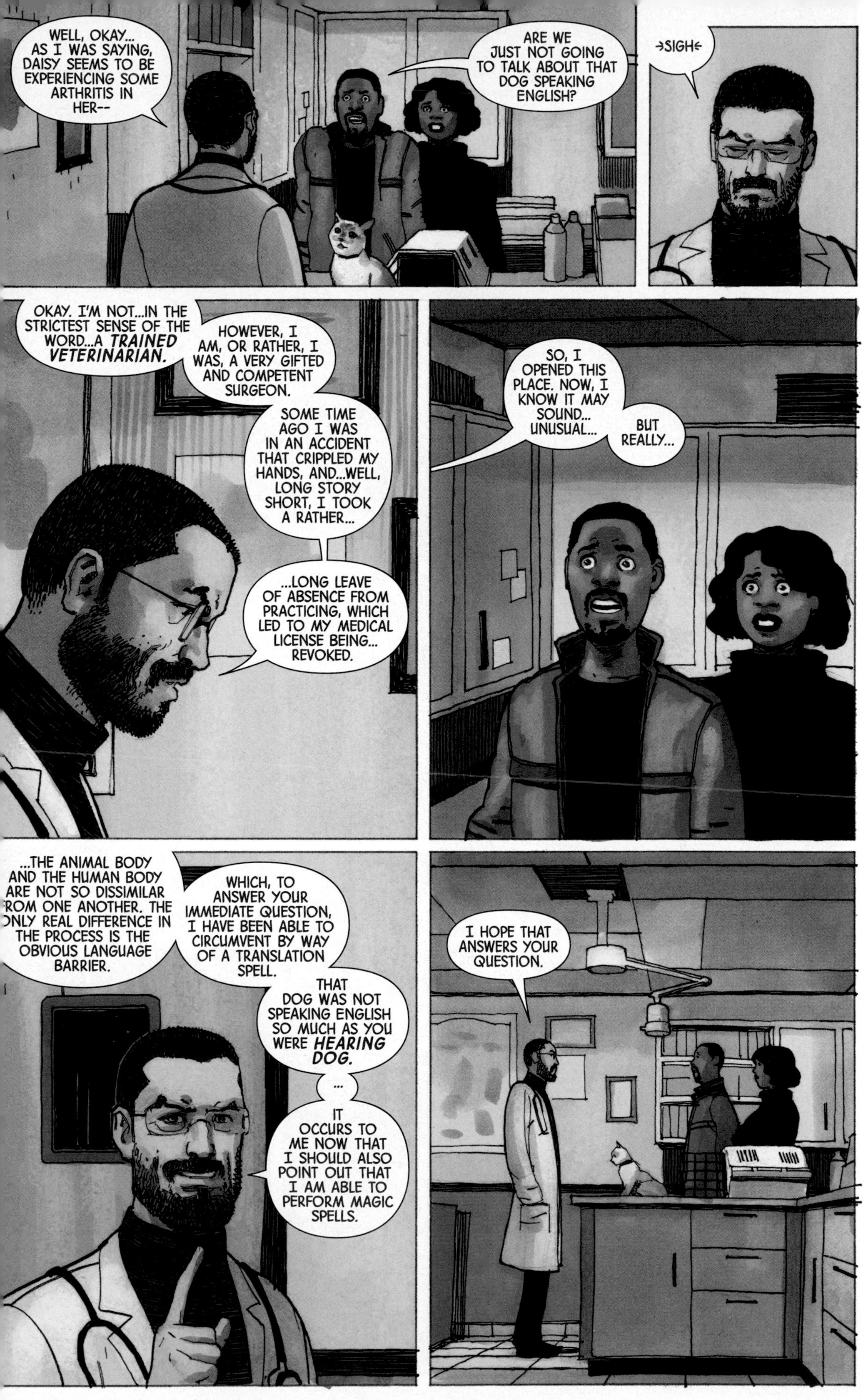
WELL, OKAY... AS I WAS SAYING, DAISY SEEMS TO BE EXPERIENCING SOME ARTHRITIS IN HER--
ARE WE JUST NOT GOING TO TALK ABOUT THAT DOG SPEAKING ENGLISH?
>SIGH<
OKAY. I'M NOT...IN THE STRICTEST SENSE OF THE WORD...A *TRAINED VETERINARIAN.*
HOWEVER, I AM, OR RATHER, I WAS, A VERY GIFTED AND COMPETENT SURGEON.
SOME TIME AGO I WAS IN AN ACCIDENT THAT CRIPPLED MY HANDS, AND...WELL, LONG STORY SHORT, I TOOK A RATHER...
...LONG LEAVE OF ABSENCE FROM PRACTICING, WHICH LED TO MY MEDICAL LICENSE BEING... REVOKED.
SO, I OPENED THIS PLACE. NOW, I KNOW IT MAY SOUND... UNUSUAL...
BUT REALLY...
...THE ANIMAL BODY AND THE HUMAN BODY ARE NOT SO DISSIMILAR FROM ONE ANOTHER. THE ONLY REAL DIFFERENCE IN THE PROCESS IS THE OBVIOUS LANGUAGE BARRIER.
WHICH, TO ANSWER YOUR IMMEDIATE QUESTION, I HAVE BEEN ABLE TO CIRCUMVENT BY WAY OF A TRANSLATION SPELL.
THAT DOG WAS NOT SPEAKING ENGLISH SO MUCH AS YOU WERE *HEARING DOG.*
...
IT OCCURS TO ME NOW THAT I SHOULD ALSO POINT OUT THAT I AM ABLE TO PERFORM MAGIC SPELLS.
I HOPE THAT ANSWERS YOUR QUESTION.

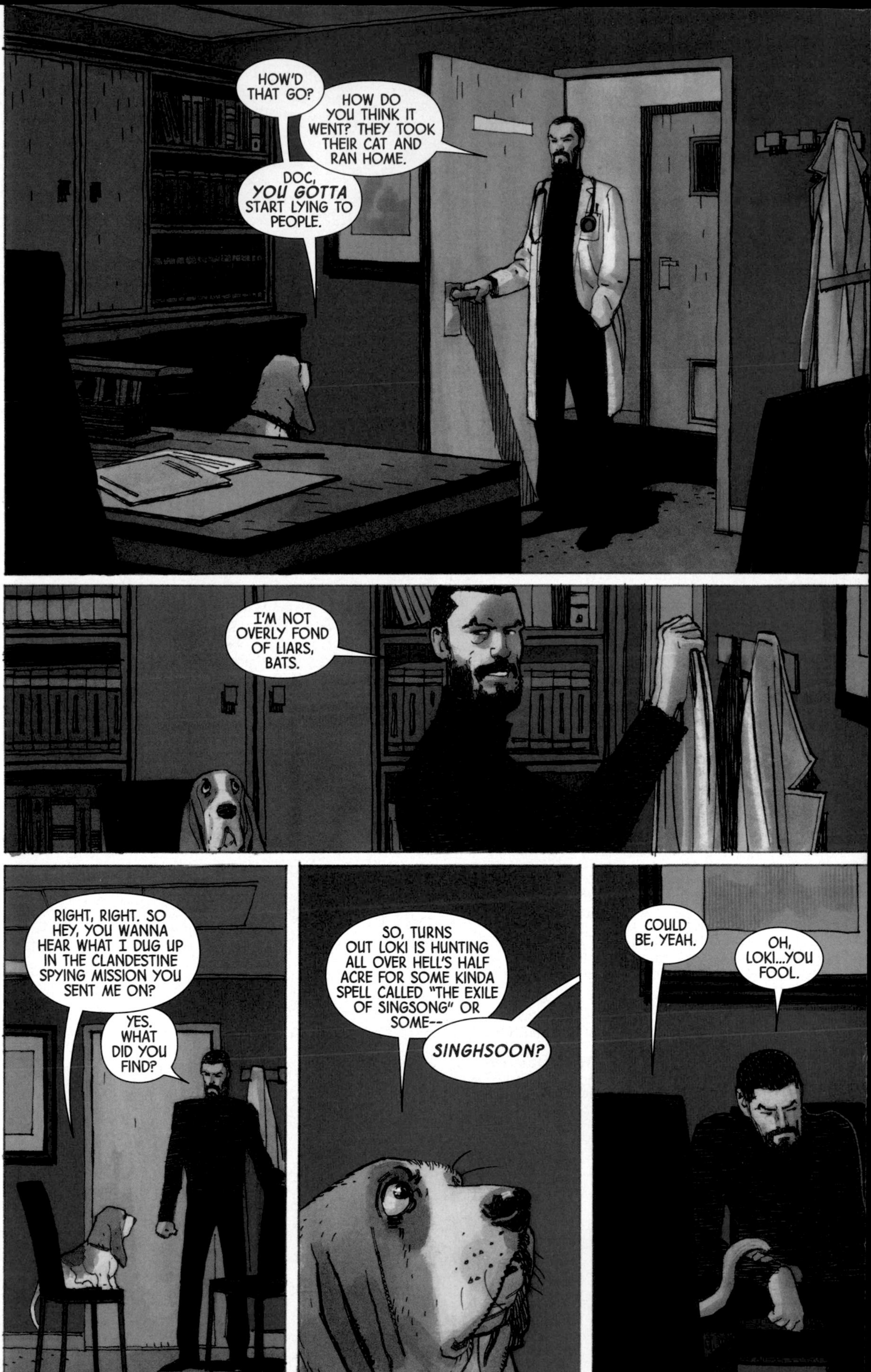

HOW'D THAT GO?
HOW DO YOU THINK IT WENT? THEY TOOK THEIR CAT AND RAN HOME.
DOC, *YOU GOTTA* START LYING TO PEOPLE.
I'M NOT OVERLY FOND OF LIARS, BATS.
RIGHT, RIGHT. SO HEY, YOU WANNA HEAR WHAT I DUG UP IN THE CLANDESTINE SPYING MISSION YOU SENT ME ON?
YES. WHAT DID YOU FIND?
SO, TURNS OUT LOKI IS HUNTING ALL OVER HELL'S HALF ACRE FOR SOME KINDA SPELL CALLED "THE EXILE OF SINGSONG" OR SOME--
SINGHSOON?
COULD BE, YEAH.
OH, LOKI...YOU FOOL.

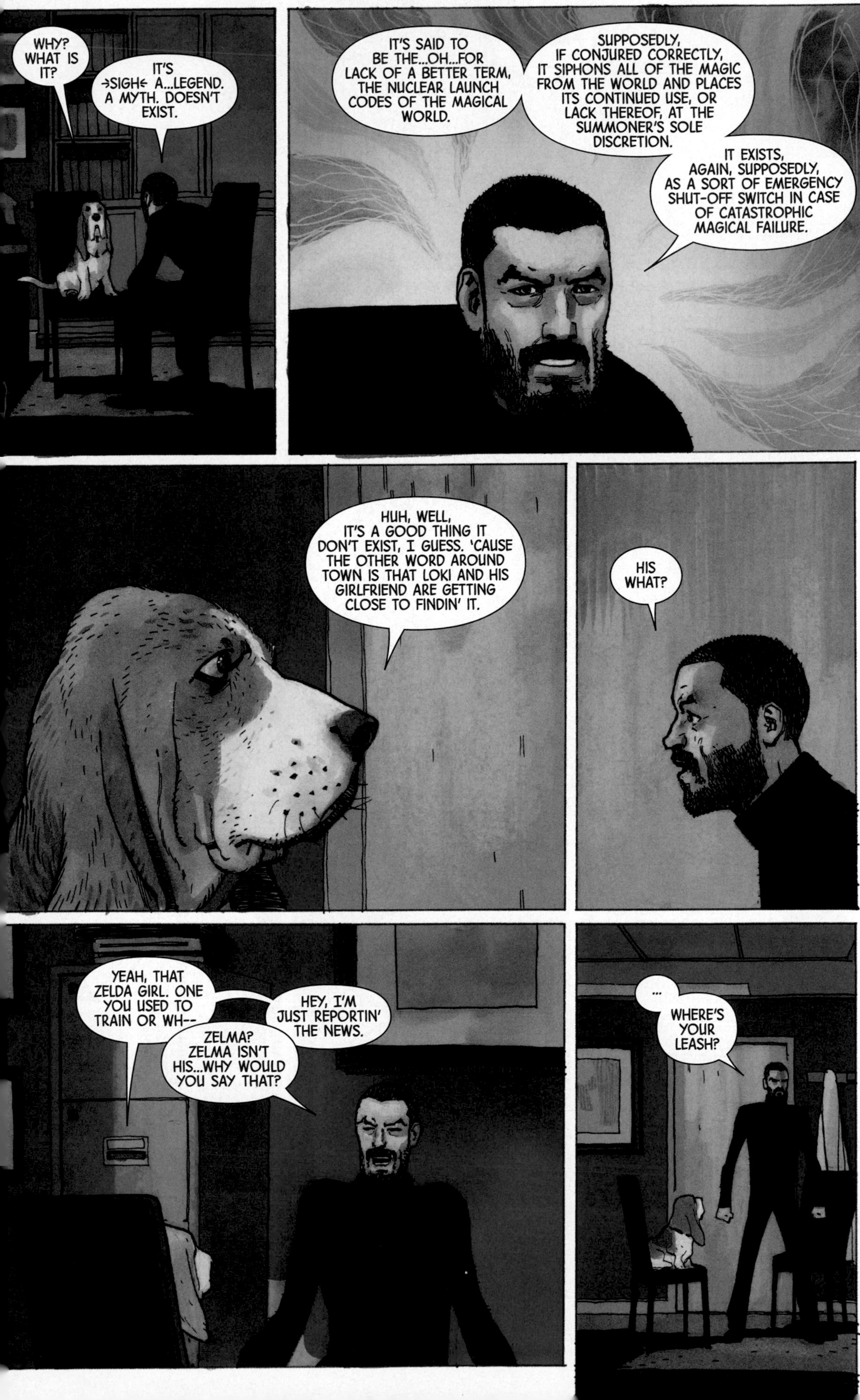
WHY? WHAT IS IT?
IT'S →SIGH← A...LEGEND. A MYTH. DOESN'T EXIST.
IT'S SAID TO BE THE...OH...FOR LACK OF A BETTER TERM, THE NUCLEAR LAUNCH CODES OF THE MAGICAL WORLD.
SUPPOSEDLY, IF CONJURED CORRECTLY, IT SIPHONS ALL OF THE MAGIC FROM THE WORLD AND PLACES ITS CONTINUED USE, OR LACK THEREOF, AT THE SUMMONER'S SOLE DISCRETION.
IT EXISTS, AGAIN, SUPPOSEDLY, AS A SORT OF EMERGENCY SHUT-OFF SWITCH IN CASE OF CATASTROPHIC MAGICAL FAILURE.
HUH, WELL, IT'S A GOOD THING IT DON'T EXIST, I GUESS. 'CAUSE THE OTHER WORD AROUND TOWN IS THAT LOKI AND HIS GIRLFRIEND ARE GETTING CLOSE TO FINDIN' IT.
HIS WHAT?
YEAH, THAT ZELDA GIRL. ONE YOU USED TO TRAIN OR WH--
ZELMA? ZELMA ISN'T HIS...WHY WOULD YOU SAY THAT?
HEY, I'M JUST REPORTIN' THE NEWS.
... WHERE'S YOUR LEASH?

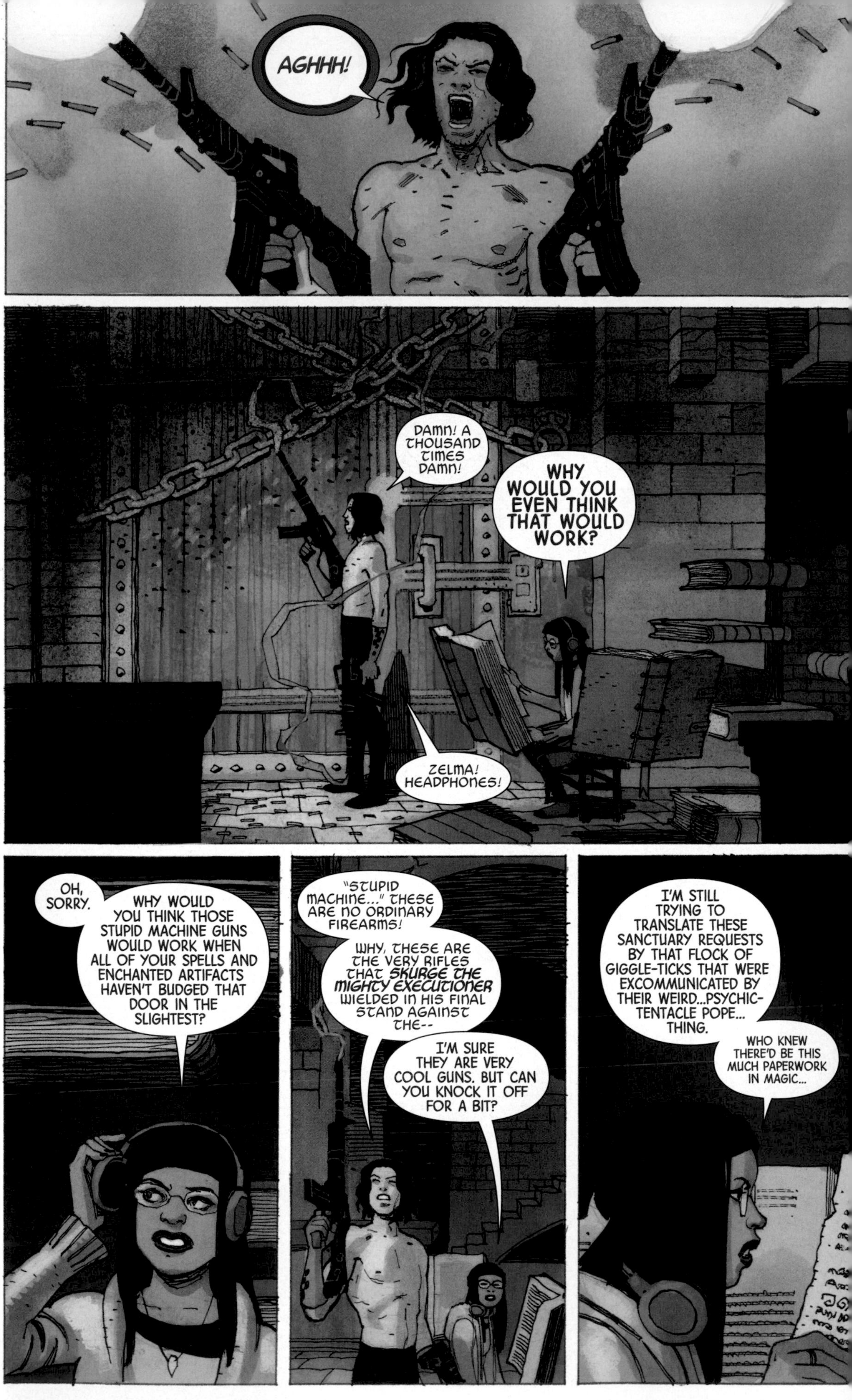
AGHHH!
DAMN! A THOUSAND TIMES DAMN!
WHY WOULD YOU EVEN THINK THAT WOULD WORK?
ZELMA! HEADPHONES!
OH, SORRY.
WHY WOULD YOU THINK THOSE STUPID MACHINE GUNS WOULD WORK WHEN ALL OF YOUR SPELLS AND ENCHANTED ARTIFACTS HAVEN'T BUDGED THAT DOOR IN THE SLIGHTEST?
"STUPID MACHINE..." THESE ARE NO ORDINARY FIREARMS!
WHY, THESE ARE THE VERY RIFLES THAT SKURGE THE MIGHTY EXECUTIONER WIELDED IN HIS FINAL STAND AGAINST THE--
I'M SURE THEY ARE VERY COOL GUNS. BUT CAN YOU KNOCK IT OFF FOR A BIT?
I'M STILL TRYING TO TRANSLATE THESE SANCTUARY REQUESTS BY THAT FLOCK OF GIGGLE-TICKS THAT WERE EXCOMMUNICATED BY THEIR WEIRD...PSYCHIC-TENTACLE POPE... THING.
WHO KNEW THERE'D BE THIS MUCH PAPERWORK IN MAGIC...

AND, YOU KNOW, I'M HAPPY TO HELP YOU, BUT FOR THE LIFE OF ME I WILL NEVER UNDERSTAND THIS OBSESSION WITH THAT DOOR OF YOURS.

MEAN, YOU DON'T VEN KNOW IF THAT SPELL *IS* IN THERE.

MAYBE IF YOU TOLD ME WHAT THIS SINGHSOON THING *DOES, I COULD* HELP YOU FIND--

⇥SIGH⇤ I KNOW I'M OBSESSING... IT'S JUST...

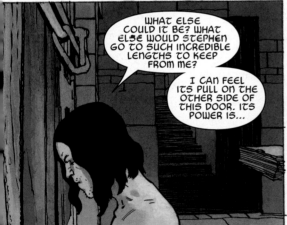

WHAT ELSE COULD IT BE? WHAT ELSE WOULD STEPHEN GO TO SUCH INCREDIBLE LENGTHS TO KEEP FROM ME?

I CAN FEEL ITS PULL ON THE OTHER SIDE OF THIS DOOR. ITS POWER IS...

OH, I SOLVED THAT GIGGLE-TICK PROBLEM, BY THE WAY.

I CREATED AN ENTIRELY NEW REALM FOR THEM TO PLAY IN INSIDE THE HEART OF A PARTICULARLY CHEERFUL DRAGON THAT I KNOW...

WHAT?! LOKI, THAT--THAT IS SOME INCREDIBLY... *EXCESSIVE MAGIC.* H-HOW ARE YOU PAYING FOR ALL OF--

IT'S FINE. IT'S TAKEN CARE OF...

I COULD HAVE DONE IT MYSELF...

I KNOW. PLEASE, DO NOT THINK THIS A LACK OF CONFIDENCE. HONESTLY, IT'S ABSURD THAT YOU STILL CALL YOURSELF AN APPRENTICE...

ZELMA, YOU...YOU ARE SO MUCH MORE...

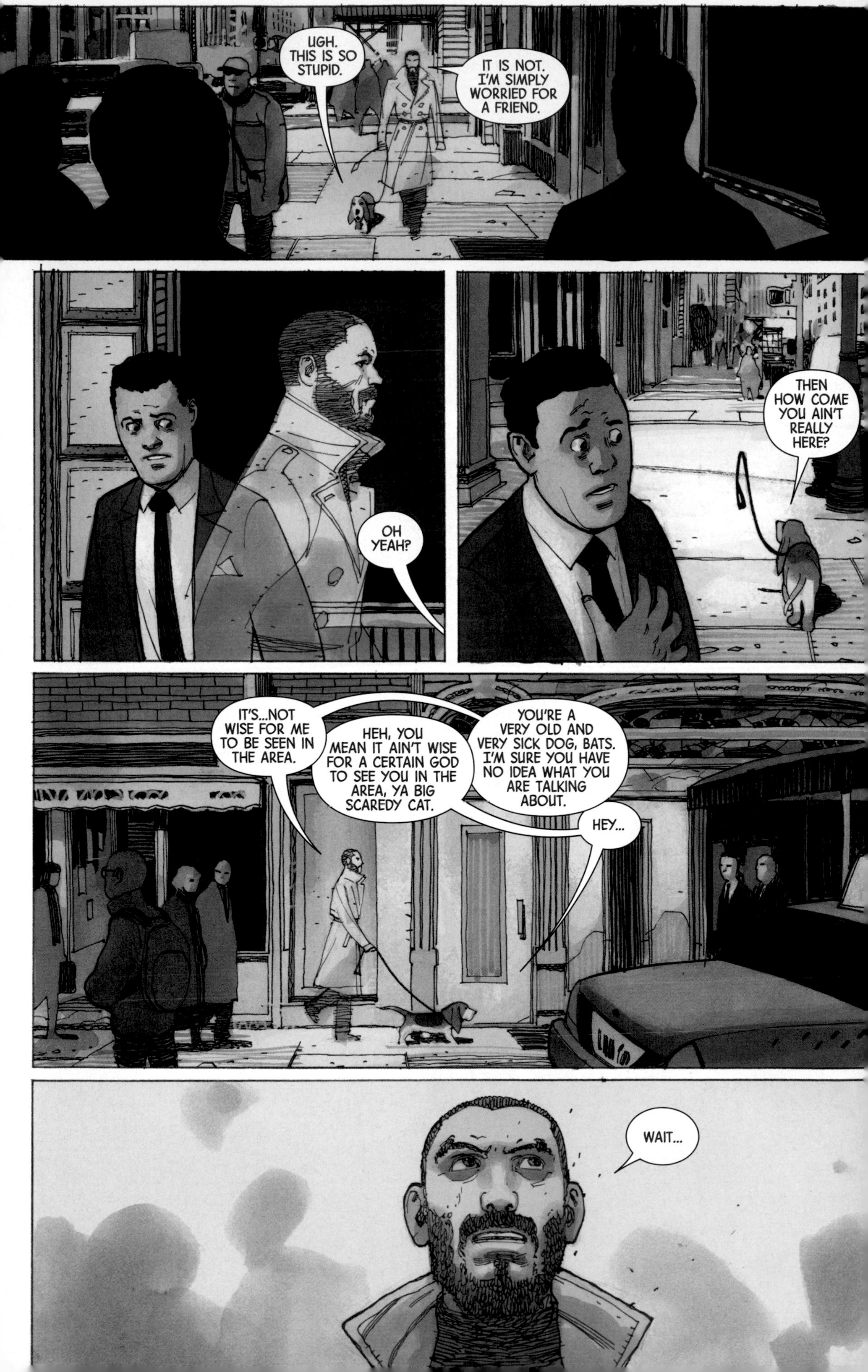
UGH. THIS IS SO STUPID.
IT IS NOT. I'M SIMPLY WORRIED FOR A FRIEND.
OH YEAH?
THEN HOW COME YOU AIN'T REALLY HERE?
IT'S...NOT WISE FOR ME TO BE SEEN IN THE AREA.
HEH, YOU MEAN IT AIN'T WISE FOR A CERTAIN GOD TO SEE YOU IN THE AREA, YA BIG SCAREDY CAT.
YOU'RE A VERY OLD AND VERY SICK DOG, BATS. I'M SURE YOU HAVE NO IDEA WHAT YOU ARE TALKING ABOUT.
HEY...
WAIT...

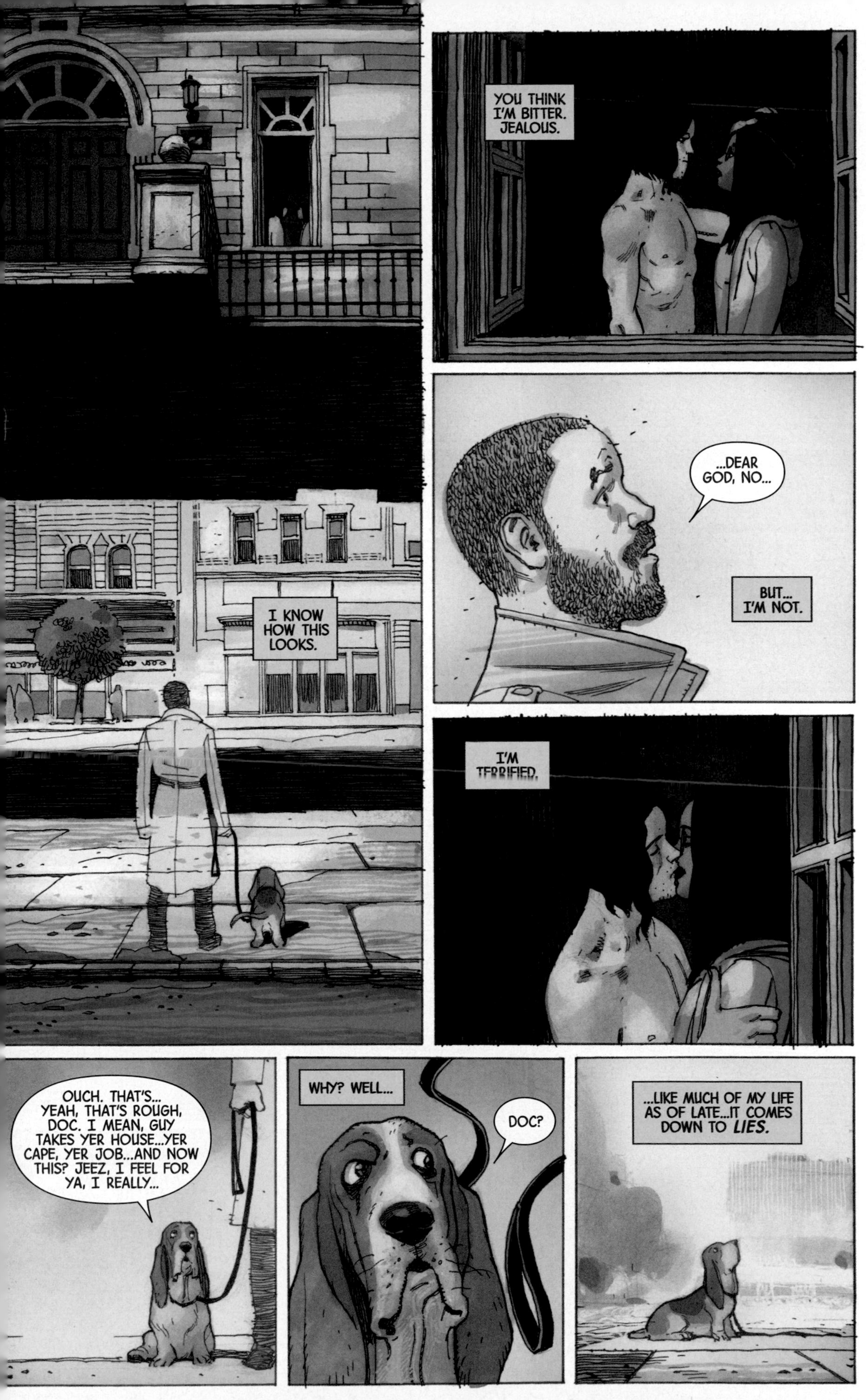
I KNOW HOW THIS LOOKS.
YOU THINK I'M BITTER. JEALOUS.
...DEAR GOD, NO...
BUT... I'M NOT.
I'M TERRIFIED.
OUCH. THAT'S... YEAH, THAT'S ROUGH, DOC. I MEAN, GUY TAKES YER HOUSE...YER CAPE, YER JOB...AND NOW THIS? JEEZ, I FEEL FOR YA, I REALLY...
WHY? WELL...
DOC?
...LIKE MUCH OF MY LIFE AS OF LATE...IT COMES DOWN TO LIES.

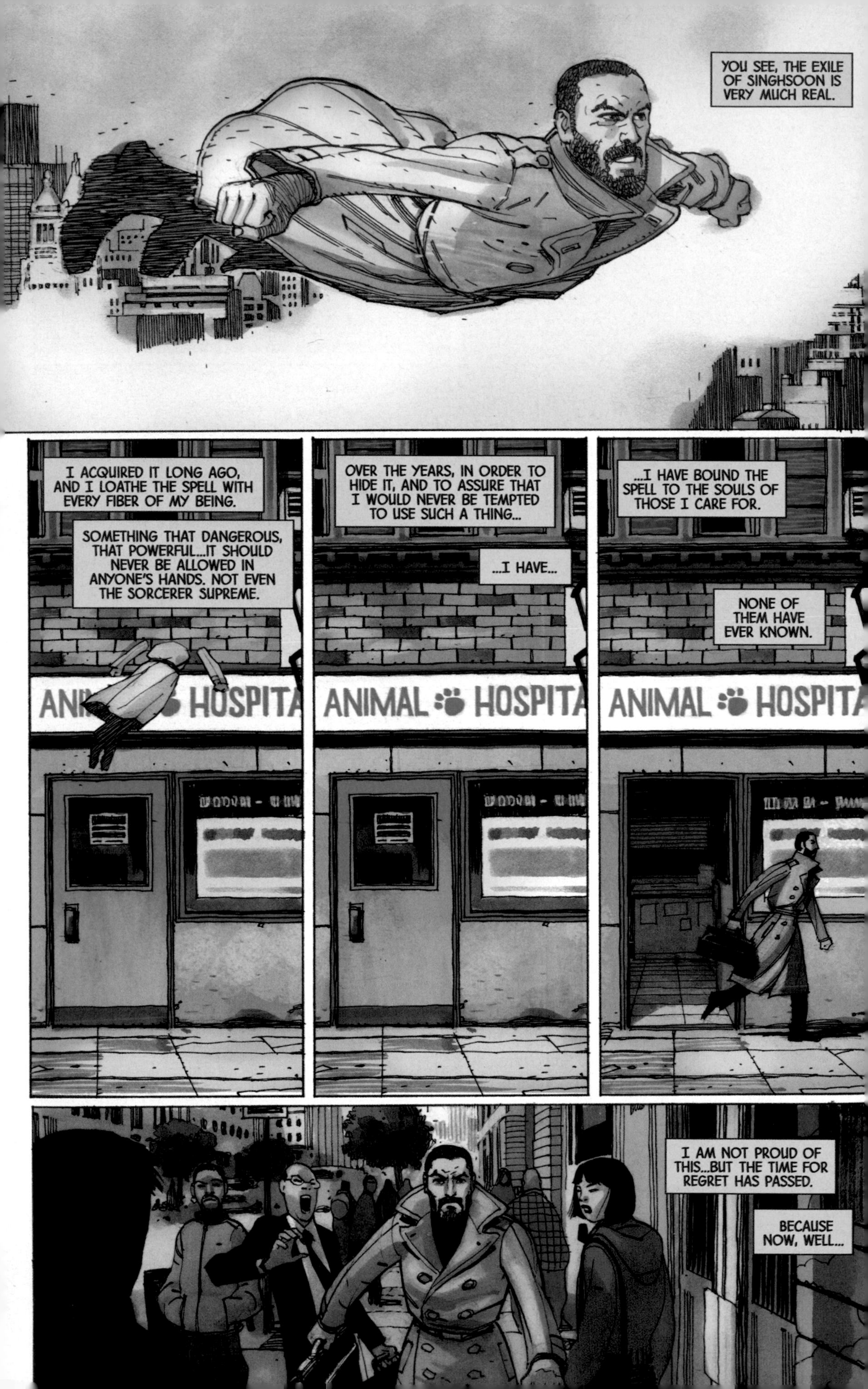
YOU SEE, THE EXILE OF SINGHSOON IS VERY MUCH REAL.
I ACQUIRED IT LONG AGO, AND I LOATHE THE SPELL WITH EVERY FIBER OF MY BEING.
SOMETHING THAT DANGEROUS, THAT POWERFUL...IT SHOULD NEVER BE ALLOWED IN ANYONE'S HANDS. NOT EVEN THE SORCERER SUPREME.
ANIMAL HOSPITA
OVER THE YEARS, IN ORDER TO HIDE IT, AND TO ASSURE THAT I WOULD NEVER BE TEMPTED TO USE SUCH A THING...
...I HAVE...
ANIMAL HOSPITA
...I HAVE BOUND THE SPELL TO THE SOULS OF THOSE I CARE FOR.
NONE OF THEM HAVE EVER KNOWN.
ANIMAL HOSPITA
I AM NOT PROUD OF THIS...BUT THE TIME FOR REGRET HAS PASSED.
BECAUSE NOW, WELL...

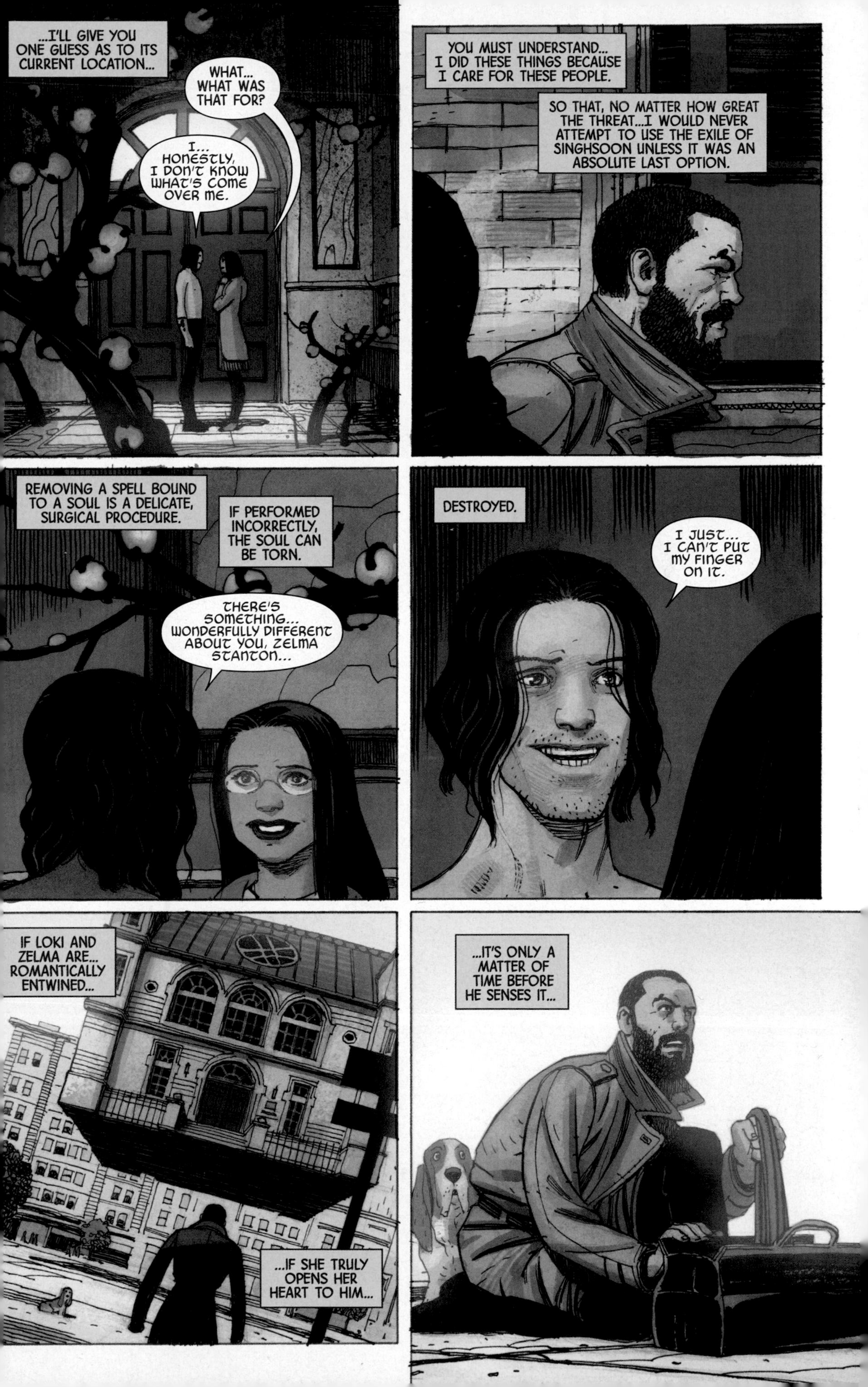

...I'LL GIVE YOU ONE GUESS AS TO ITS CURRENT LOCATION...
WHAT... WHAT WAS THAT FOR?
I... HONESTLY, I DON'T KNOW WHAT'S COME OVER ME.
YOU MUST UNDERSTAND... I DID THESE THINGS BECAUSE I CARE FOR THESE PEOPLE.
SO THAT, NO MATTER HOW GREAT THE THREAT...I WOULD NEVER ATTEMPT TO USE THE EXILE OF SINGHSOON UNLESS IT WAS AN ABSOLUTE LAST OPTION.
REMOVING A SPELL BOUND TO A SOUL IS A DELICATE, SURGICAL PROCEDURE.
IF PERFORMED INCORRECTLY, THE SOUL CAN BE TORN.
THERE'S SOMETHING... WONDERFULLY DIFFERENT ABOUT YOU, ZELMA STANTON...
DESTROYED.
I JUST... I CAN'T PUT MY FINGER ON IT.
IF LOKI AND ZELMA ARE... ROMANTICALLY ENTWINED...
...IF SHE TRULY OPENS HER HEART TO HIM...
...IT'S ONLY A MATTER OF TIME BEFORE HE SENSES IT...

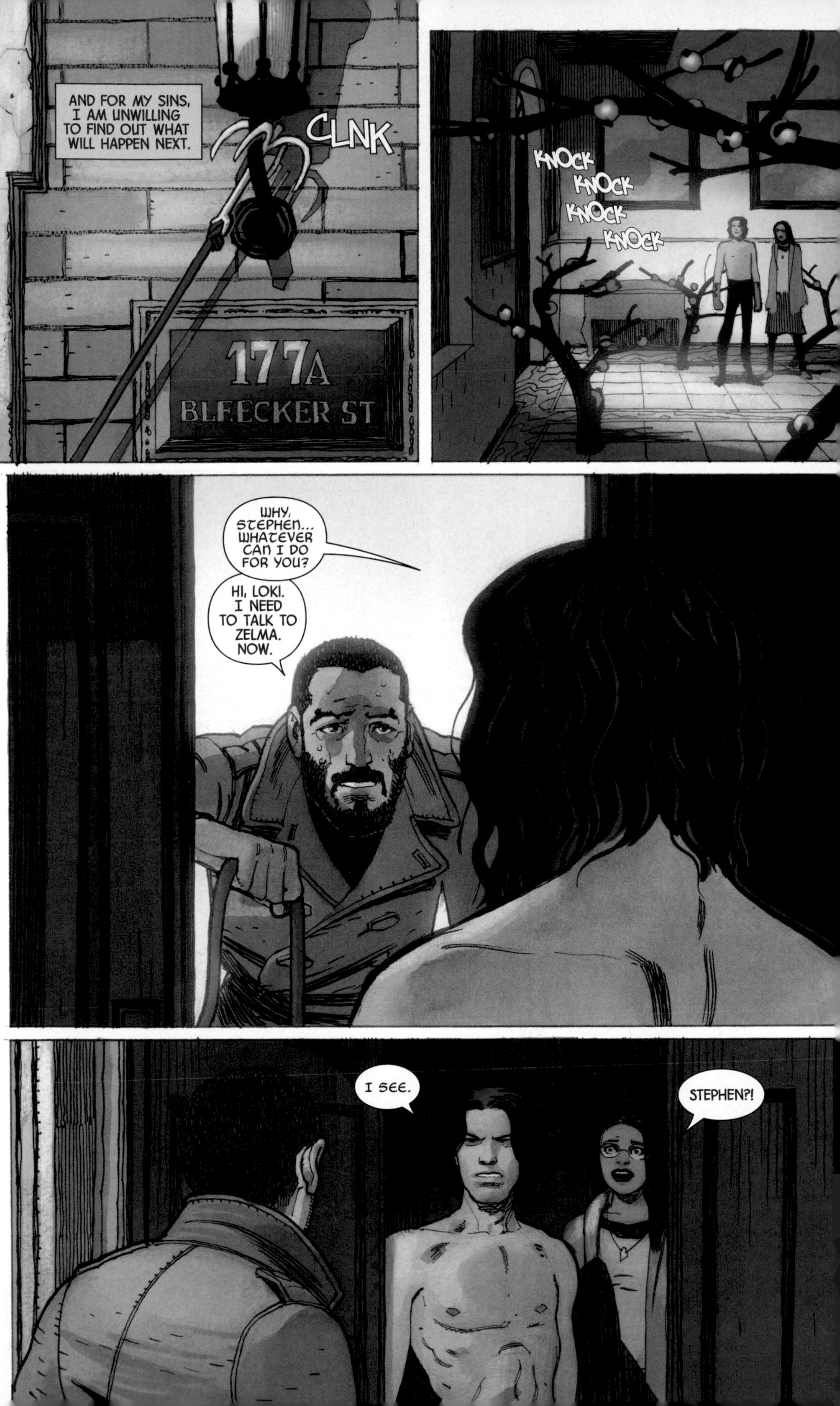
AND FOR MY SINS, I AM UNWILLING TO FIND OUT WHAT WILL HAPPEN NEXT.
CLNK
177A
BLEECKER ST
KNOCK
KNOCK
KNOCK
KNOCK
WHY, STEPHEN... WHATEVER CAN I DO FOR YOU?
HI, LOKI. I NEED TO TALK TO ZELMA. NOW.
I SEE.
STEPHEN?!

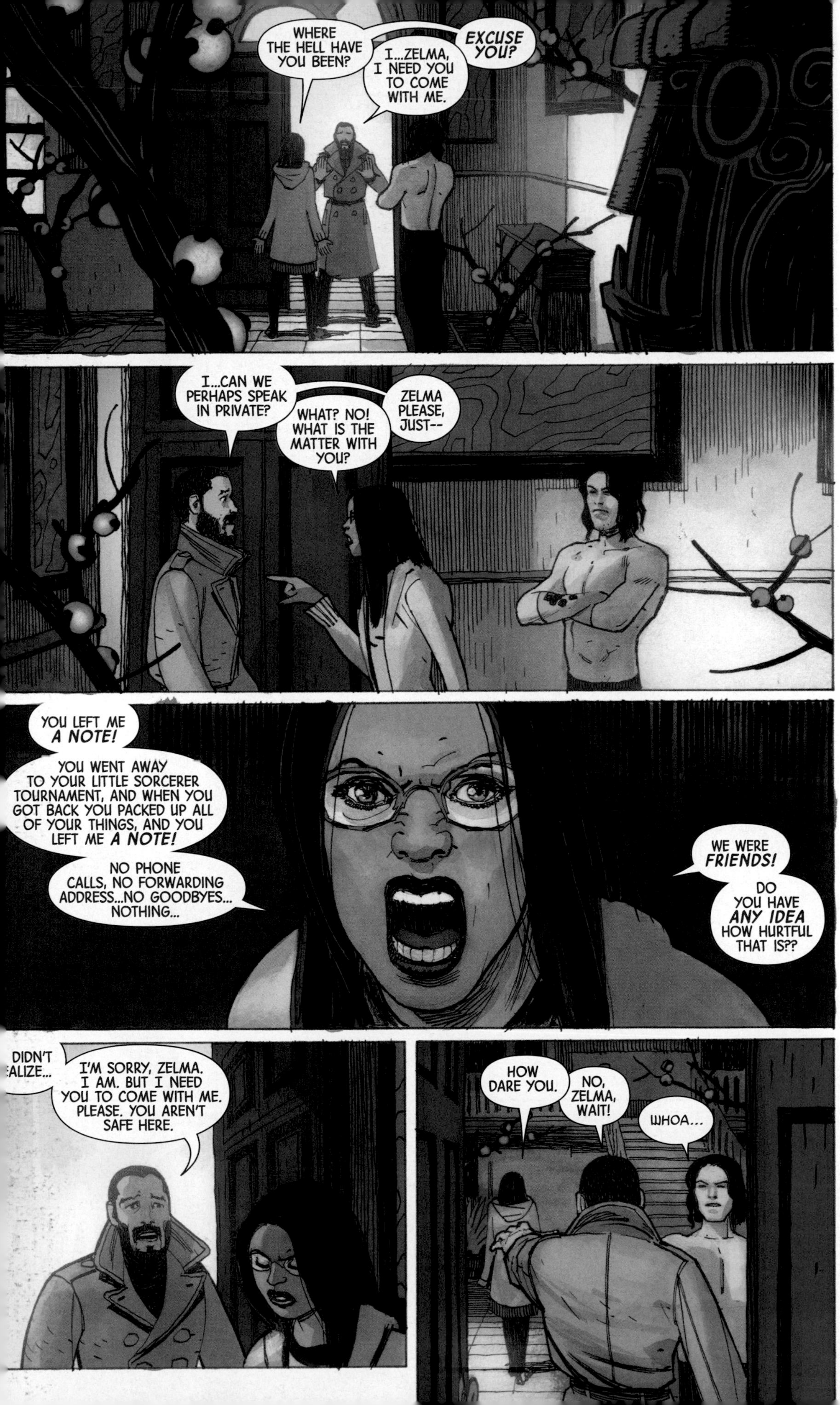
WHERE THE HELL HAVE YOU BEEN?
I...ZELMA, I NEED YOU TO COME WITH ME.
EXCUSE YOU?
I...CAN WE PERHAPS SPEAK IN PRIVATE?
WHAT? NO! WHAT IS THE MATTER WITH YOU?
ZELMA PLEASE, JUST--
YOU LEFT ME A NOTE!
YOU WENT AWAY TO YOUR LITTLE SORCERER TOURNAMENT, AND WHEN YOU GOT BACK YOU PACKED UP ALL OF YOUR THINGS, AND YOU LEFT ME A NOTE!
NO PHONE CALLS, NO FORWARDING ADDRESS...NO GOODBYES... NOTHING...
WE WERE FRIENDS!
DO YOU HAVE ANY IDEA HOW HURTFUL THAT IS??
DIDN'T EALIZE...
I'M SORRY, ZELMA. I AM. BUT I NEED YOU TO COME WITH ME. PLEASE. YOU AREN'T SAFE HERE.
HOW DARE YOU.
NO, ZELMA, WAIT!
WHOA...

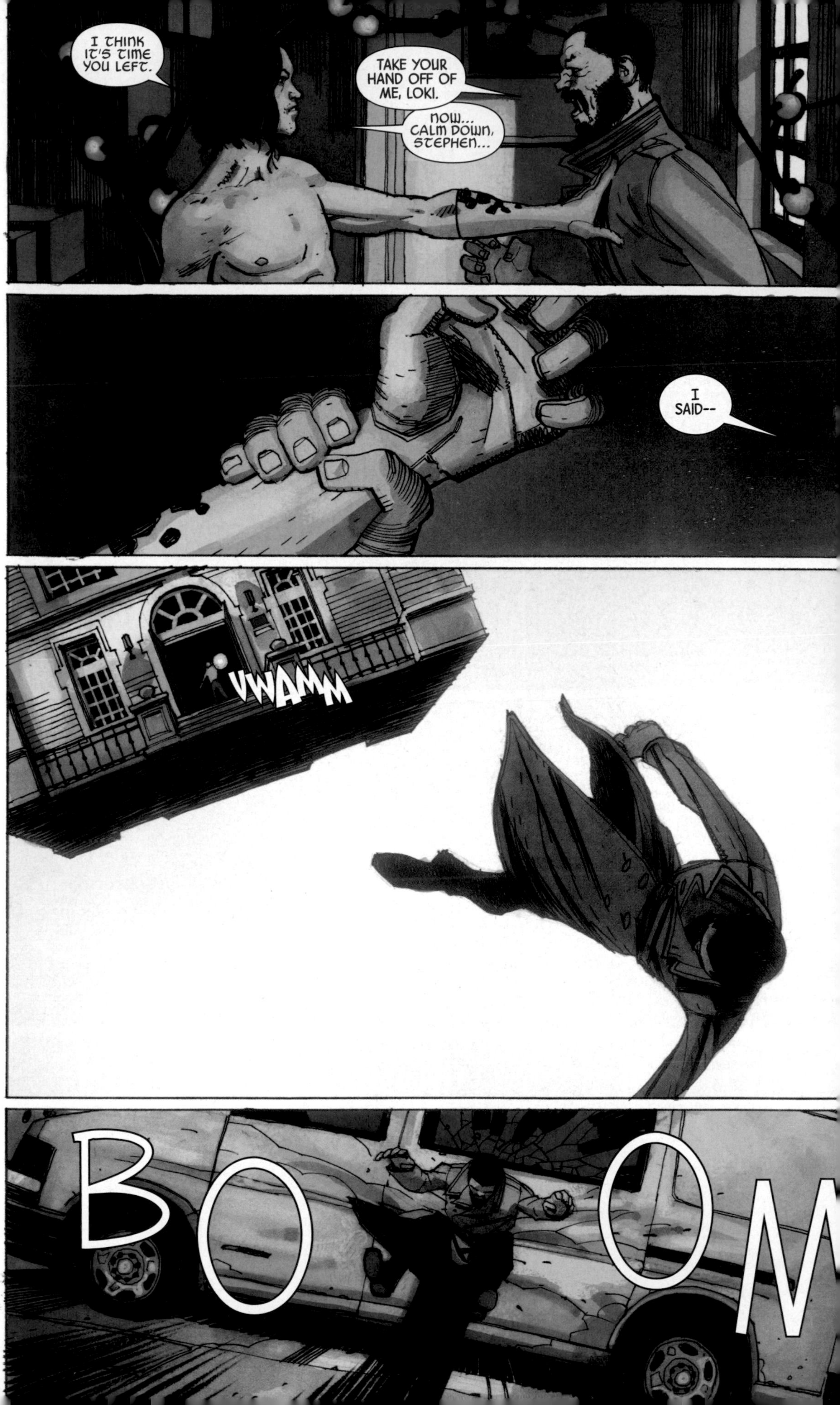
I THINK IT'S TIME YOU LEFT.
TAKE YOUR HAND OFF OF ME, LOKI.
NOW... CALM DOWN, STEPHEN...
I SAID--
VWAMM
BOOM

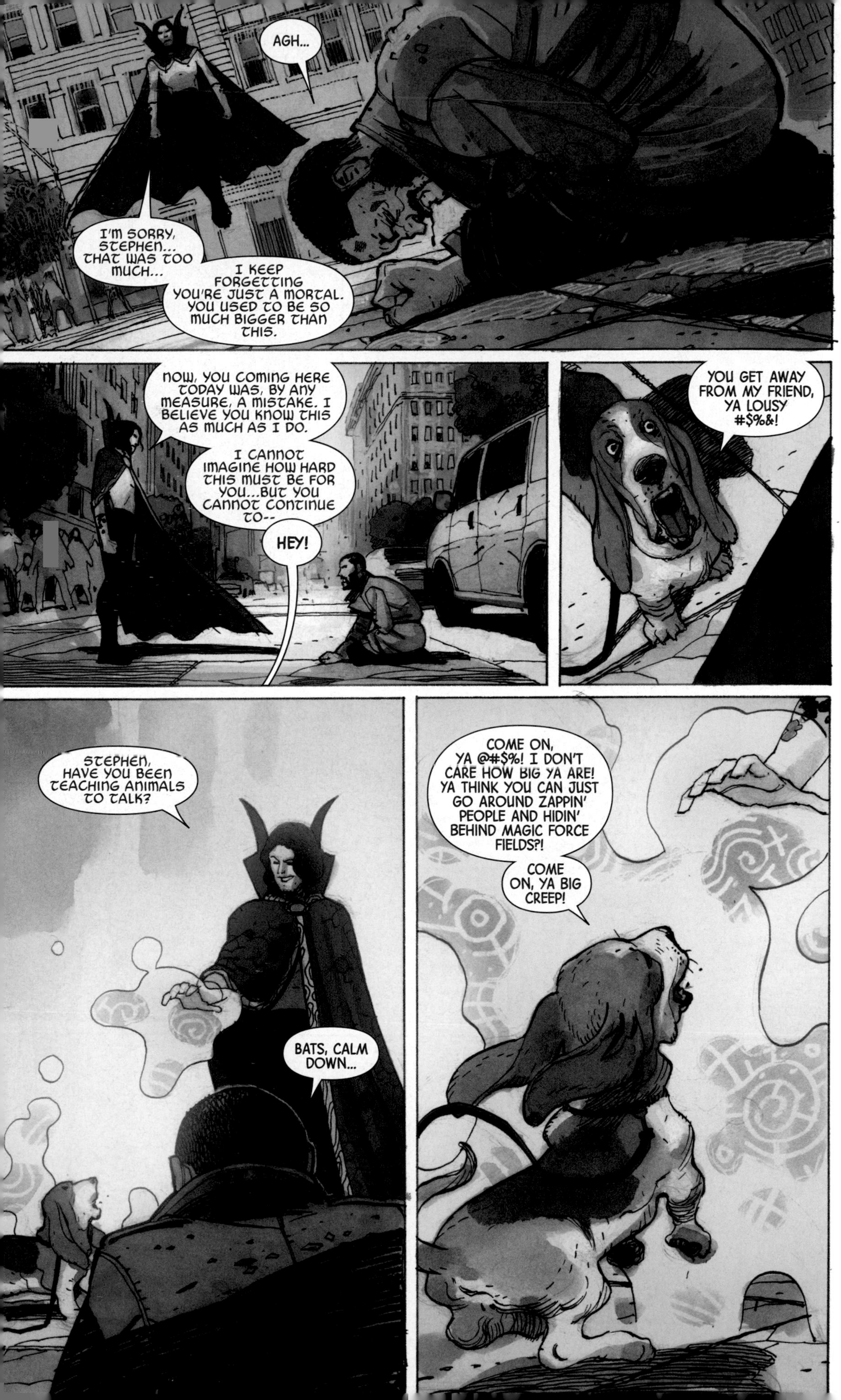
AGH...
I'M SORRY, STEPHEN... THAT WAS TOO MUCH...
I KEEP FORGETTING YOU'RE JUST A MORTAL. YOU USED TO BE SO MUCH BIGGER THAN THIS.
NOW, YOU COMING HERE TODAY WAS, BY ANY MEASURE, A MISTAKE. I BELIEVE YOU KNOW THIS AS MUCH AS I DO.
I CANNOT IMAGINE HOW HARD THIS MUST BE FOR YOU...BUT YOU CANNOT CONTINUE TO--
HEY!
YOU GET AWAY FROM MY FRIEND, YA LOUSY #$%&!
STEPHEN, HAVE YOU BEEN TEACHING ANIMALS TO TALK?
BATS, CALM DOWN...
COME ON, YA @#$%! I DON'T CARE HOW BIG YA ARE! YA THINK YOU CAN JUST GO AROUND ZAPPIN' PEOPLE AND HIDIN' BEHIND MAGIC FORCE FIELDS?!
COME ON, YA BIG CREEP!

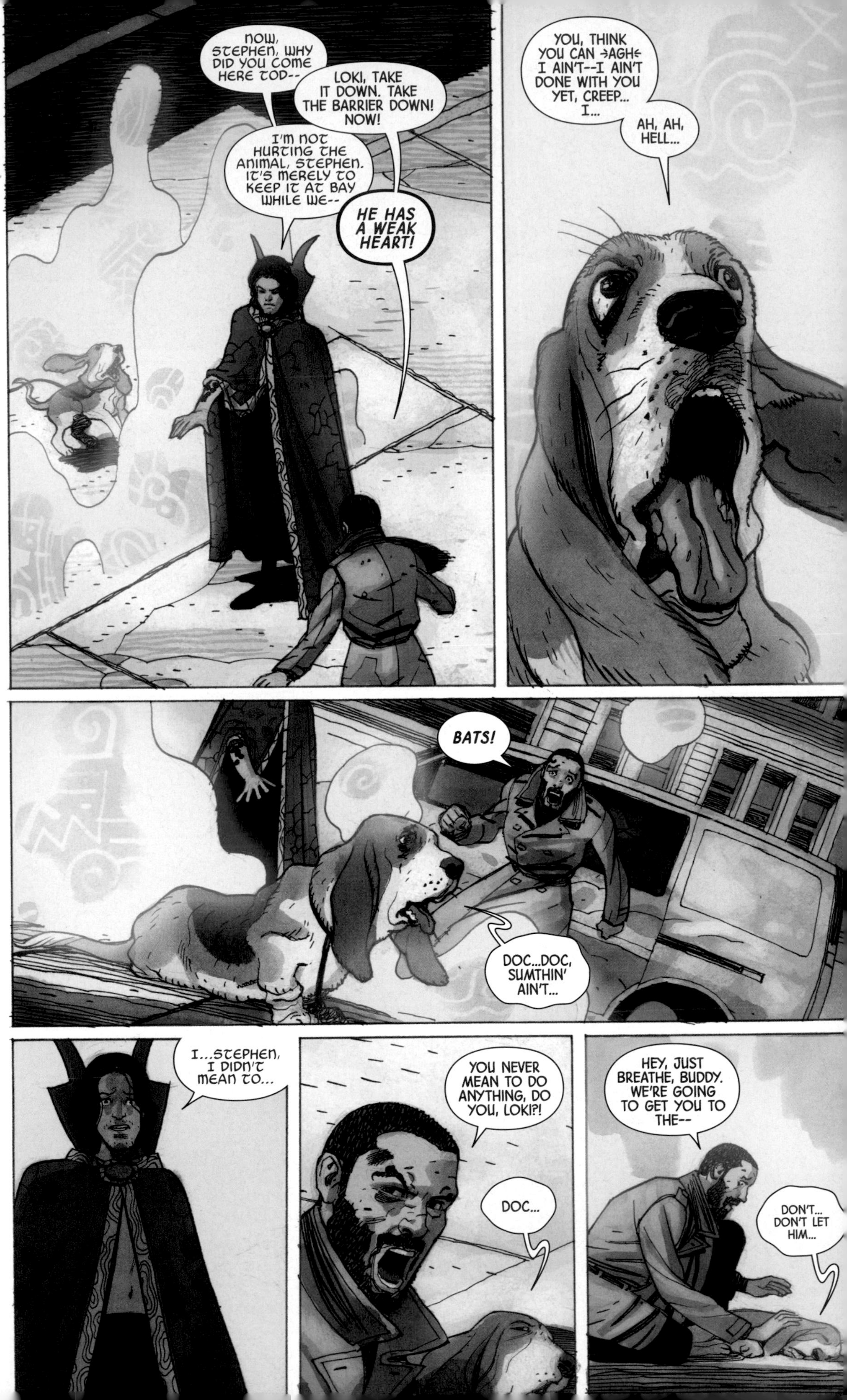
NOW, STEPHEN, WHY DID YOU COME HERE TOD--
LOKI, TAKE IT DOWN. TAKE THE BARRIER DOWN! NOW!
I'M NOT HURTING THE ANIMAL, STEPHEN. IT'S MERELY TO KEEP IT AT BAY WHILE WE--
HE HAS A WEAK HEART!
YOU, THINK YOU CAN ⋺AGH⋹ I AIN'T--I AIN'T DONE WITH YOU YET, CREEP... I...
AH, AH, HELL...
BATS!
DOC...DOC, SUMTHIN' AIN'T...
I...STEPHEN, I DIDN'T MEAN TO...
YOU NEVER MEAN TO DO ANYTHING, DO YOU, LOKI?!
DOC...
HEY, JUST BREATHE, BUDDY. WE'RE GOING TO GET YOU TO THE--
DON'T... DON'T LET HIM...

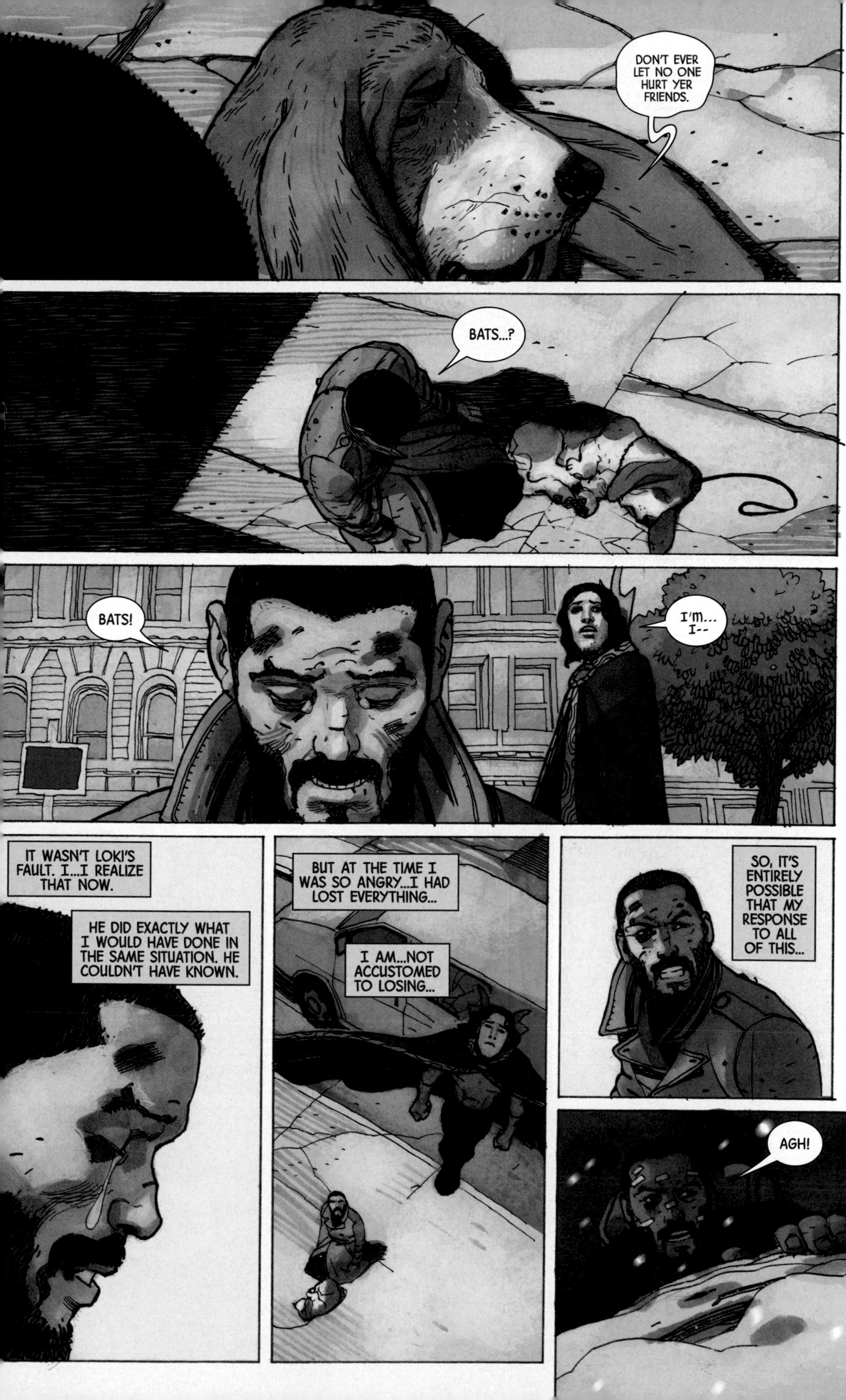
DON'T EVER LET NO ONE HURT YER FRIENDS.
BATS...?
BATS!
I'M... I--
IT WASN'T LOKI'S FAULT. I...I REALIZE THAT NOW.
HE DID EXACTLY WHAT I WOULD HAVE DONE IN THE SAME SITUATION. HE COULDN'T HAVE KNOWN.
BUT AT THE TIME I WAS SO ANGRY...I HAD LOST EVERYTHING...
I AM...NOT ACCUSTOMED TO LOSING...
SO, IT'S ENTIRELY POSSIBLE THAT MY RESPONSE TO ALL OF THIS...
AGH!

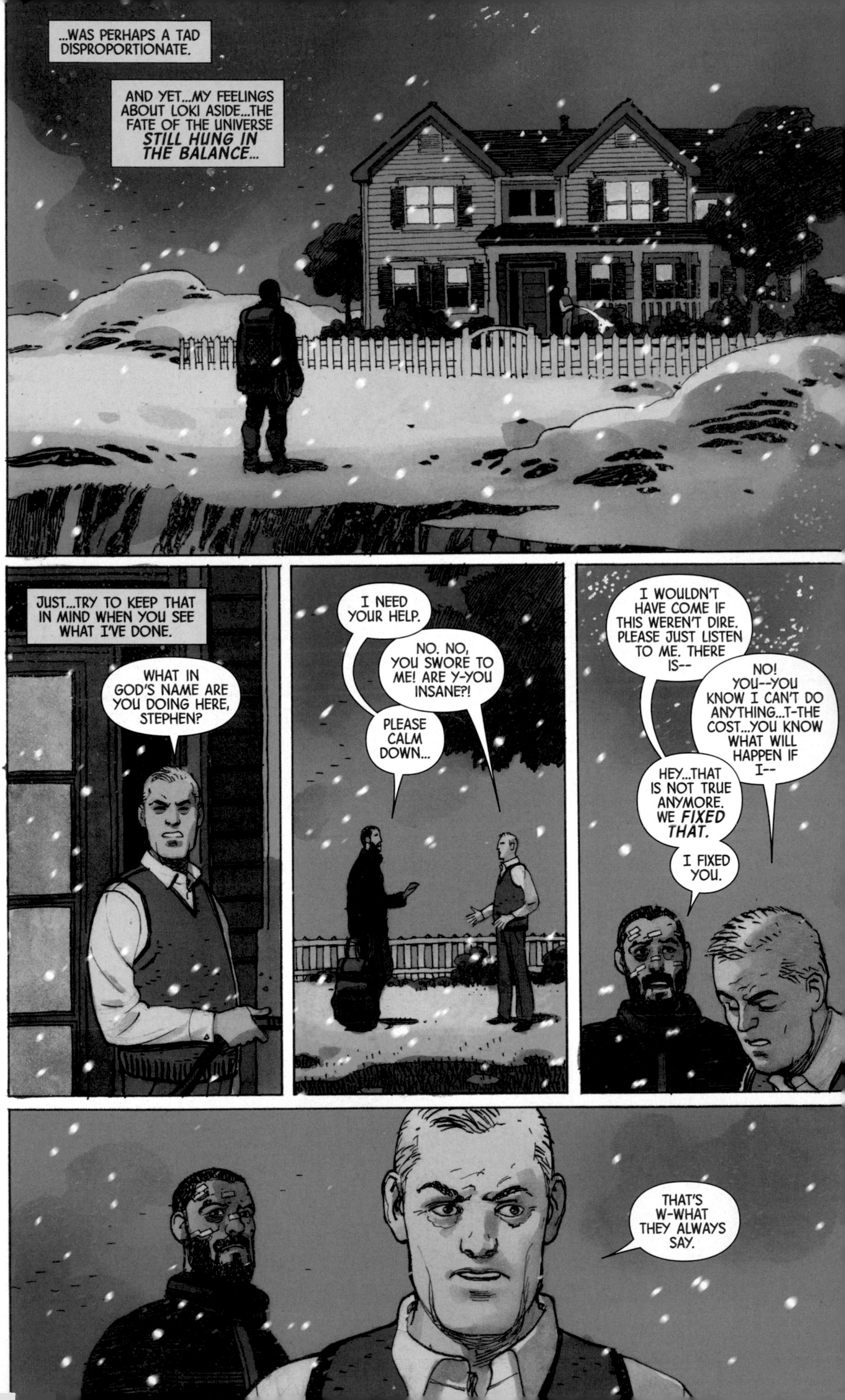
...WAS PERHAPS A TAD DISPROPORTIONATE.
AND YET...MY FEELINGS ABOUT LOKI ASIDE...THE FATE OF THE UNIVERSE STILL HUNG IN THE BALANCE...
JUST...TRY TO KEEP THAT IN MIND WHEN YOU SEE WHAT I'VE DONE.
WHAT IN GOD'S NAME ARE YOU DOING HERE, STEPHEN?
I NEED YOUR HELP.
NO. NO, YOU SWORE TO ME! ARE Y-YOU INSANE?!
PLEASE CALM DOWN...
I WOULDN'T HAVE COME IF THIS WEREN'T DIRE. PLEASE JUST LISTEN TO ME. THERE IS--
NO! YOU--YOU KNOW I CAN'T DO ANYTHING...T-THE COST...YOU KNOW WHAT WILL HAPPEN IF I--
HEY...THAT IS NOT TRUE ANYMORE. WE FIXED THAT.
I FIXED YOU.
THAT'S W-WHAT THEY ALWAYS SAY.

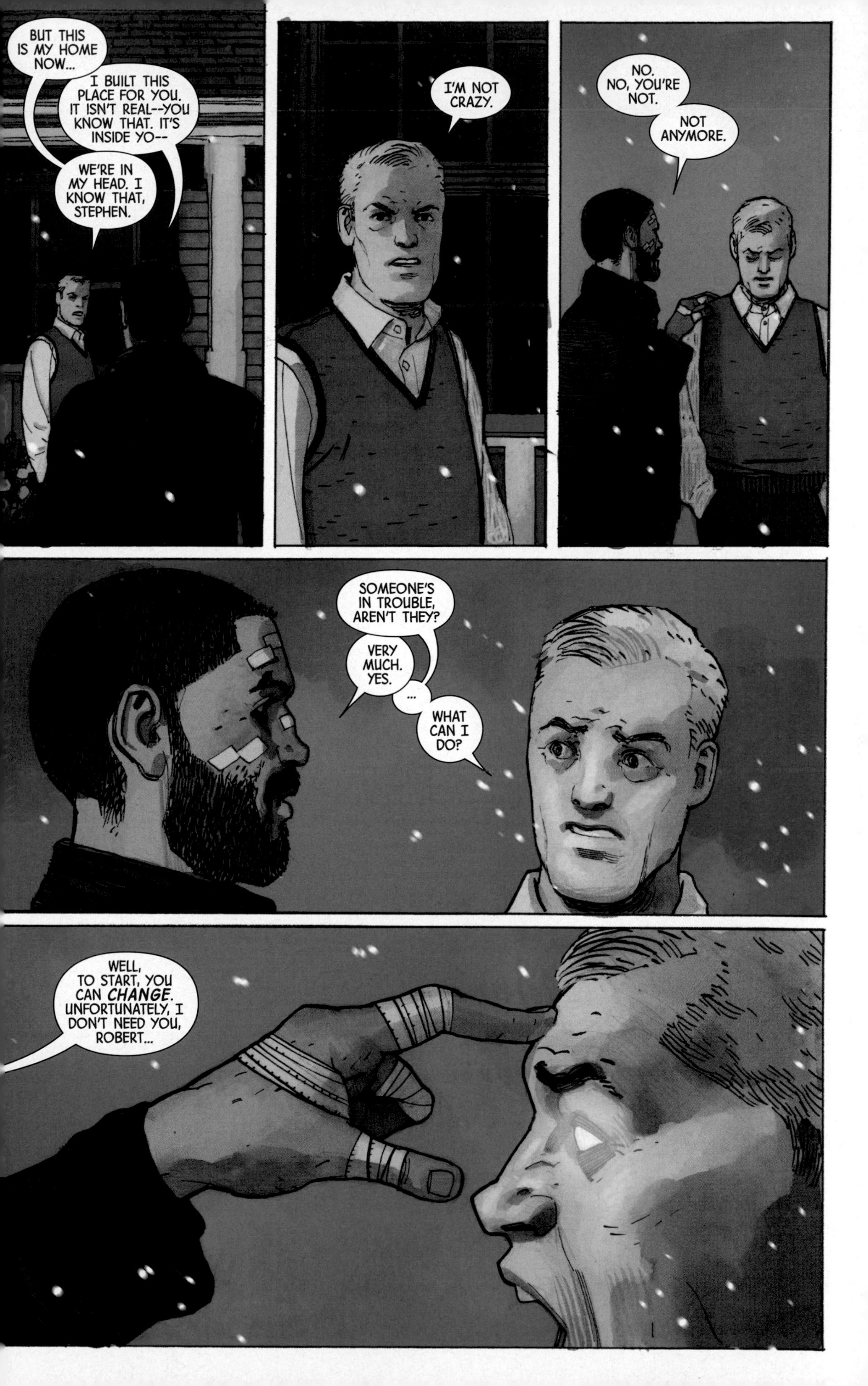
BUT THIS IS MY HOME NOW...
I BUILT THIS PLACE FOR YOU. IT ISN'T REAL--YOU KNOW THAT. IT'S INSIDE YO--
WE'RE IN MY HEAD. I KNOW THAT, STEPHEN.
I'M NOT CRAZY.
NO. NO, YOU'RE NOT.
NOT ANYMORE.
SOMEONE'S IN TROUBLE, AREN'T THEY?
VERY MUCH. YES.
...
WHAT CAN I DO?
WELL, TO START, YOU CAN CHANGE. UNFORTUNATELY, I DON'T NEED YOU, ROBERT...

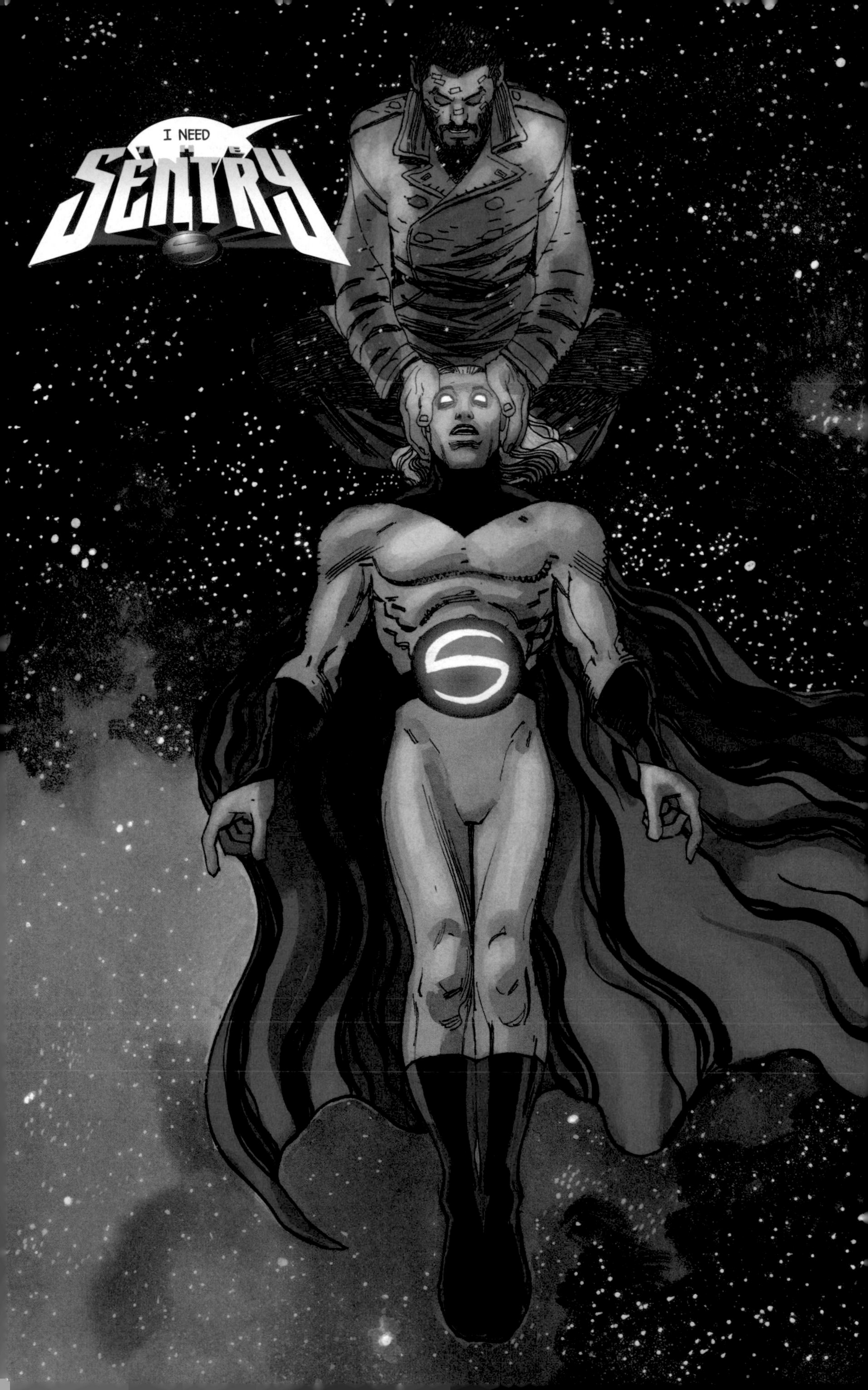
I NEED
THE
SENTRY

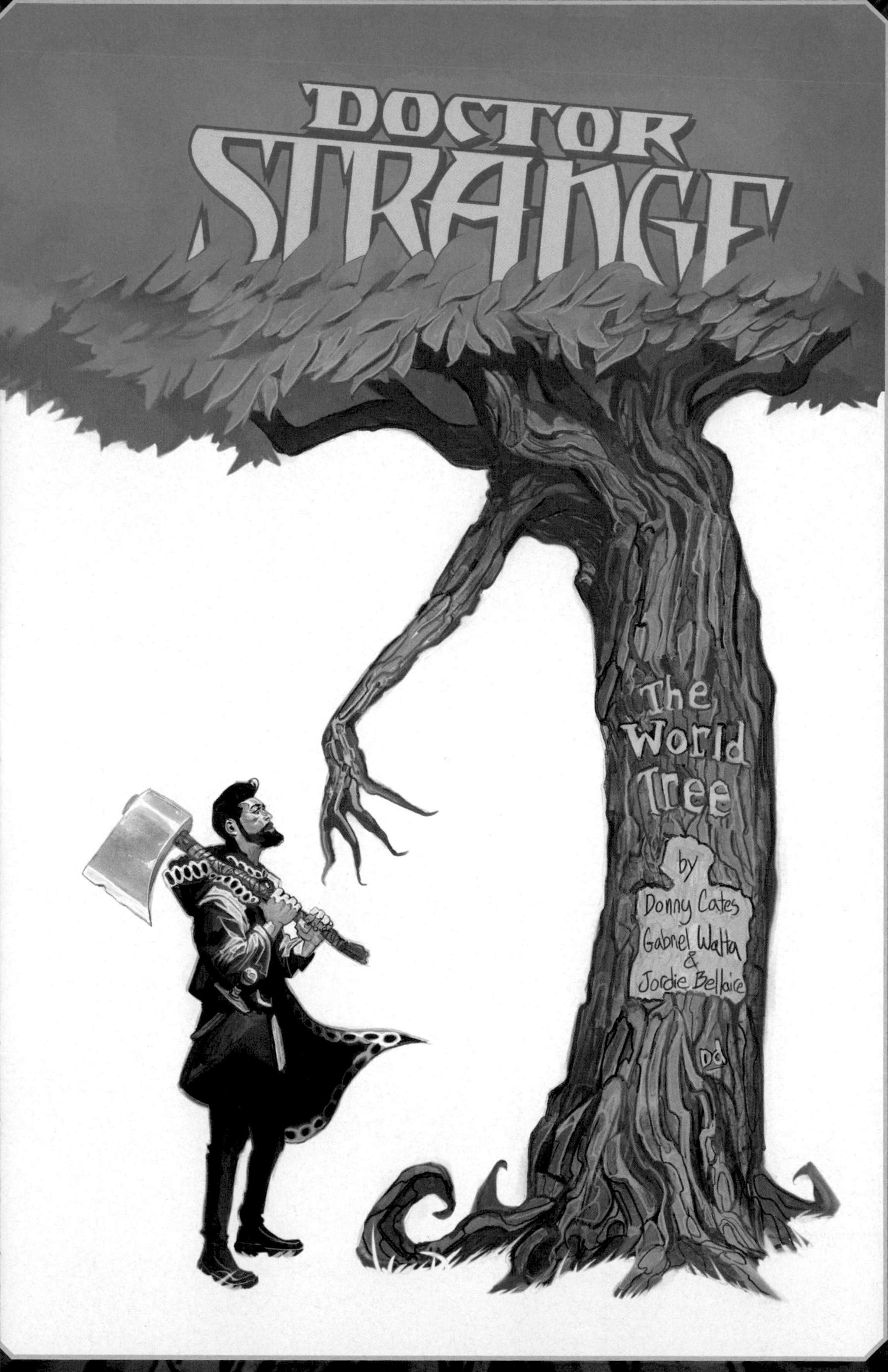
DOCTOR STRANGE
The World Tree
by
Donny Cates
Gabriel Walta
&
Jordie Bellaire
DC

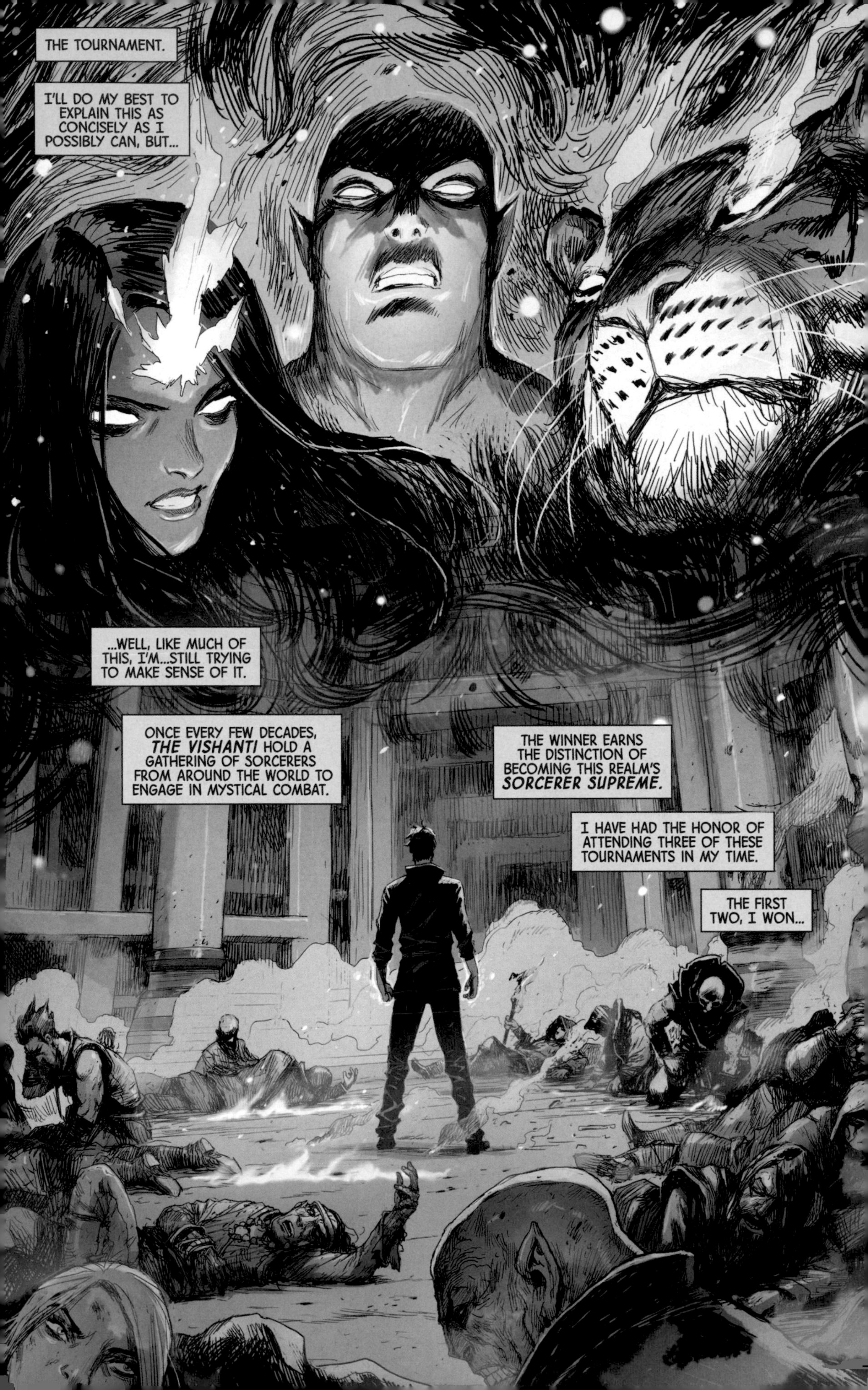
THE TOURNAMENT.
I'LL DO MY BEST TO EXPLAIN THIS AS CONCISELY AS I POSSIBLY CAN, BUT...
...WELL, LIKE MUCH OF THIS, I'M...STILL TRYING TO MAKE SENSE OF IT.
ONCE EVERY FEW DECADES, THE VISHANTI HOLD A GATHERING OF SORCERERS FROM AROUND THE WORLD TO ENGAGE IN MYSTICAL COMBAT.
THE WINNER EARNS THE DISTINCTION OF BECOMING THIS REALM'S SORCERER SUPREME.
I HAVE HAD THE HONOR OF ATTENDING THREE OF THESE TOURNAMENTS IN MY TIME.
THE FIRST TWO, I WON...

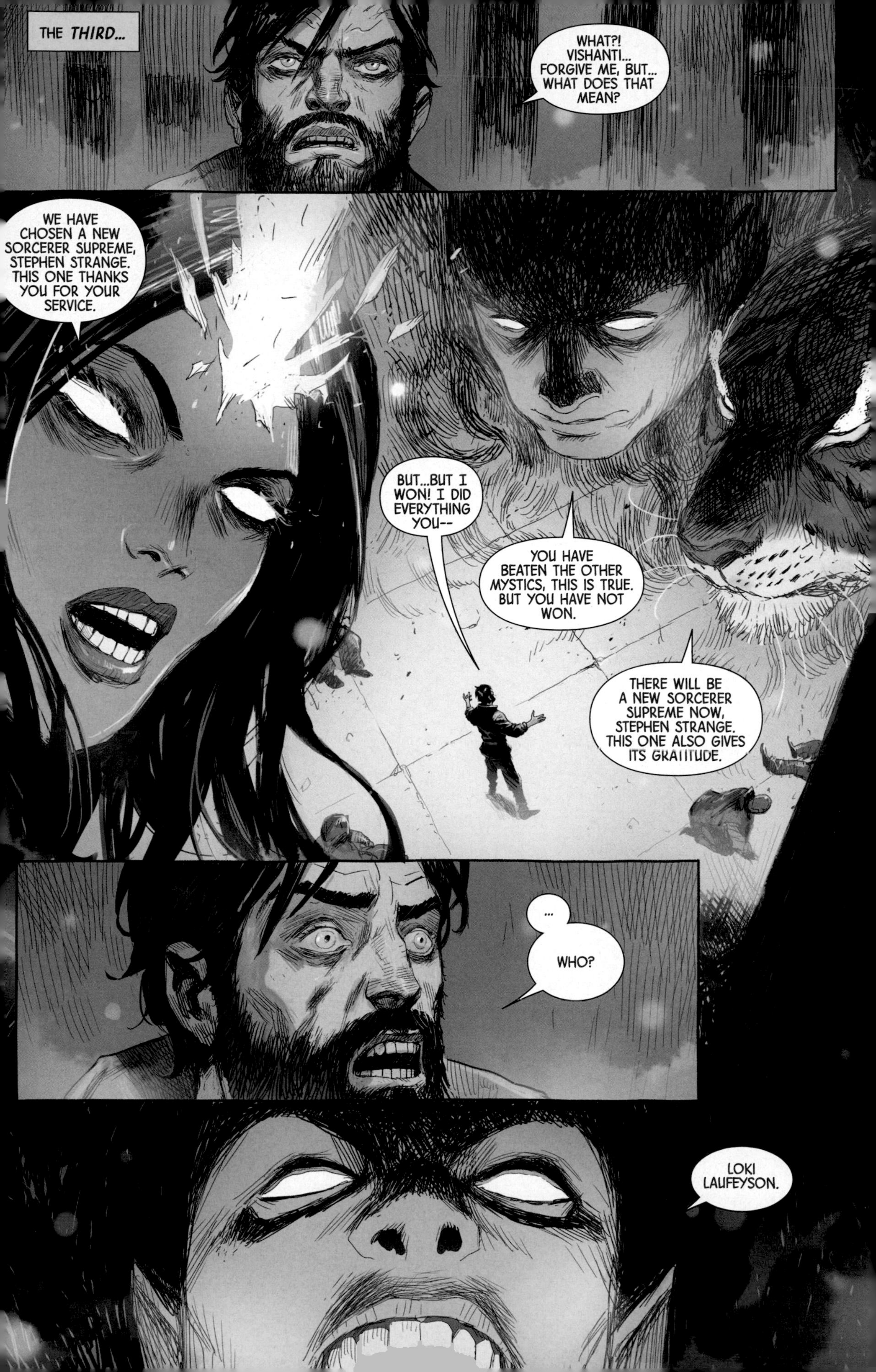
THE THIRD...
WHAT?! VISHANTI... FORGIVE ME, BUT... WHAT DOES THAT MEAN?
WE HAVE CHOSEN A NEW SORCERER SUPREME, STEPHEN STRANGE. THIS ONE THANKS YOU FOR YOUR SERVICE.
BUT...BUT I WON! I DID EVERYTHING YOU--
YOU HAVE BEATEN THE OTHER MYSTICS, THIS IS TRUE. BUT YOU HAVE NOT WON.
THERE WILL BE A NEW SORCERER SUPREME NOW, STEPHEN STRANGE. THIS ONE ALSO GIVES ITS GRATITUDE.
...
WHO?
LOKI LAUFEYSON.

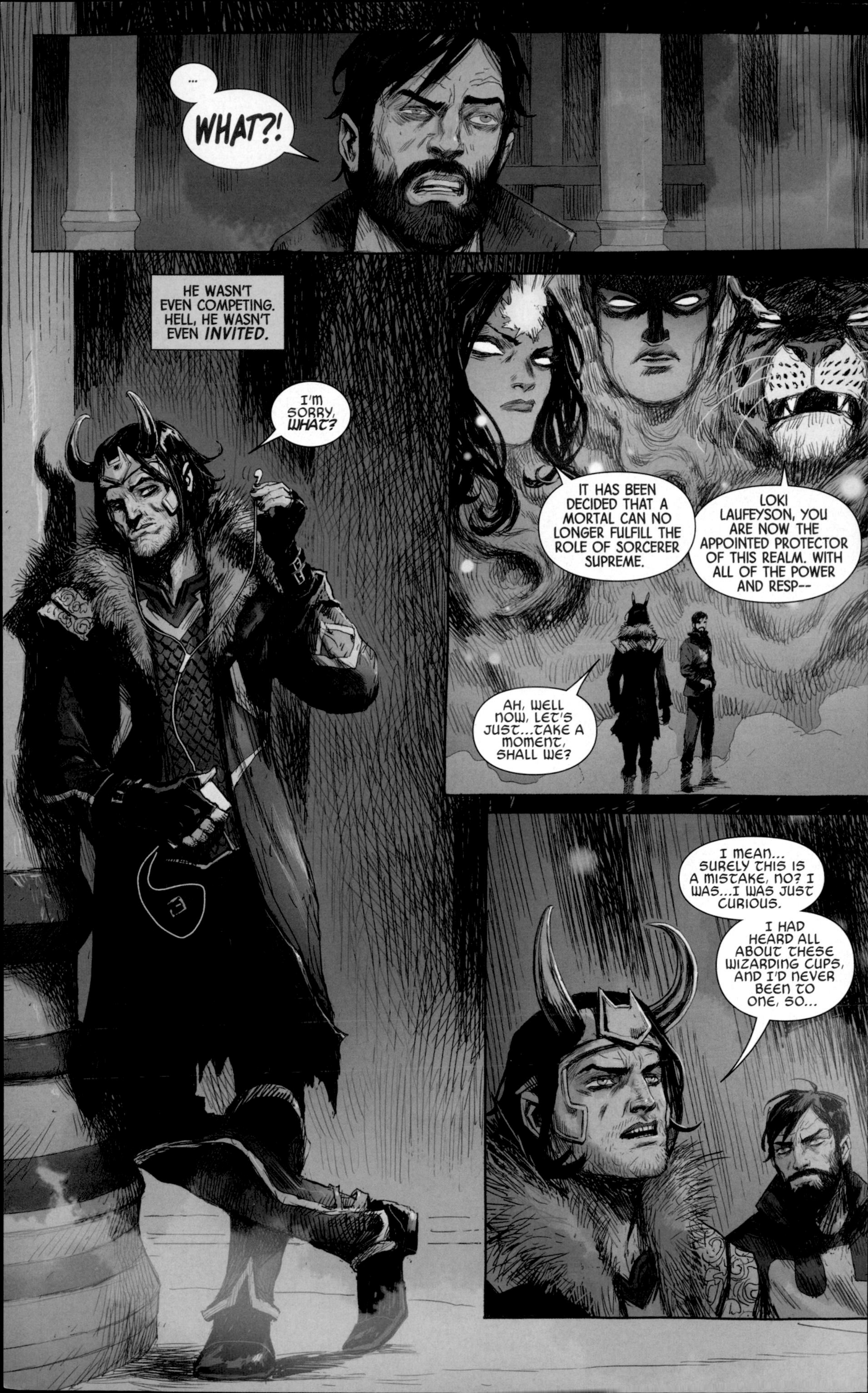

...
WHAT?!
HE WASN'T EVEN COMPETING. HELL, HE WASN'T EVEN *INVITED.*
I'M SORRY, *WHAT?*
IT HAS BEEN DECIDED THAT A MORTAL CAN NO LONGER FULFILL THE ROLE OF SORCERER SUPREME.
LOKI LAUFEYSON, YOU ARE NOW THE APPOINTED PROTECTOR OF THIS REALM. WITH ALL OF THE POWER AND RESP--
AH, WELL NOW, LET'S JUST...TAKE A MOMENT, SHALL WE?
I MEAN... SURELY THIS IS A MISTAKE, NO? I WAS...I WAS JUST CURIOUS.
I HAD HEARD ALL ABOUT THESE WIZARDING CUPS, AND I'D NEVER BEEN TO ONE, SO...

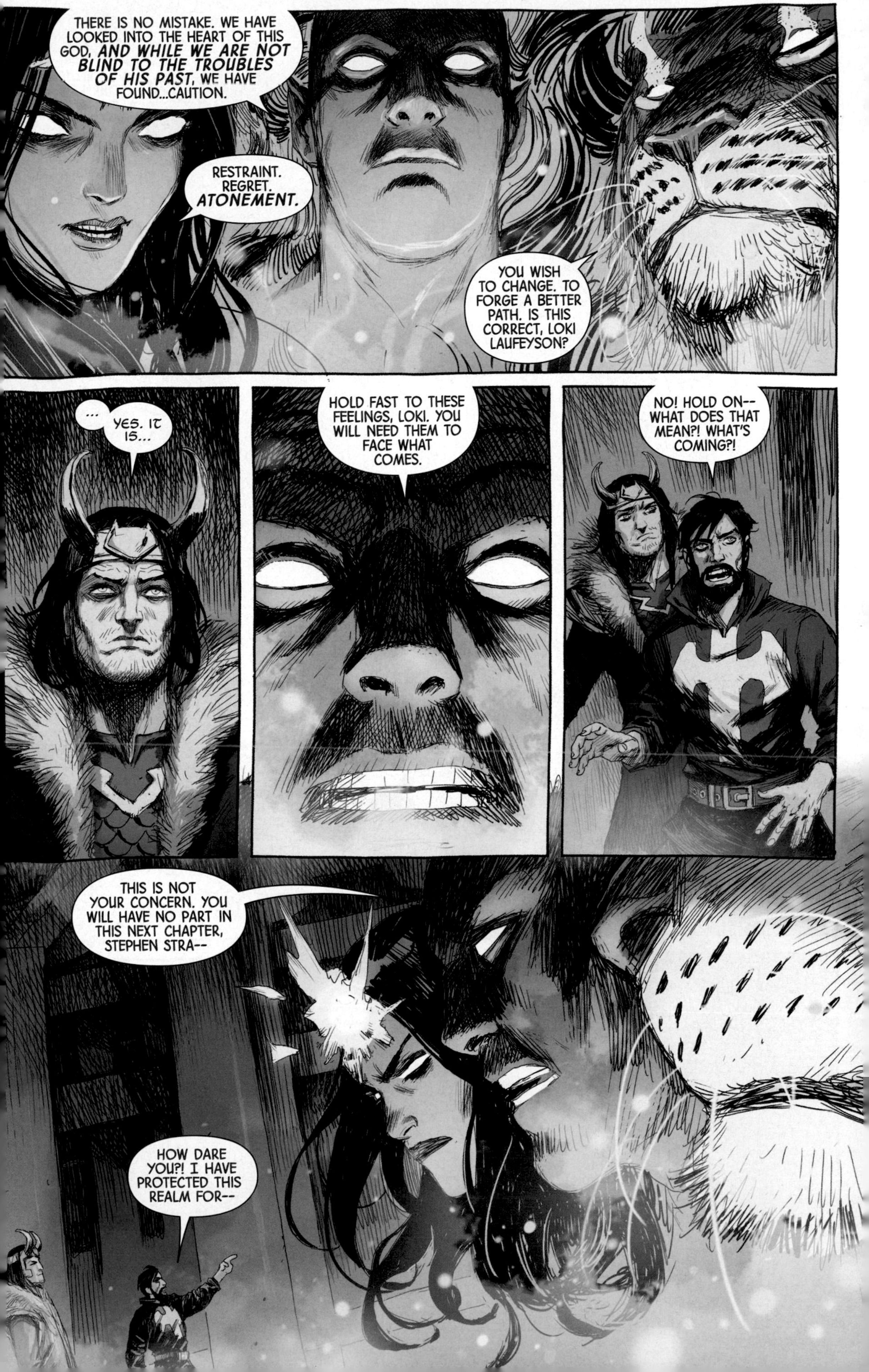

THERE IS NO MISTAKE. WE HAVE LOOKED INTO THE HEART OF THIS GOD, ***AND WHILE WE ARE NOT BLIND TO THE TROUBLES OF HIS PAST***, WE HAVE FOUND...CAUTION.
RESTRAINT. REGRET. ***ATONEMENT.***
YOU WISH TO CHANGE. TO FORGE A BETTER PATH. IS THIS CORRECT, LOKI LAUFEYSON?
... YES. IT IS...
HOLD FAST TO THESE FEELINGS, LOKI. YOU WILL NEED THEM TO FACE WHAT COMES.
NO! HOLD ON-- WHAT DOES THAT MEAN?! WHAT'S COMING?!
THIS IS NOT YOUR CONCERN. YOU WILL HAVE NO PART IN THIS NEXT CHAPTER, STEPHEN STRA--
HOW DARE YOU?! I HAVE PROTECTED THIS REALM FOR--

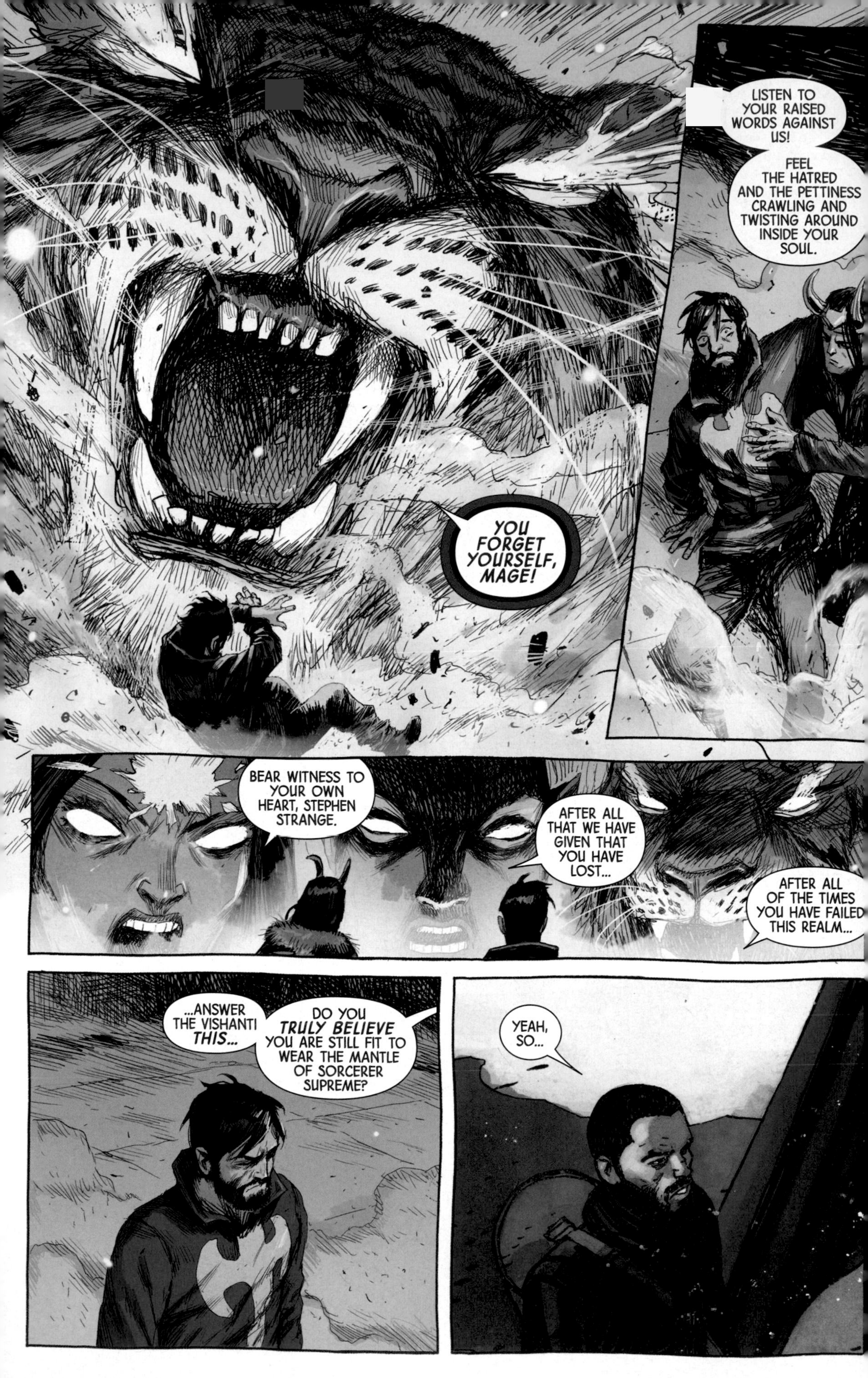
YOU FORGET YOURSELF, MAGE!
LISTEN TO YOUR RAISED WORDS AGAINST US!
FEEL THE HATRED AND THE PETTINESS CRAWLING AND TWISTING AROUND INSIDE YOUR SOUL.
BEAR WITNESS TO YOUR OWN HEART, STEPHEN STRANGE.
AFTER ALL THAT WE HAVE GIVEN THAT YOU HAVE LOST...
AFTER ALL OF THE TIMES YOU HAVE FAILED THIS REALM...
...ANSWER THE VISHANTI THIS...
DO YOU TRULY BELIEVE YOU ARE STILL FIT TO WEAR THE MANTLE OF SORCERER SUPREME?
YEAH, SO...

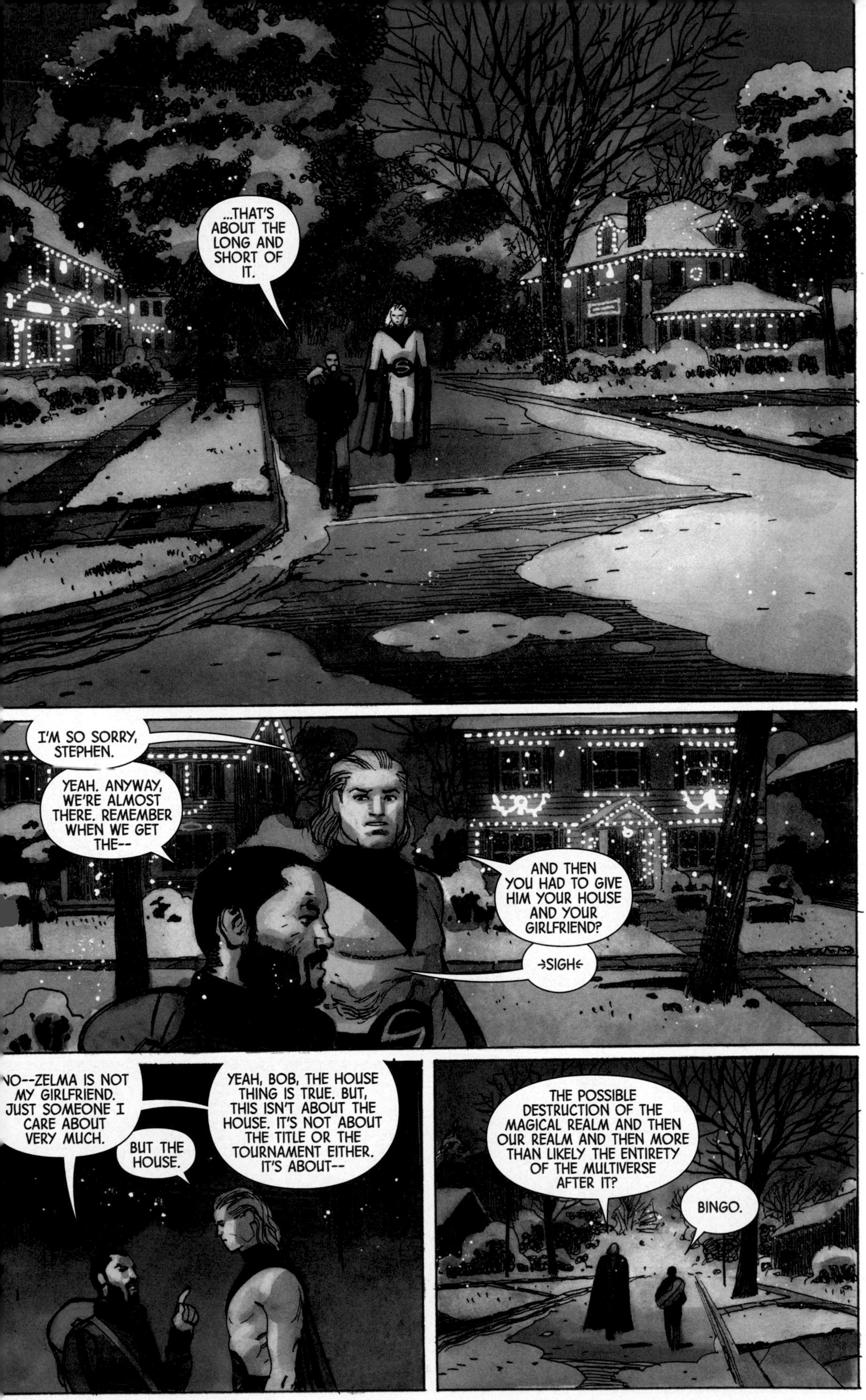
...THAT'S ABOUT THE LONG AND SHORT OF IT.
I'M SO SORRY, STEPHEN.
YEAH. ANYWAY, WE'RE ALMOST THERE. REMEMBER WHEN WE GET THE--
AND THEN YOU HAD TO GIVE HIM YOUR HOUSE AND YOUR GIRLFRIEND?
→SIGH←
NO--ZELMA IS NOT MY GIRLFRIEND. JUST SOMEONE I CARE ABOUT VERY MUCH.
BUT THE HOUSE.
YEAH, BOB, THE HOUSE THING IS TRUE. BUT, THIS ISN'T ABOUT THE HOUSE. IT'S NOT ABOUT THE TITLE OR THE TOURNAMENT EITHER. IT'S ABOUT--
THE POSSIBLE DESTRUCTION OF THE MAGICAL REALM AND THEN OUR REALM AND THEN MORE THAN LIKELY THE ENTIRETY OF THE MULTIVERSE AFTER IT?
BINGO.

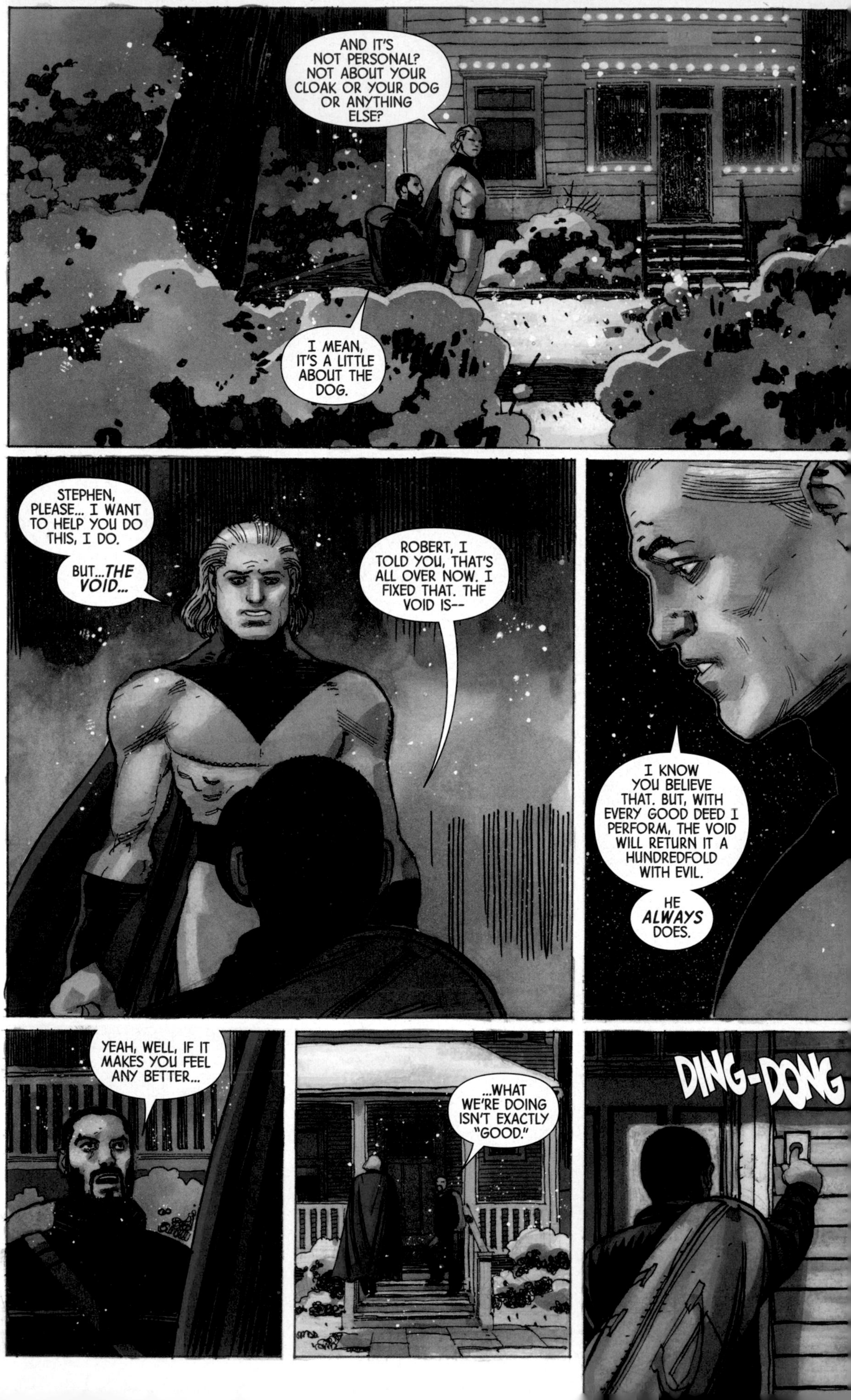
AND IT'S NOT PERSONAL? NOT ABOUT YOUR CLOAK OR YOUR DOG OR ANYTHING ELSE?
I MEAN, IT'S A LITTLE ABOUT THE DOG.
STEPHEN, PLEASE... I WANT TO HELP YOU DO THIS, I DO.
BUT... *THE VOID*...
ROBERT, I TOLD YOU, THAT'S ALL OVER NOW. I FIXED THAT. THE VOID IS--
I KNOW YOU BELIEVE THAT. BUT, WITH EVERY GOOD DEED I PERFORM, THE VOID WILL RETURN IT A HUNDREDFOLD WITH EVIL.
HE *ALWAYS* DOES.
YEAH, WELL, IF IT MAKES YOU FEEL ANY BETTER...
...WHAT WE'RE DOING ISN'T EXACTLY "GOOD."
DING-DONG

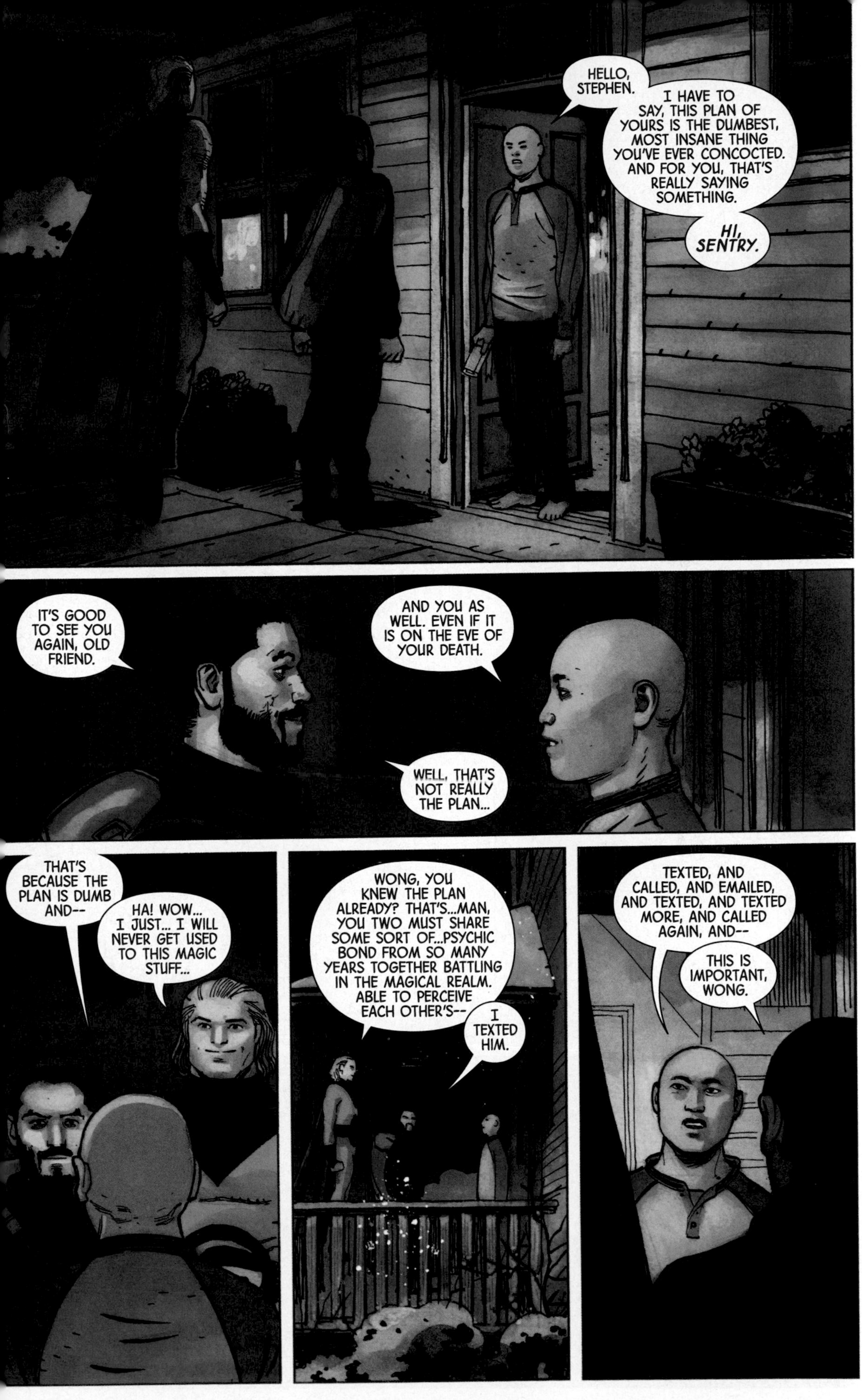
HELLO, STEPHEN.
I HAVE TO SAY, THIS PLAN OF YOURS IS THE DUMBEST, MOST INSANE THING YOU'VE EVER CONCOCTED. AND FOR YOU, THAT'S REALLY SAYING SOMETHING.
HI, SENTRY.
IT'S GOOD TO SEE YOU AGAIN, OLD FRIEND.
AND YOU AS WELL. EVEN IF IT IS ON THE EVE OF YOUR DEATH.
WELL, THAT'S NOT REALLY THE PLAN...
THAT'S BECAUSE THE PLAN IS DUMB AND--
HA! WOW... I JUST... I WILL NEVER GET USED TO THIS MAGIC STUFF...
WONG, YOU KNEW THE PLAN ALREADY? THAT'S...MAN, YOU TWO MUST SHARE SOME SORT OF...PSYCHIC BOND FROM SO MANY YEARS TOGETHER BATTLING IN THE MAGICAL REALM. ABLE TO PERCEIVE EACH OTHER'S--
I TEXTED HIM.
TEXTED, AND CALLED, AND EMAILED, AND TEXTED, AND TEXTED MORE, AND CALLED AGAIN, AND--
THIS IS IMPORTANT, WONG.

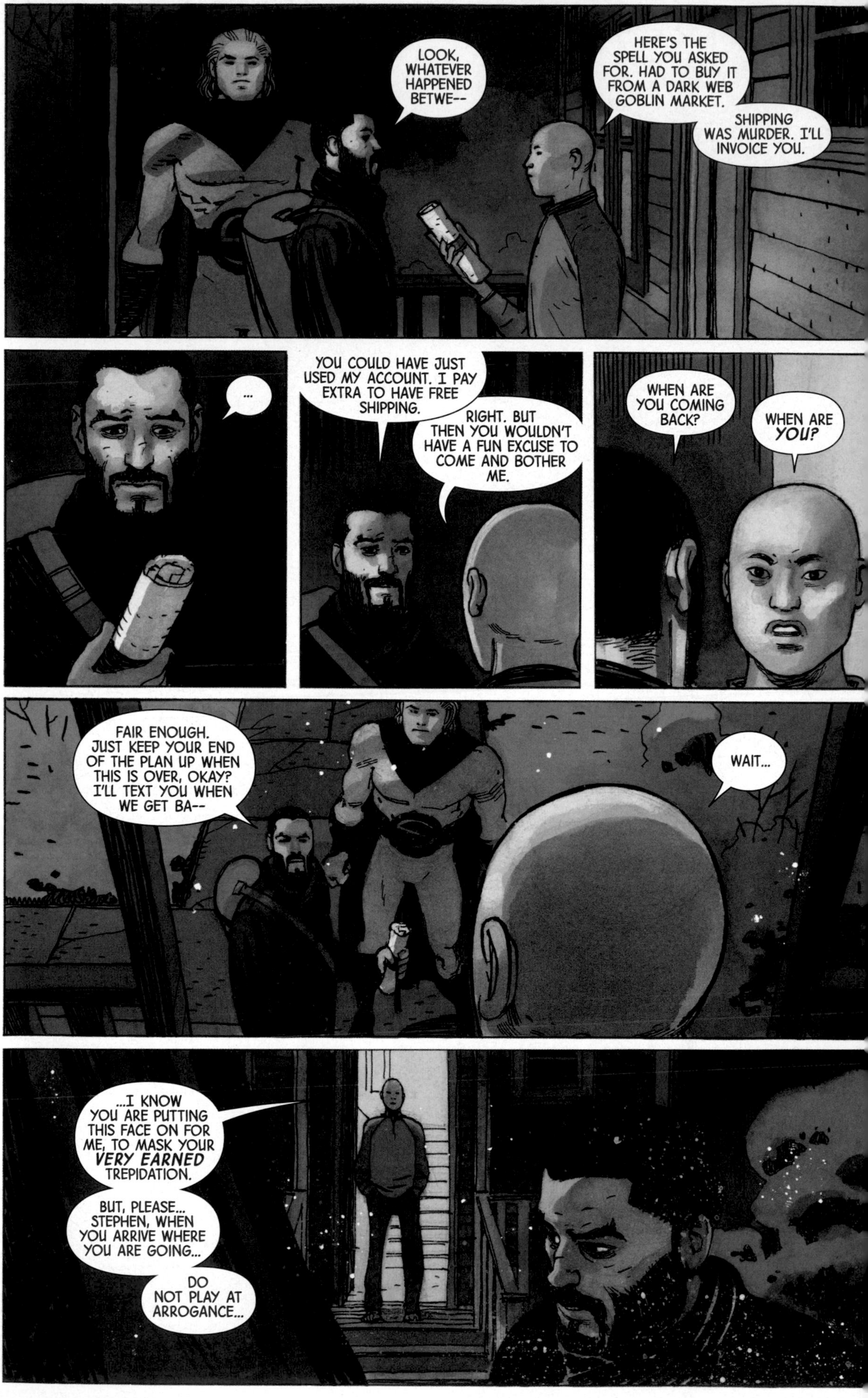
LOOK, WHATEVER HAPPENED BETWE--
HERE'S THE SPELL YOU ASKED FOR. HAD TO BUY IT FROM A DARK WEB GOBLIN MARKET.
SHIPPING WAS MURDER. I'LL INVOICE YOU.
...
YOU COULD HAVE JUST USED MY ACCOUNT. I PAY EXTRA TO HAVE FREE SHIPPING.
RIGHT. BUT THEN YOU WOULDN'T HAVE A FUN EXCUSE TO COME AND BOTHER ME.
WHEN ARE YOU COMING BACK?
WHEN ARE *YOU?*
FAIR ENOUGH. JUST KEEP YOUR END OF THE PLAN UP WHEN THIS IS OVER, OKAY? I'LL TEXT YOU WHEN WE GET BA--
WAIT...
...I KNOW YOU ARE PUTTING THIS FACE ON FOR ME, TO MASK YOUR *VERY EARNED* TREPIDATION.
BUT, PLEASE... STEPHEN, WHEN YOU ARRIVE WHERE YOU ARE GOING...
DO NOT PLAY AT ARROGANCE...

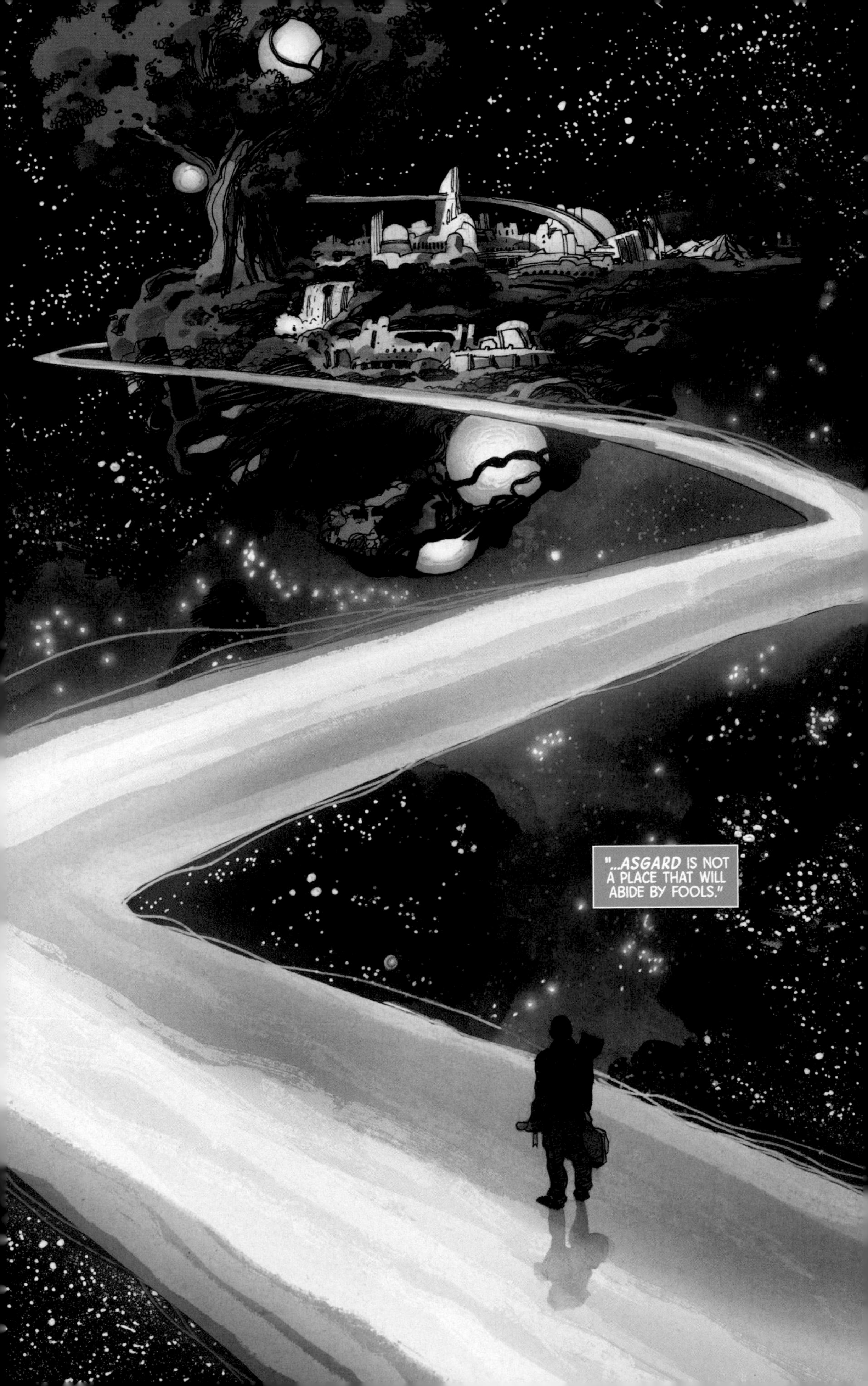
"...ASGARD IS NOT A PLACE THAT WILL ABIDE BY FOOLS."

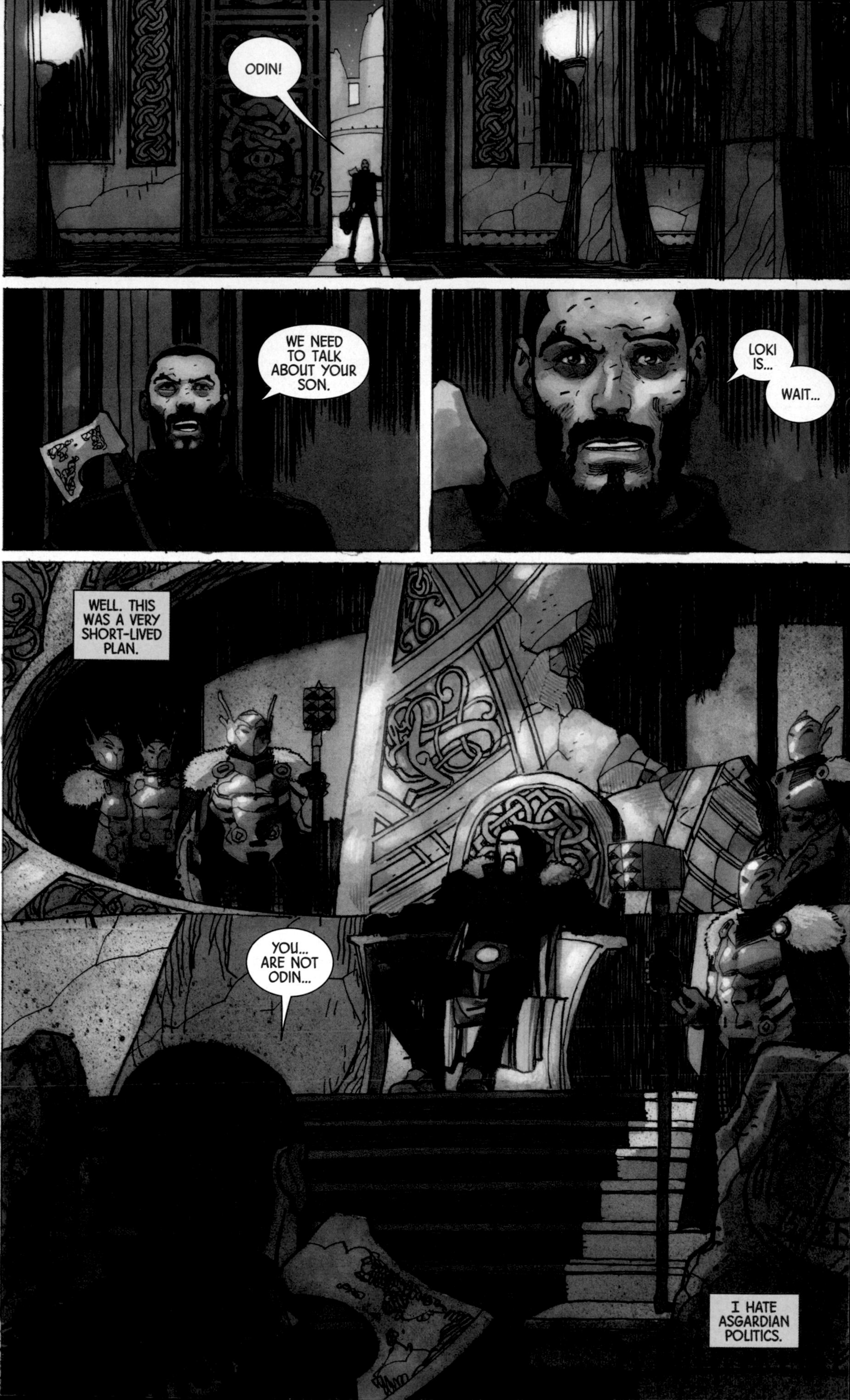
ODIN!
WE NEED TO TALK ABOUT YOUR SON.
LOKI IS...
WAIT...
WELL. THIS WAS A VERY SHORT-LIVED PLAN.
YOU... ARE NOT ODIN...
I HATE ASGARDIAN POLITICS.

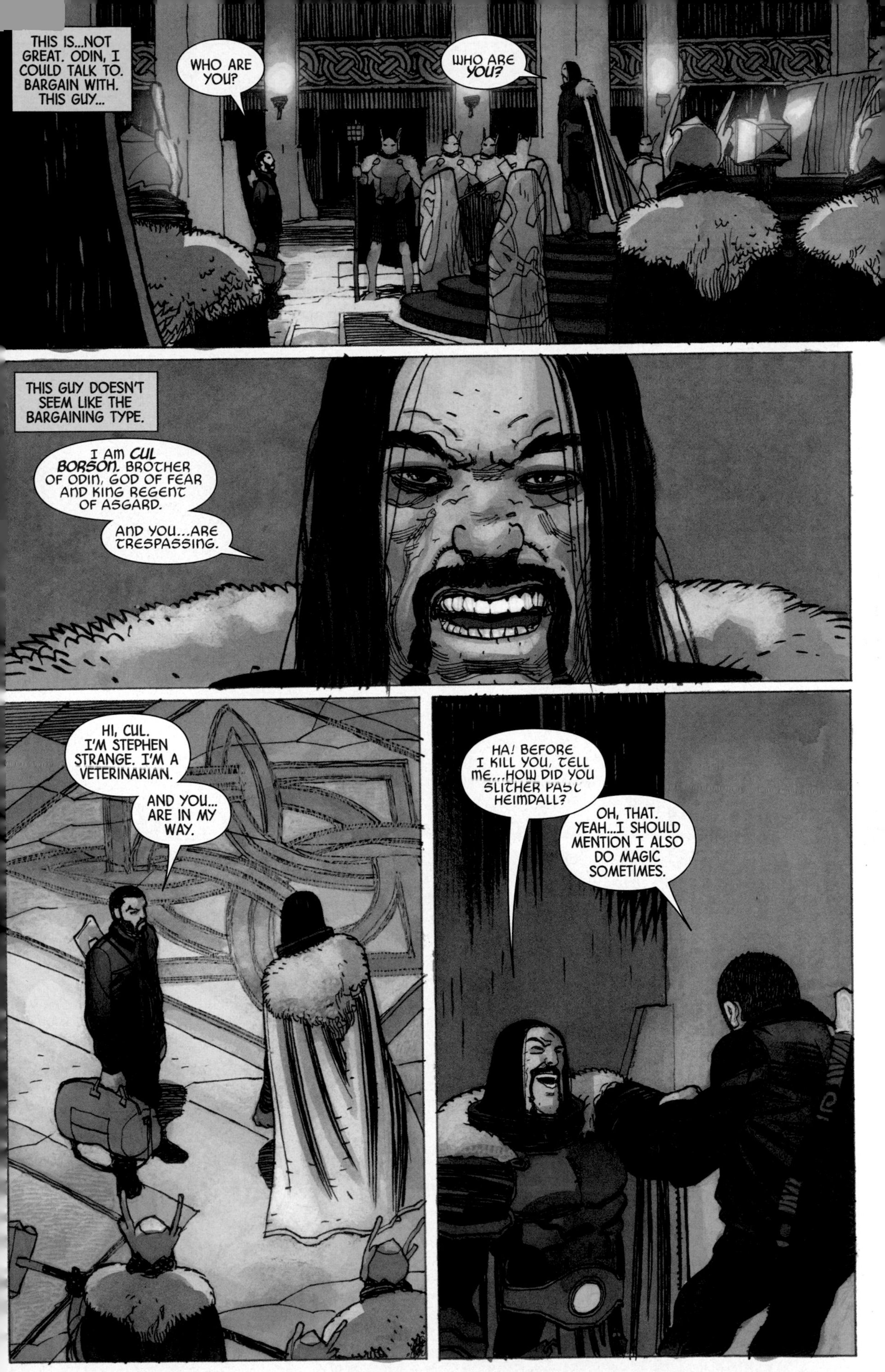
THIS IS...NOT GREAT. ODIN, I COULD TALK TO. BARGAIN WITH. THIS GUY...
WHO ARE YOU?
WHO ARE YOU?
THIS GUY DOESN'T SEEM LIKE THE BARGAINING TYPE.
I AM CUL BORSON. BROTHER OF ODIN, GOD OF FEAR AND KING REGENT OF ASGARD.
AND YOU...ARE TRESPASSING.
HI, CUL. I'M STEPHEN STRANGE. I'M A VETERINARIAN.
AND YOU... ARE IN MY WAY.
HA! BEFORE I KILL YOU, TELL ME...HOW DID YOU SLITHER PAST HEIMDALL?
OH, THAT. YEAH...I SHOULD MENTION I ALSO DO MAGIC SOMETIMES.

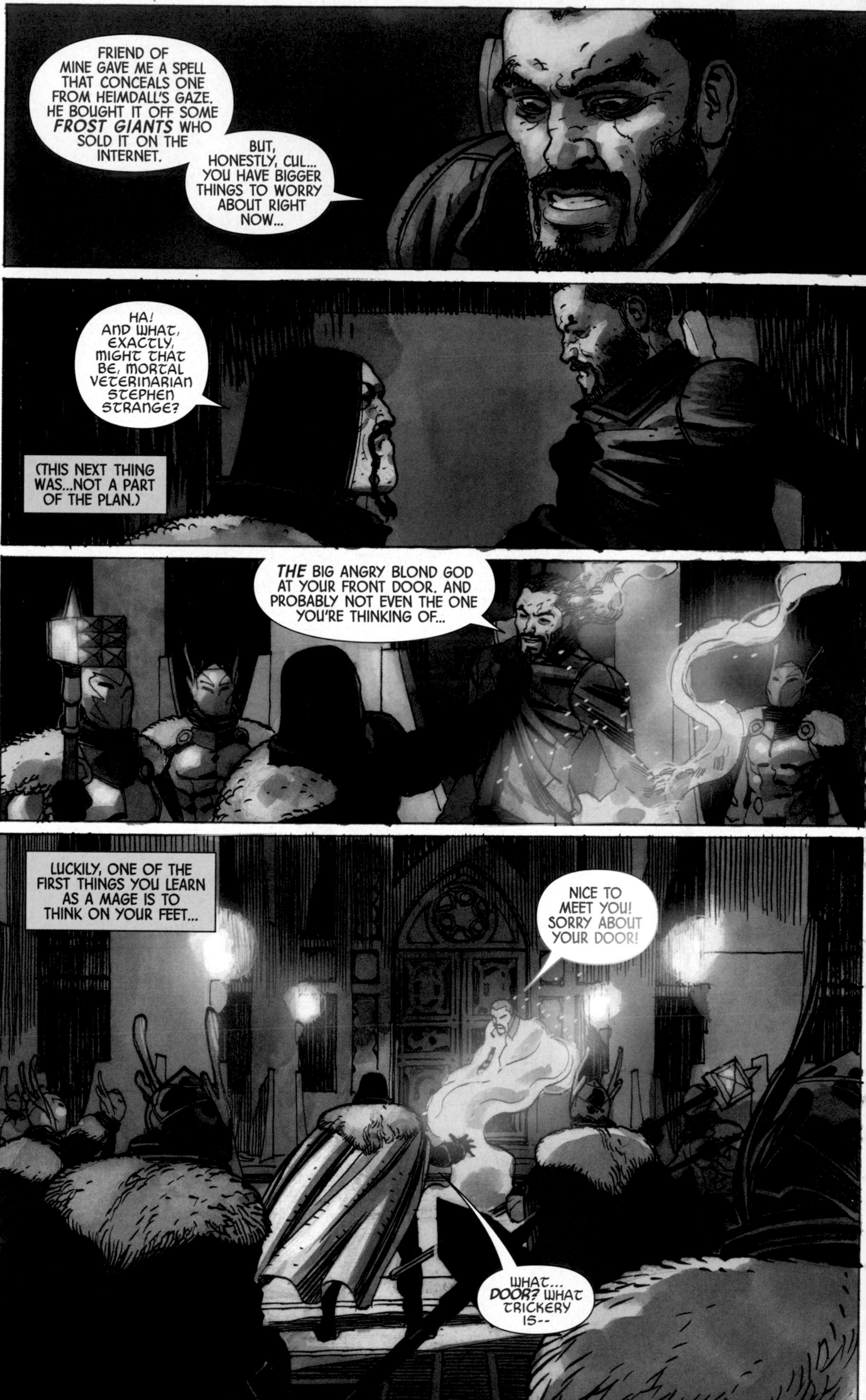
FRIEND OF MINE GAVE ME A SPELL THAT CONCEALS ONE FROM HEIMDALL'S GAZE. HE BOUGHT IT OFF SOME FROST GIANTS WHO SOLD IT ON THE INTERNET.
BUT, HONESTLY, CUL... YOU HAVE BIGGER THINGS TO WORRY ABOUT RIGHT NOW...
HA! AND WHAT, EXACTLY, MIGHT THAT BE, MORTAL VETERINARIAN STEPHEN STRANGE?
(THIS NEXT THING WAS...NOT A PART OF THE PLAN.)
THE BIG ANGRY BLOND GOD AT YOUR FRONT DOOR. AND PROBABLY NOT EVEN THE ONE YOU'RE THINKING OF...
LUCKILY, ONE OF THE FIRST THINGS YOU LEARN AS A MAGE IS TO THINK ON YOUR FEET...
NICE TO MEET YOU! SORRY ABOUT YOUR DOOR!
WHAT... DOOR? WHAT TRICKERY IS--

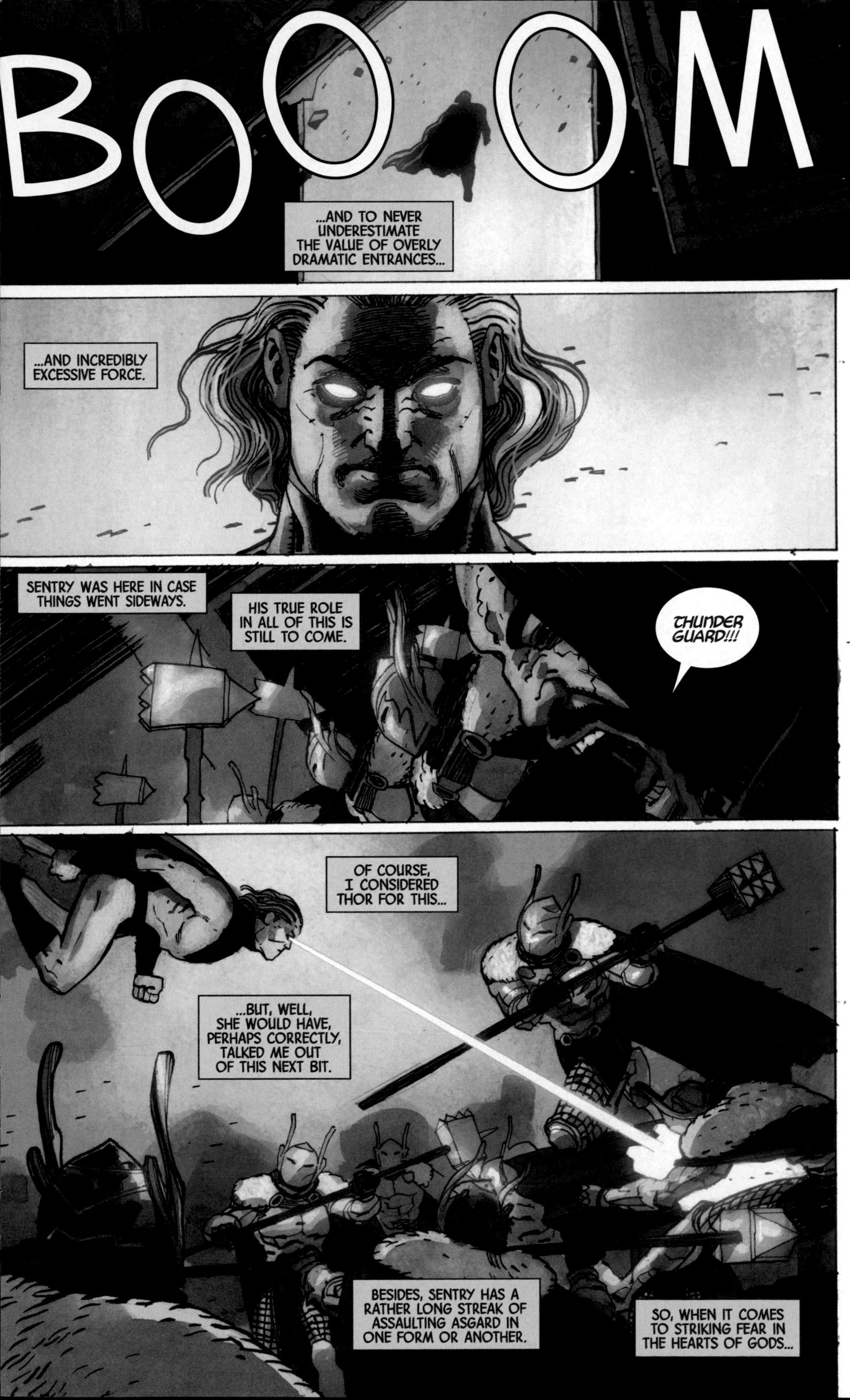
BOOOM
...AND TO NEVER UNDERESTIMATE THE VALUE OF OVERLY DRAMATIC ENTRANCES...
...AND INCREDIBLY EXCESSIVE FORCE.
SENTRY WAS HERE IN CASE THINGS WENT SIDEWAYS.
HIS TRUE ROLE IN ALL OF THIS IS STILL TO COME.
THUNDER GUARD!!!
OF COURSE, I CONSIDERED THOR FOR THIS...
...BUT, WELL, SHE WOULD HAVE, PERHAPS CORRECTLY, TALKED ME OUT OF THIS NEXT BIT.
BESIDES, SENTRY HAS A RATHER LONG STREAK OF ASSAULTING ASGARD IN ONE FORM OR ANOTHER.
SO, WHEN IT COMES TO STRIKING FEAR IN THE HEARTS OF GODS...

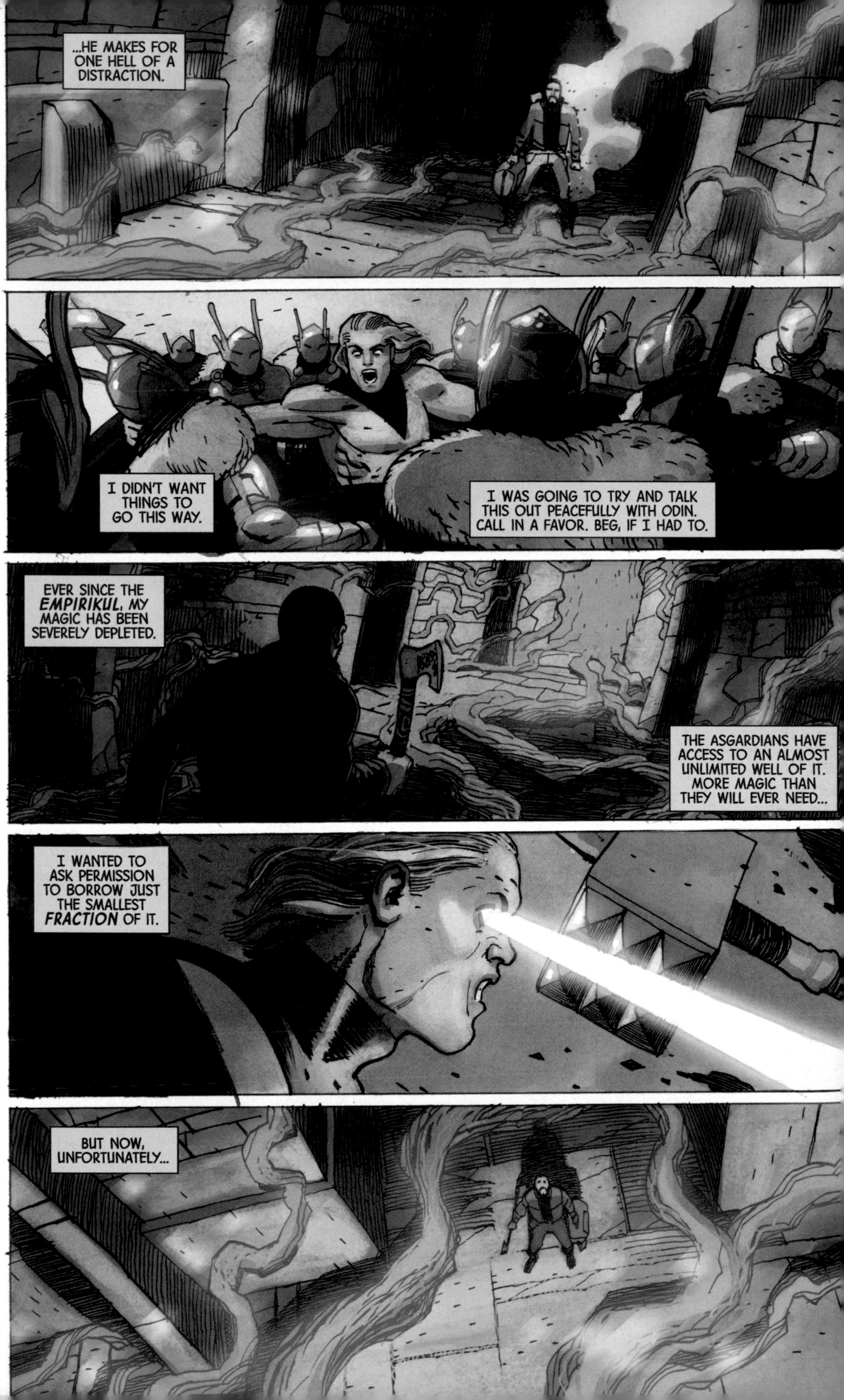

...HE MAKES FOR ONE HELL OF A DISTRACTION.
I DIDN'T WANT THINGS TO GO THIS WAY.
I WAS GOING TO TRY AND TALK THIS OUT PEACEFULLY WITH ODIN. CALL IN A FAVOR. BEG, IF I HAD TO.
EVER SINCE THE *EMPIRIKUL*, MY MAGIC HAS BEEN SEVERELY DEPLETED.
THE ASGARDIANS HAVE ACCESS TO AN ALMOST UNLIMITED WELL OF IT. MORE MAGIC THAN THEY WILL EVER NEED...
I WANTED TO ASK PERMISSION TO BORROW JUST THE SMALLEST *FRACTION* OF IT.
BUT NOW, UNFORTUNATELY...

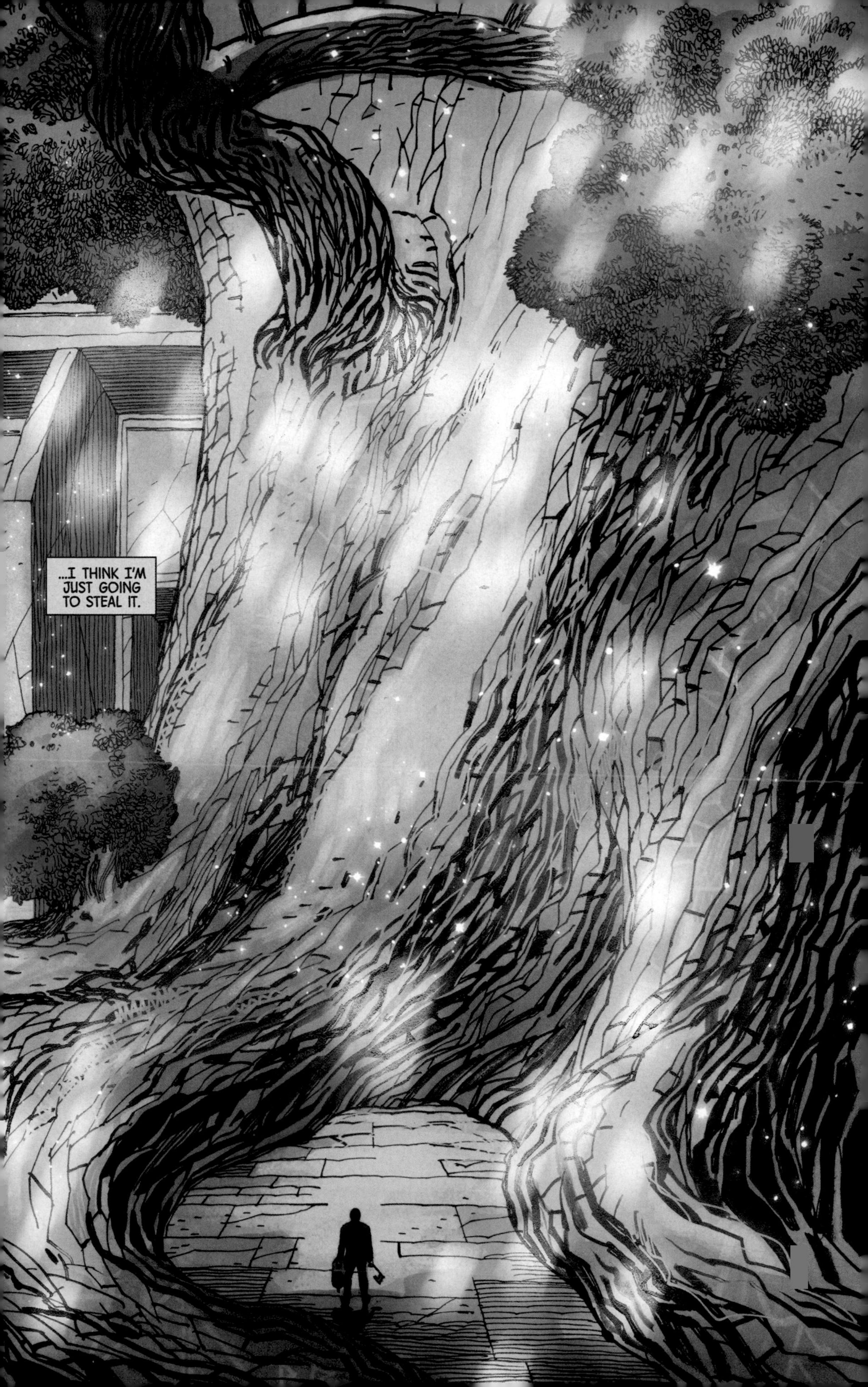
...I THINK I'M JUST GOING TO STEAL IT.

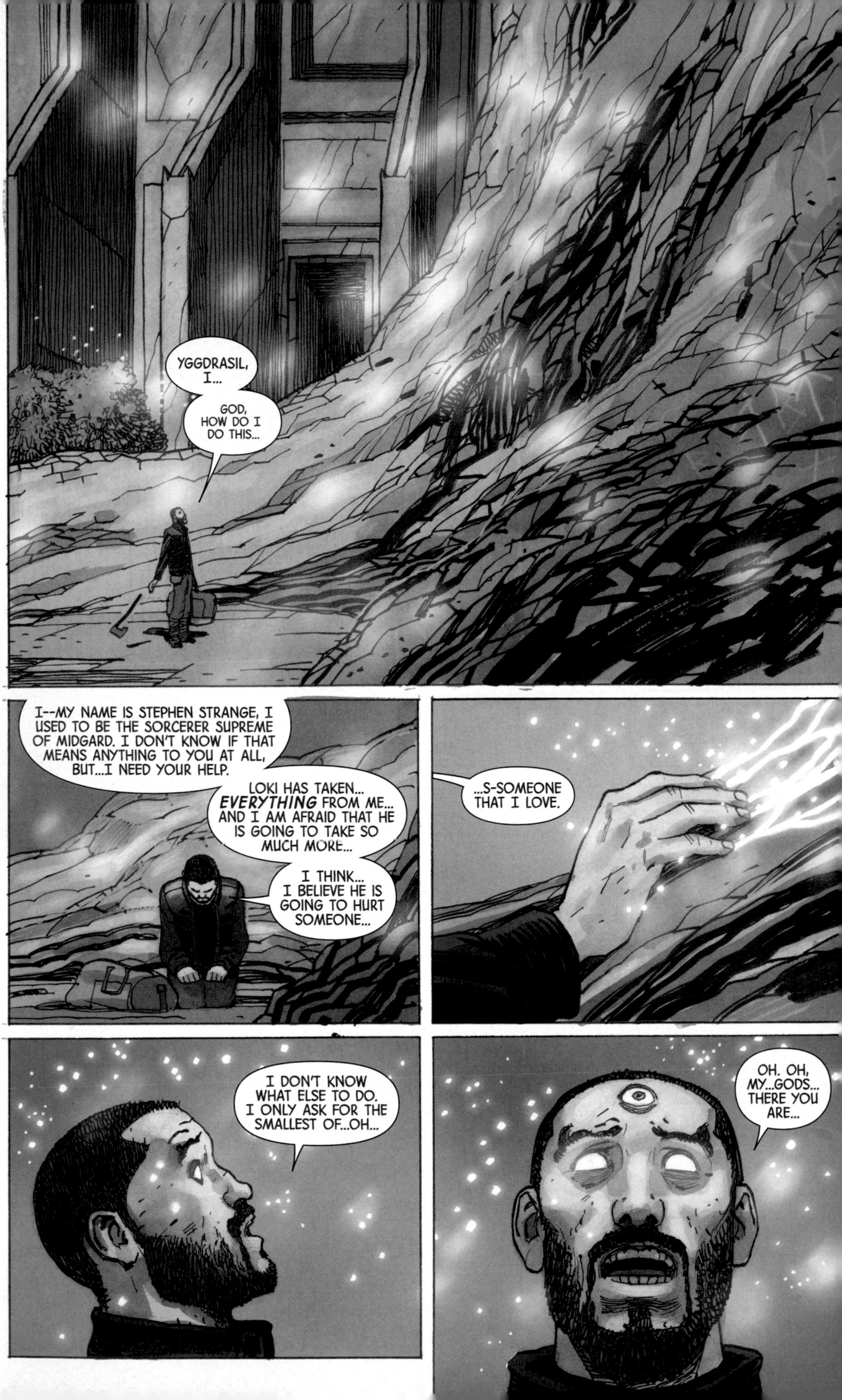
YGGDRASIL, I...
GOD, HOW DO I DO THIS...
I--MY NAME IS STEPHEN STRANGE, I USED TO BE THE SORCERER SUPREME OF MIDGARD. I DON'T KNOW IF THAT MEANS ANYTHING TO YOU AT ALL, BUT...I NEED YOUR HELP.
LOKI HAS TAKEN... *EVERYTHING* FROM ME... AND I AM AFRAID THAT HE IS GOING TO TAKE SO MUCH MORE...
I THINK... I BELIEVE HE IS GOING TO HURT SOMEONE...
...S-SOMEONE THAT I LOVE.
I DON'T KNOW WHAT ELSE TO DO. I ONLY ASK FOR THE SMALLEST OF...OH...
OH. OH, MY...GODS... THERE YOU ARE...

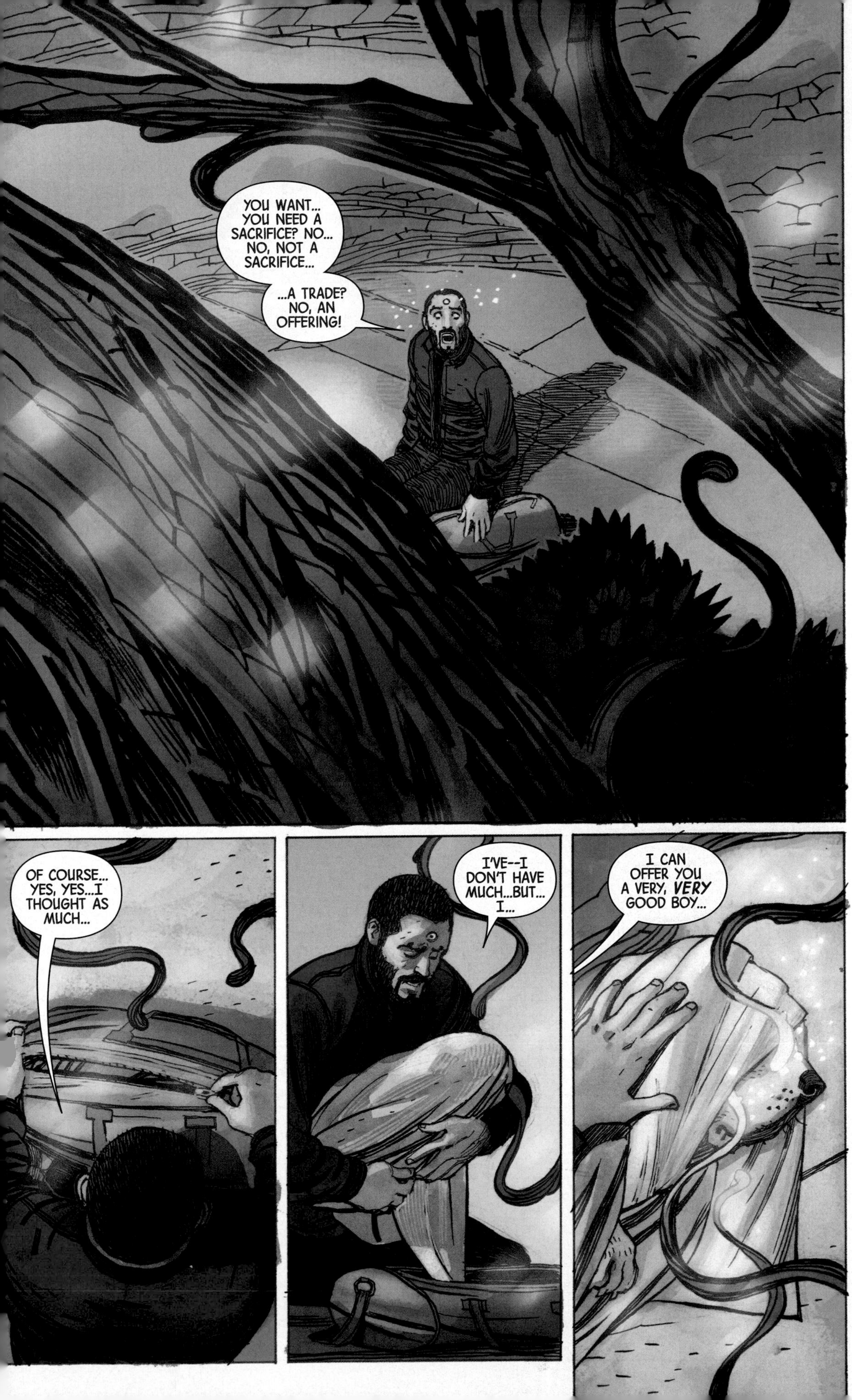
YOU WANT... YOU NEED A SACRIFICE? NO... NO, NOT A SACRIFICE...
...A TRADE? NO, AN OFFERING!
OF COURSE... YES, YES...I THOUGHT AS MUCH...
I'VE--I DON'T HAVE MUCH...BUT... I...
I CAN OFFER YOU A VERY, *VERY* GOOD BOY...

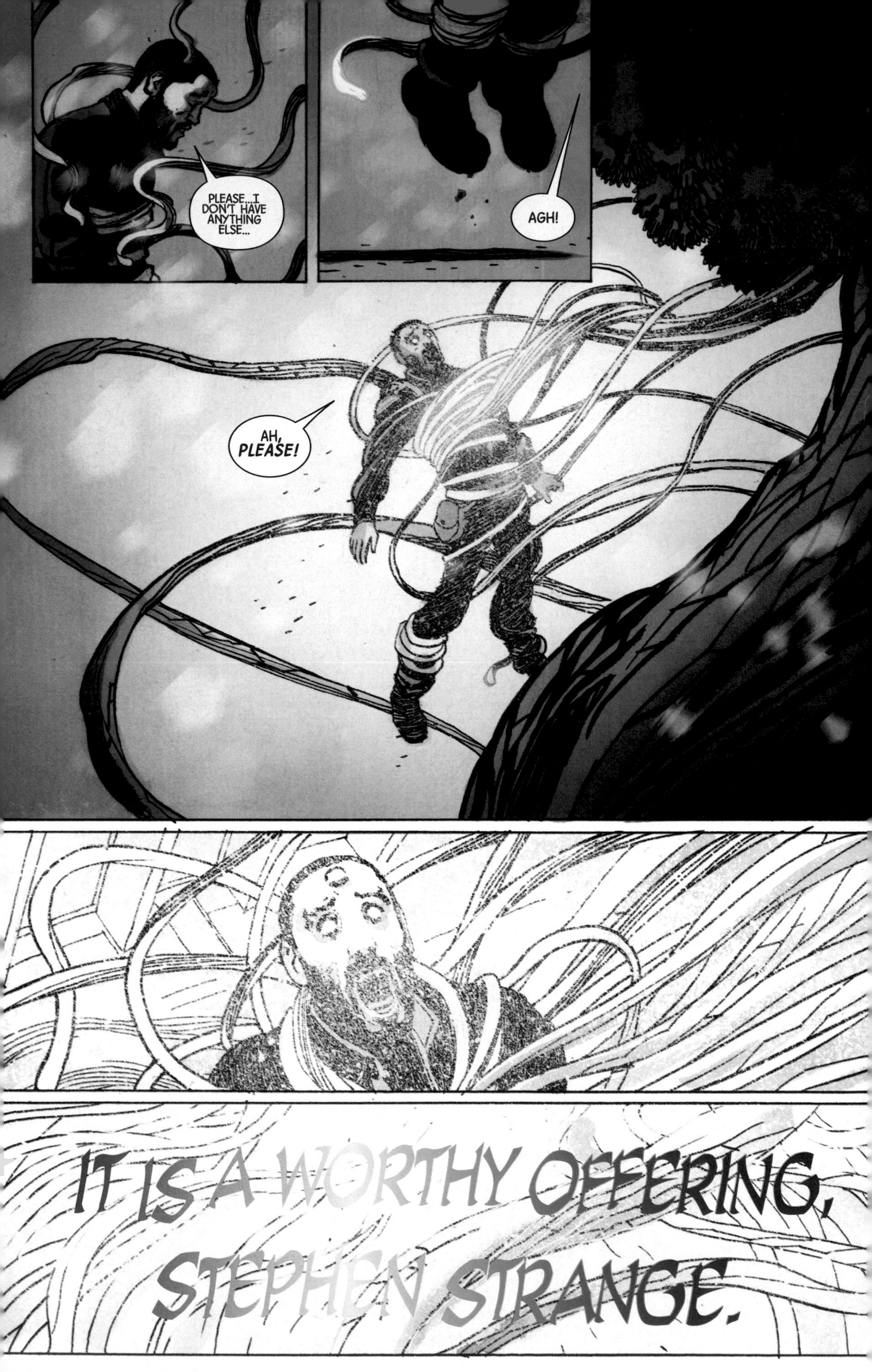
PLEASE...I DON'T HAVE ANYTHING ELSE...
AGH!
AH, PLEASE!
IT IS A WORTHY OFFERING, STEPHEN STRANGE.

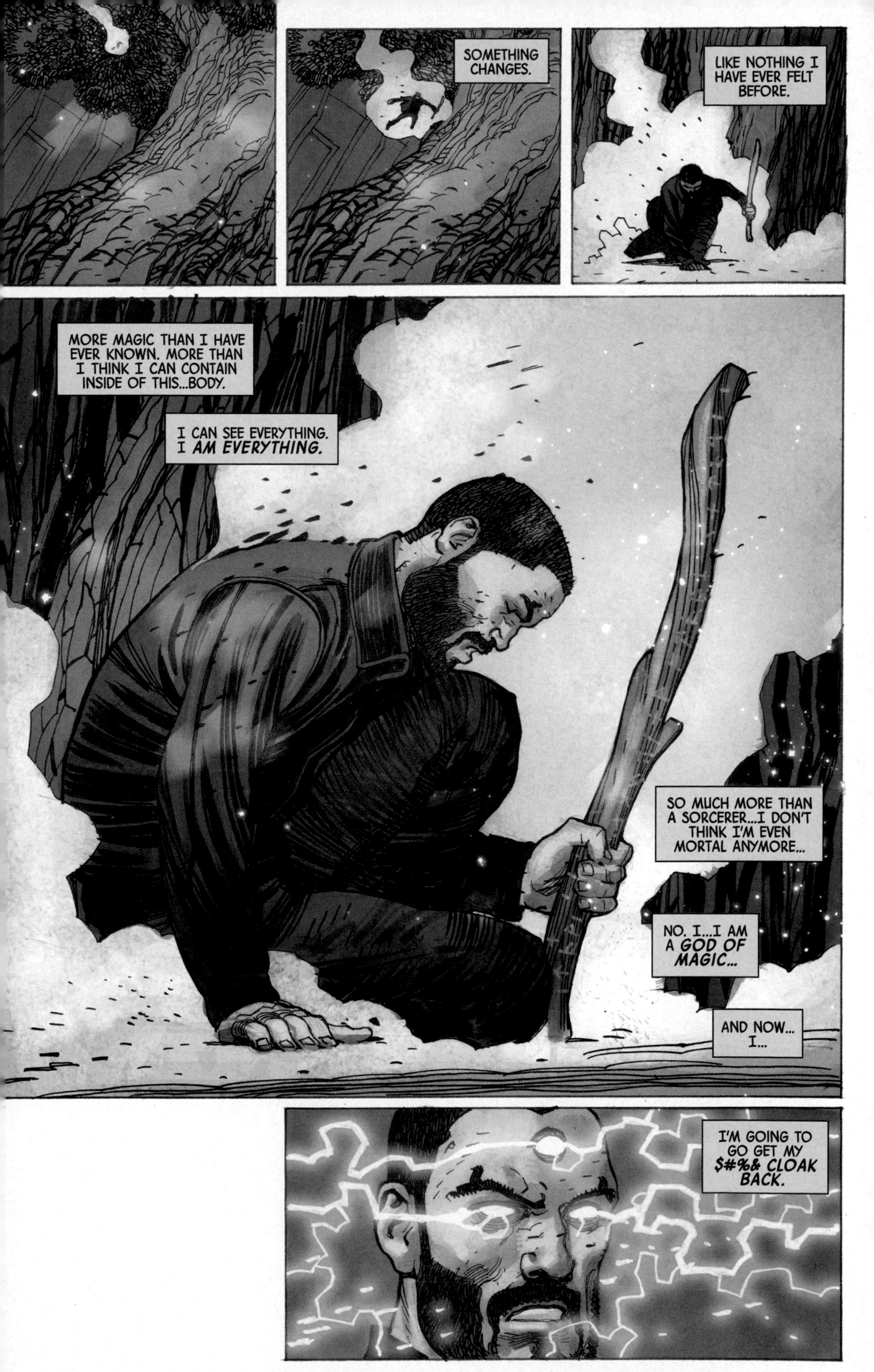
SOMETHING CHANGES.
LIKE NOTHING I HAVE EVER FELT BEFORE.
MORE MAGIC THAN I HAVE EVER KNOWN. MORE THAN I THINK I CAN CONTAIN INSIDE OF THIS...BODY.
I CAN SEE EVERYTHING. I *AM EVERYTHING.*
SO MUCH MORE THAN A SORCERER...I DON'T THINK I'M EVEN MORTAL ANYMORE...
NO. I...I AM A *GOD OF MAGIC...*
AND NOW... I...
I'M GOING TO GO GET MY *$#%& CLOAK BACK.*

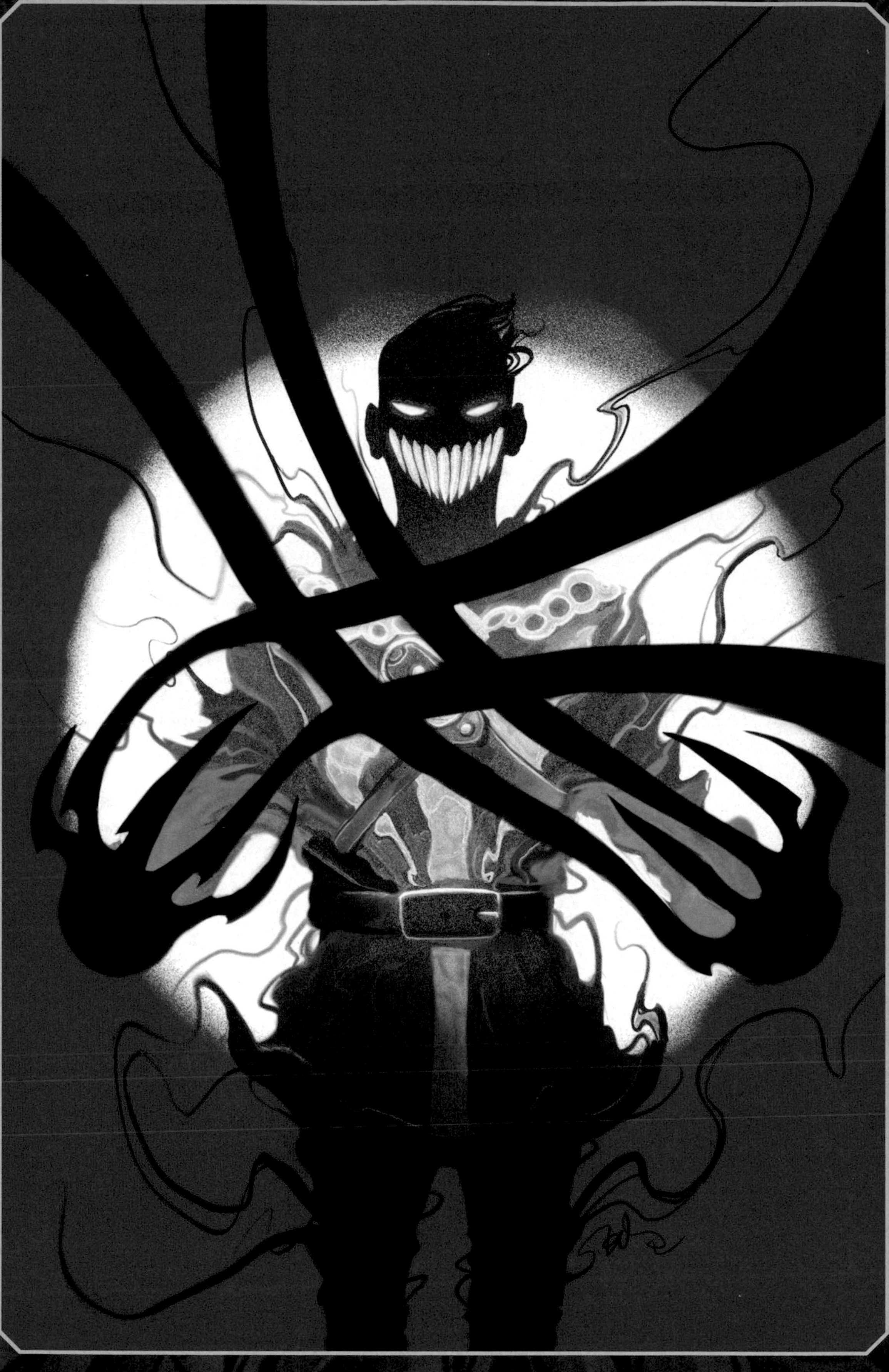

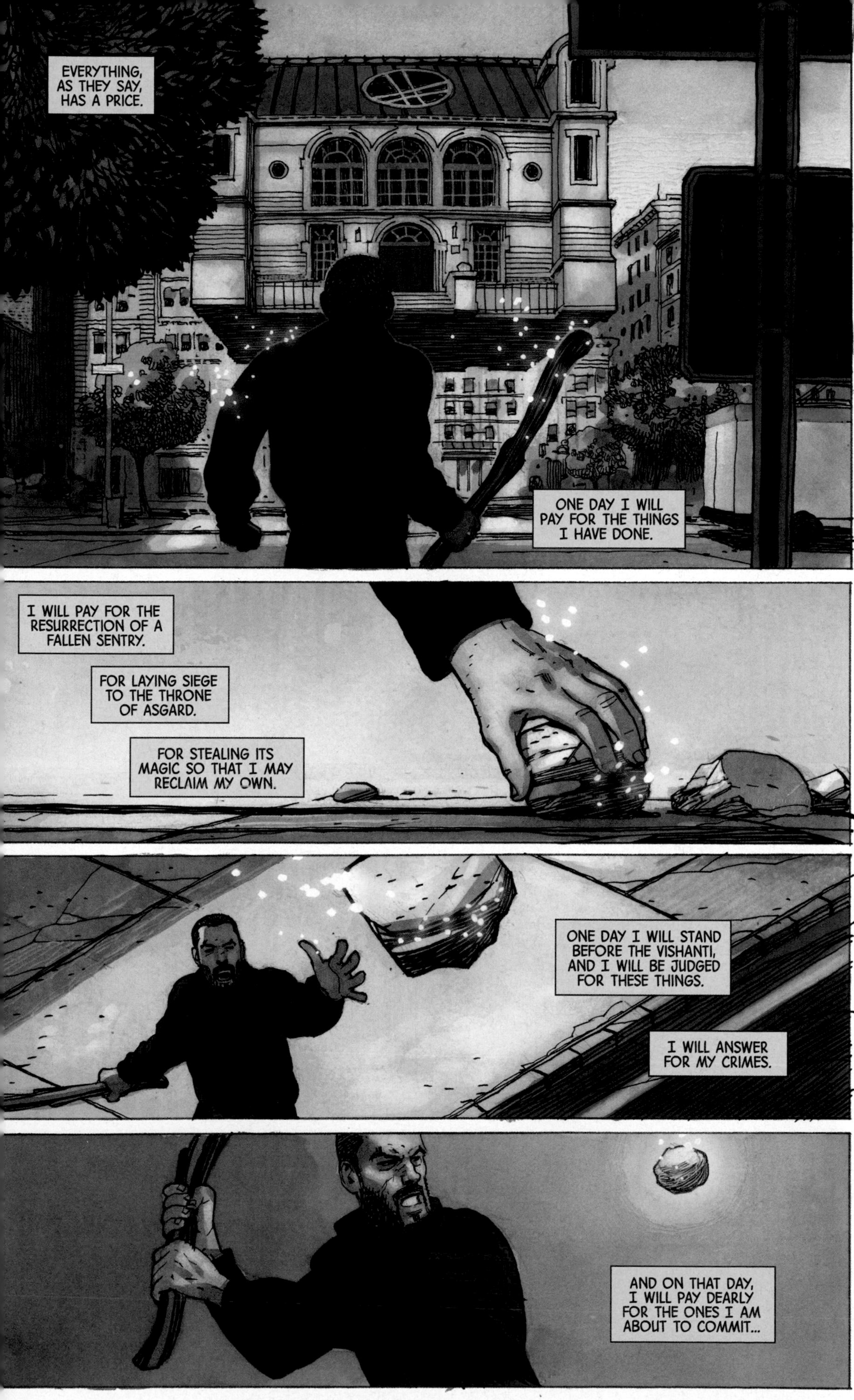
EVERYTHING, AS THEY SAY, HAS A PRICE.
ONE DAY I WILL PAY FOR THE THINGS I HAVE DONE.
I WILL PAY FOR THE RESURRECTION OF A FALLEN SENTRY.
FOR LAYING SIEGE TO THE THRONE OF ASGARD.
FOR STEALING ITS MAGIC SO THAT I MAY RECLAIM MY OWN.
ONE DAY I WILL STAND BEFORE THE VISHANTI, AND I WILL BE JUDGED FOR THESE THINGS.
I WILL ANSWER FOR MY CRIMES.
AND ON THAT DAY, I WILL PAY DEARLY FOR THE ONES I AM ABOUT TO COMMIT...

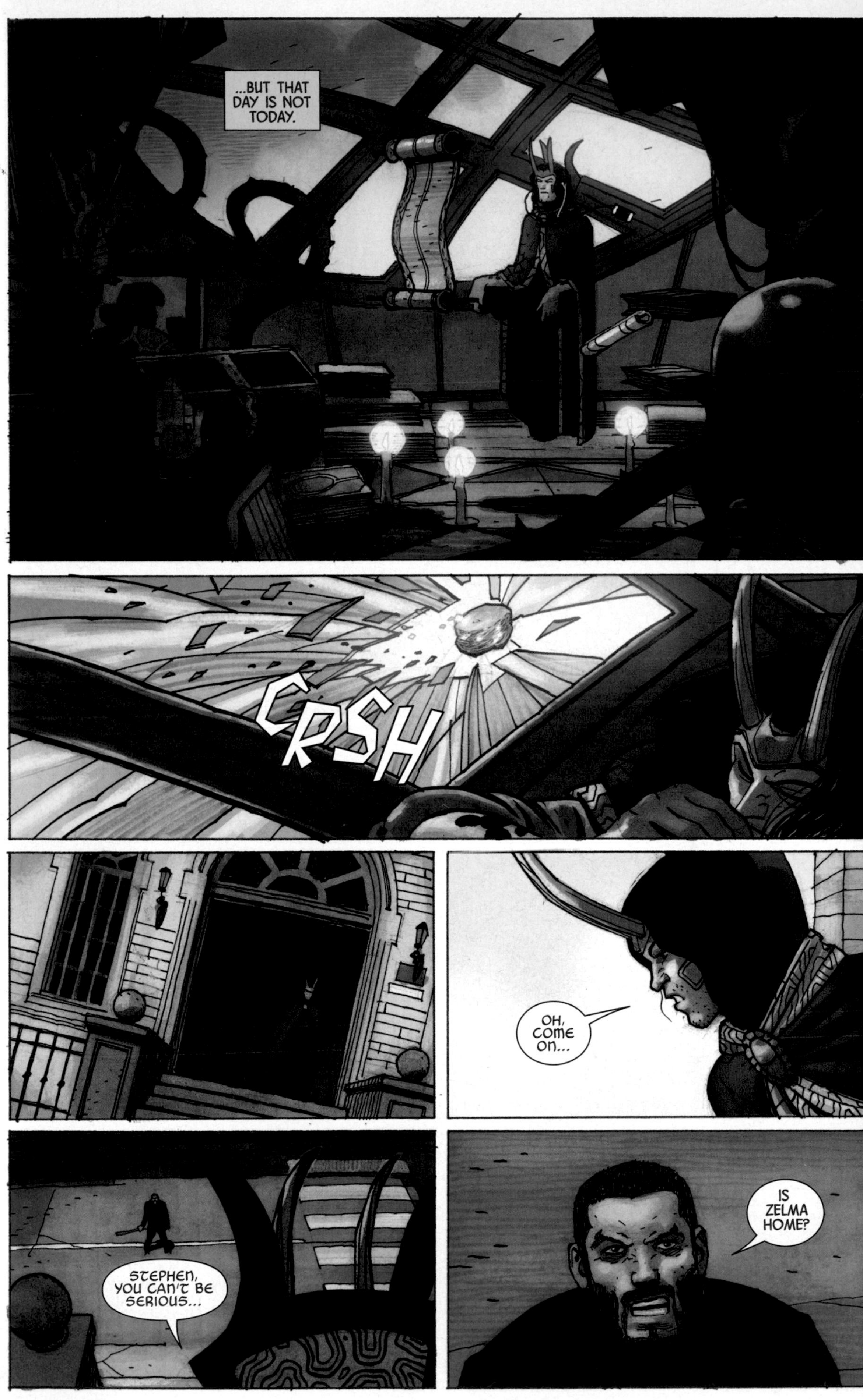
...BUT THAT DAY IS NOT TODAY.
CRSH
OH, COME ON...
STEPHEN, YOU CAN'T BE SERIOUS...
IS ZELMA HOME?

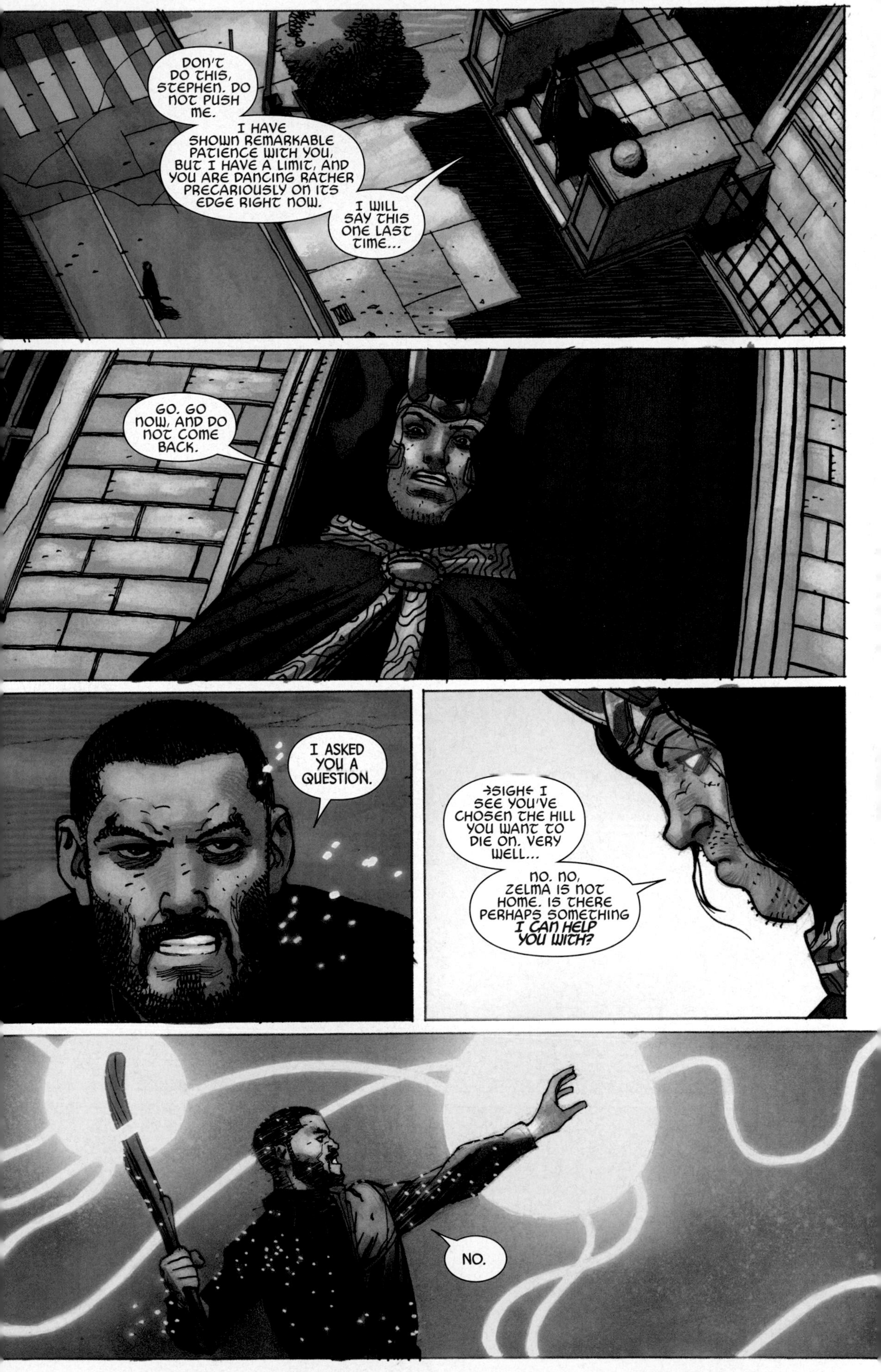

DON'T DO THIS, STEPHEN. DO NOT PUSH ME.
I HAVE SHOWN REMARKABLE PATIENCE WITH YOU, BUT I HAVE A LIMIT, AND YOU ARE DANCING RATHER PRECARIOUSLY ON ITS EDGE RIGHT NOW.
I WILL SAY THIS ONE LAST TIME...
GO. GO NOW, AND DO NOT COME BACK.
I ASKED YOU A QUESTION.
›SIGH‹ I SEE YOU'VE CHOSEN THE HILL YOU WANT TO DIE ON. VERY WELL...
NO. NO, ZELMA IS NOT HOME. IS THERE PERHAPS SOMETHING *I CAN HELP YOU WITH?*
NO.

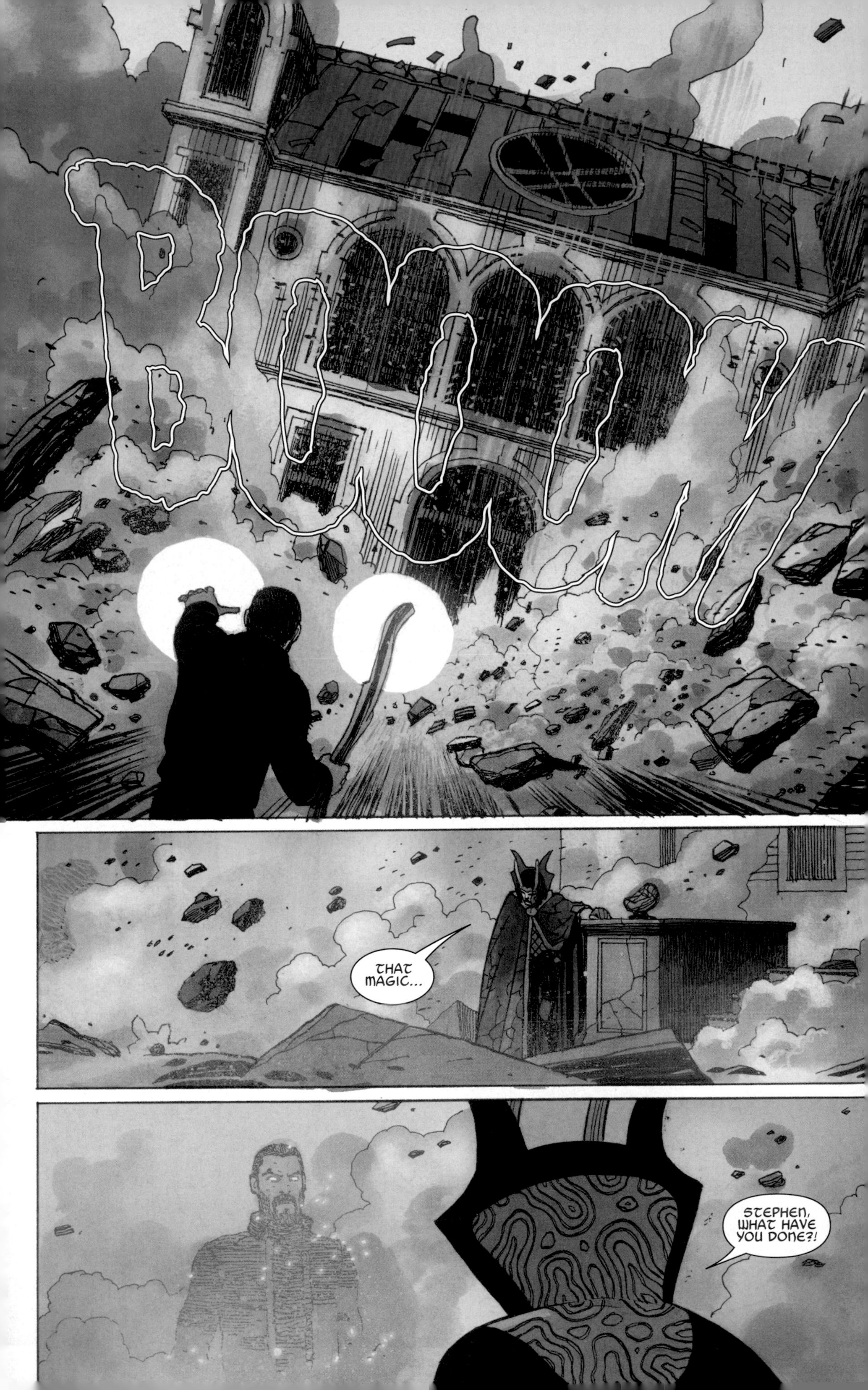
THAT MAGIC...
STEPHEN, WHAT HAVE YOU DONE?!

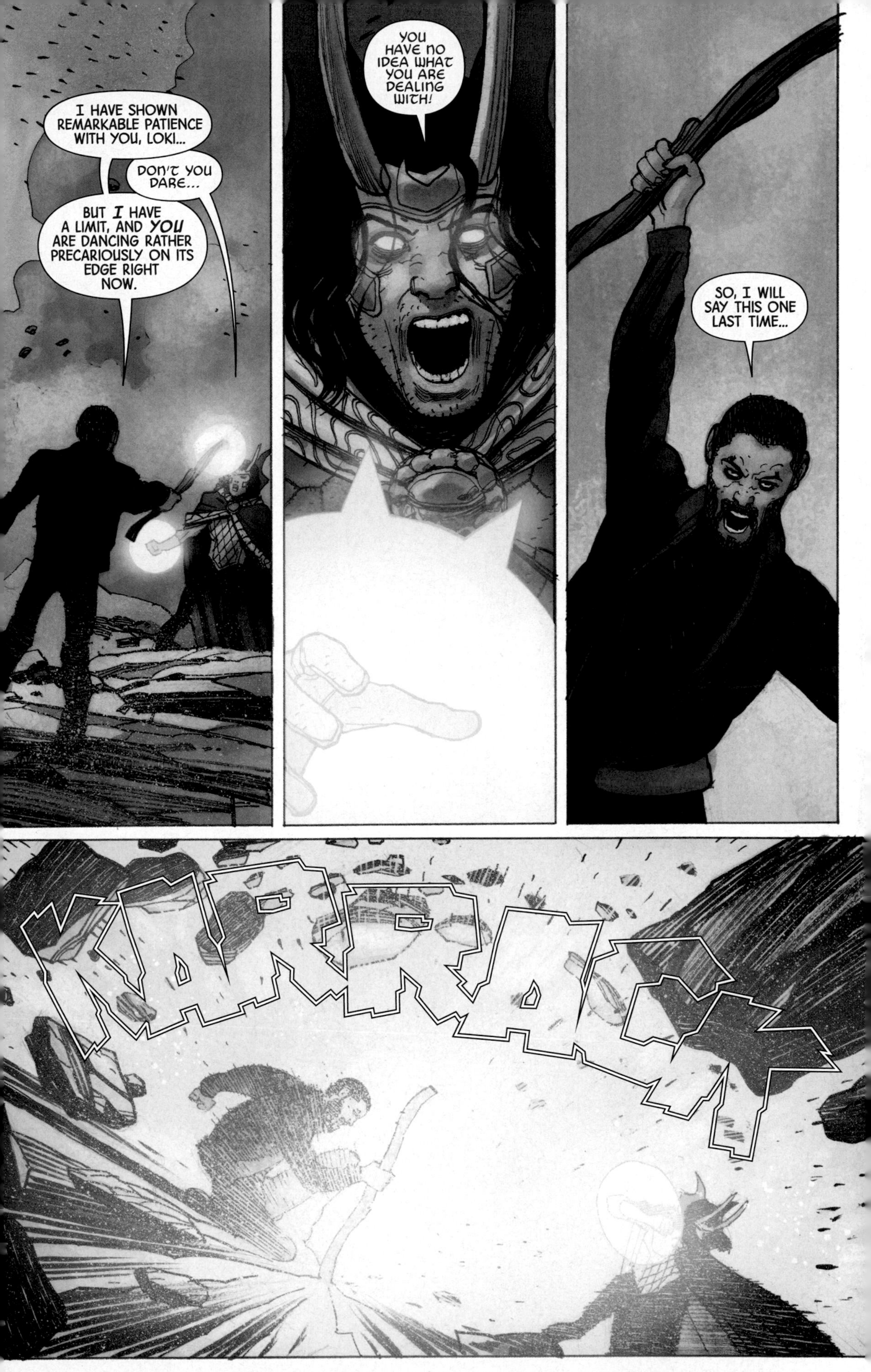
I HAVE SHOWN REMARKABLE PATIENCE WITH YOU, LOKI...
DON'T YOU DARE...
BUT I HAVE A LIMIT, AND YOU ARE DANCING RATHER PRECARIOUSLY ON ITS EDGE RIGHT NOW.
YOU HAVE NO IDEA WHAT YOU ARE DEALING WITH!
SO, I WILL SAY THIS ONE LAST TIME...
KA-RACK

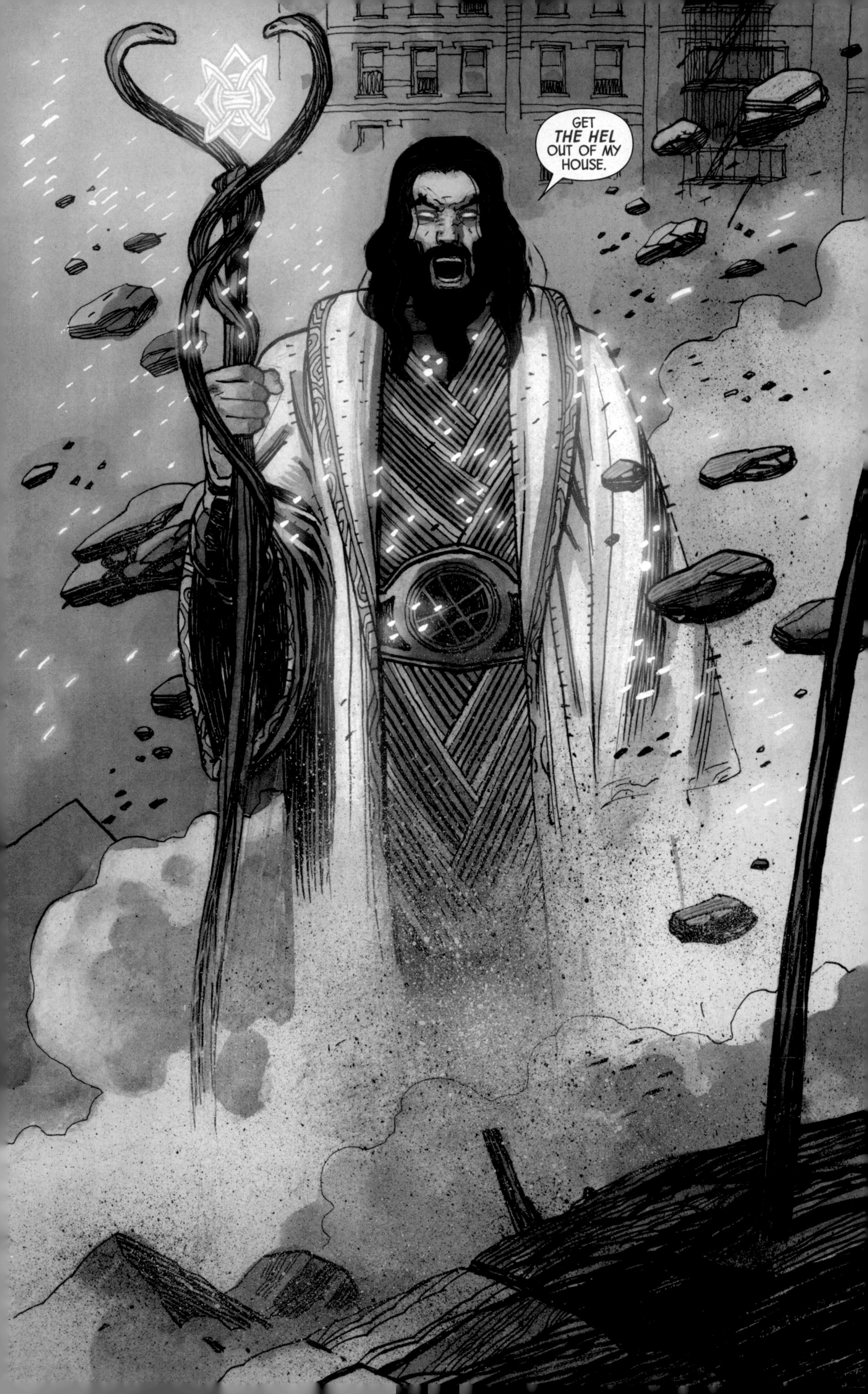
GET THE HEL OUT OF MY HOUSE.

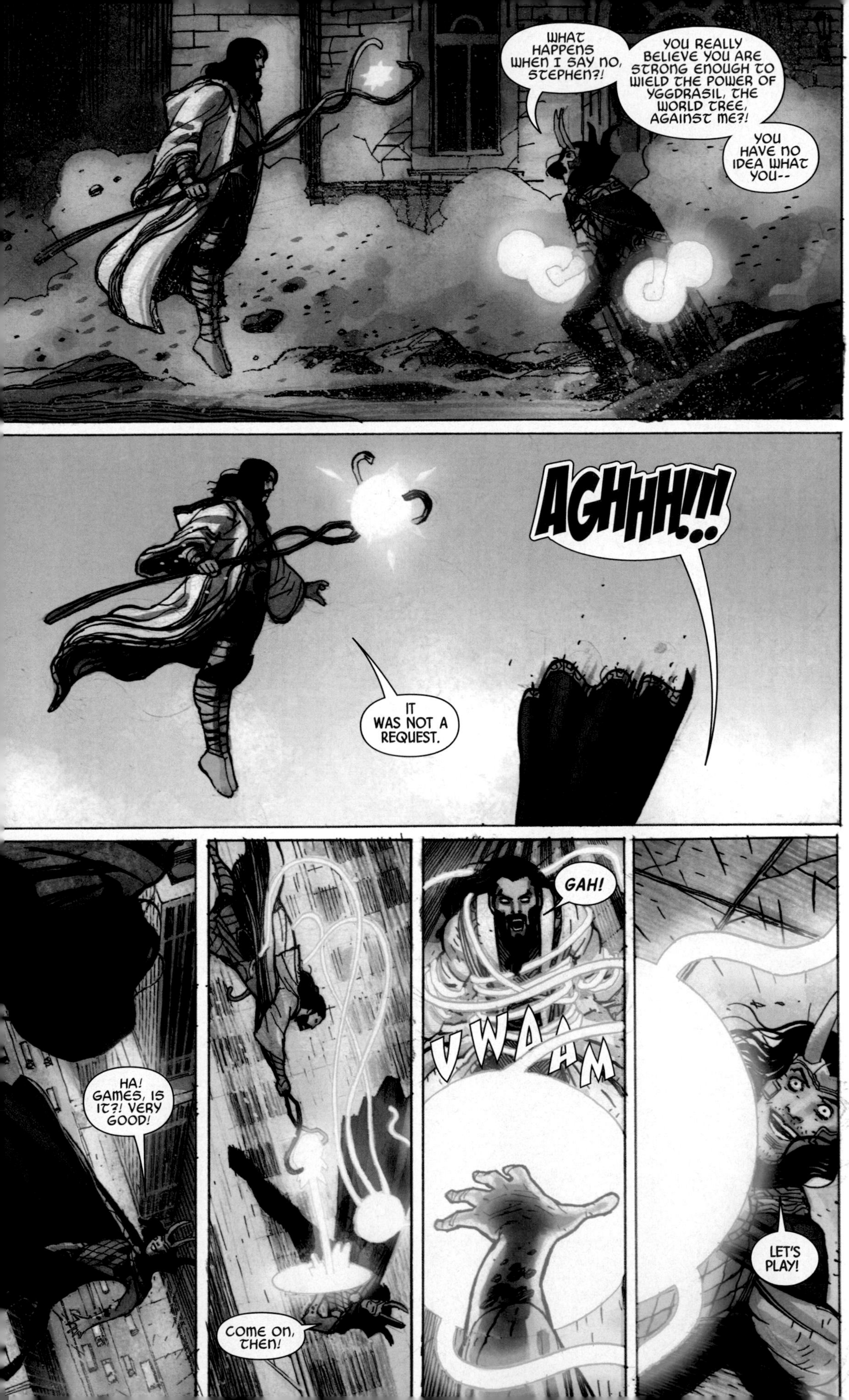

WHAT HAPPENS WHEN I SAY NO, STEPHEN?!
YOU REALLY BELIEVE YOU ARE STRONG ENOUGH TO WIELD THE POWER OF YGGDRASIL, THE WORLD TREE, AGAINST ME?!
YOU HAVE NO IDEA WHAT YOU--
AGHHH!!!
IT WAS NOT A REQUEST.
HA! GAMES, IS IT?! VERY GOOD!
COME ON, THEN!
GAH!
VWAAM
LET'S PLAY!

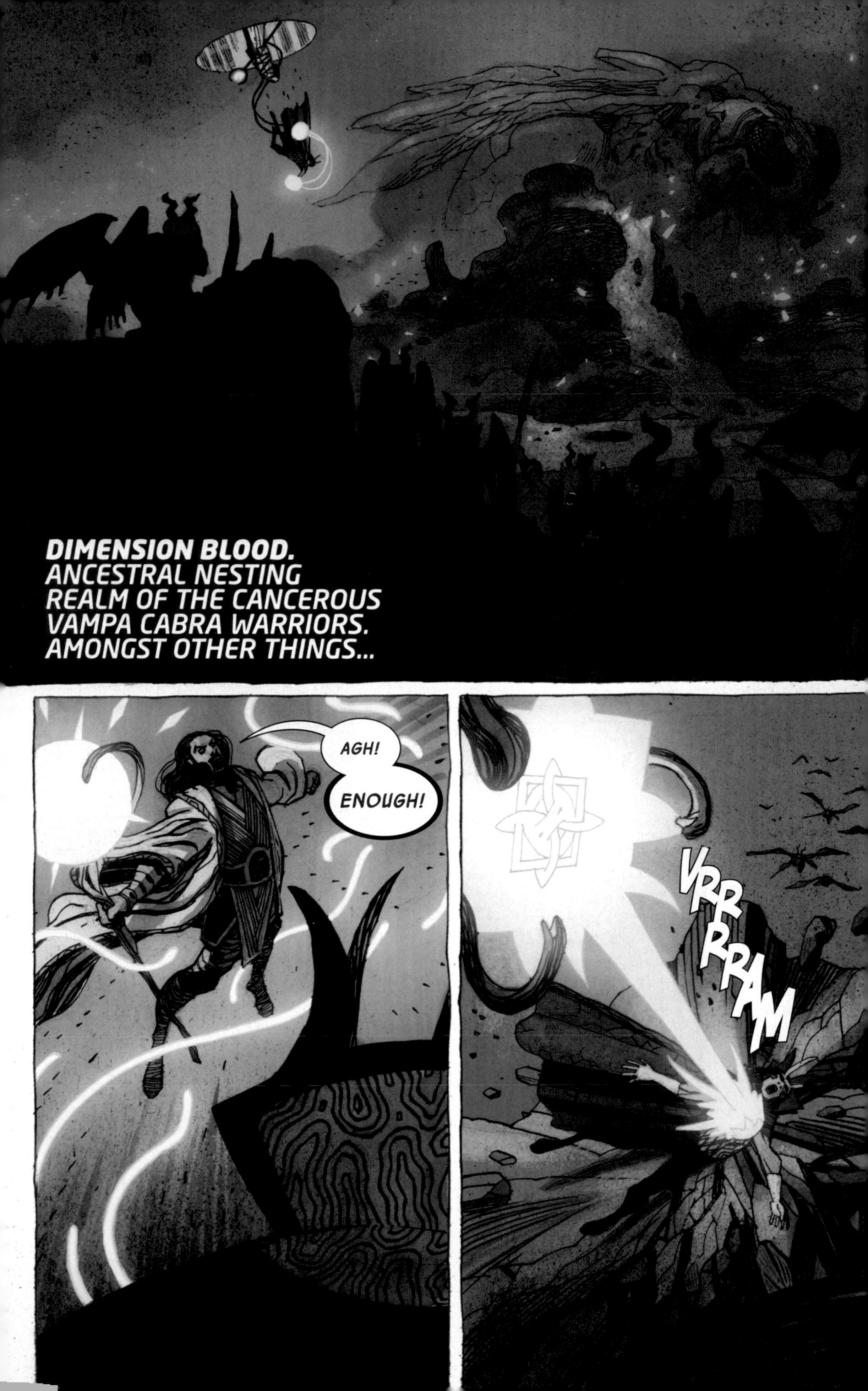
DIMENSION BLOOD.
ANCESTRAL NESTING REALM OF THE CANCEROUS VAMPA CABRA WARRIORS. AMONGST OTHER THINGS...
AGH!
ENOUGH!
VRRRRAM

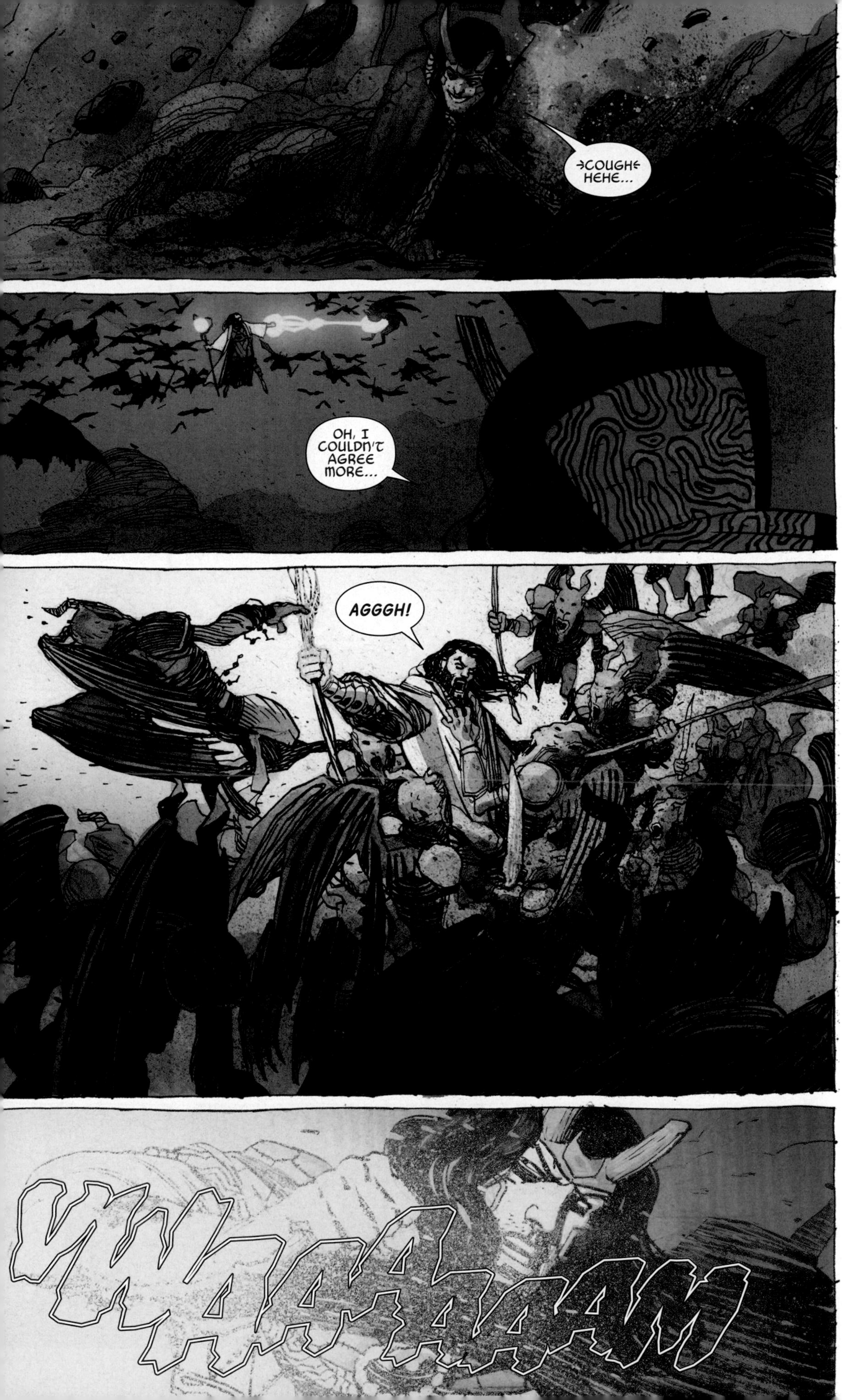
COUGH HEHE...
OH, I COULDN'T AGREE MORE...
AGGGH!
WHAAAAM

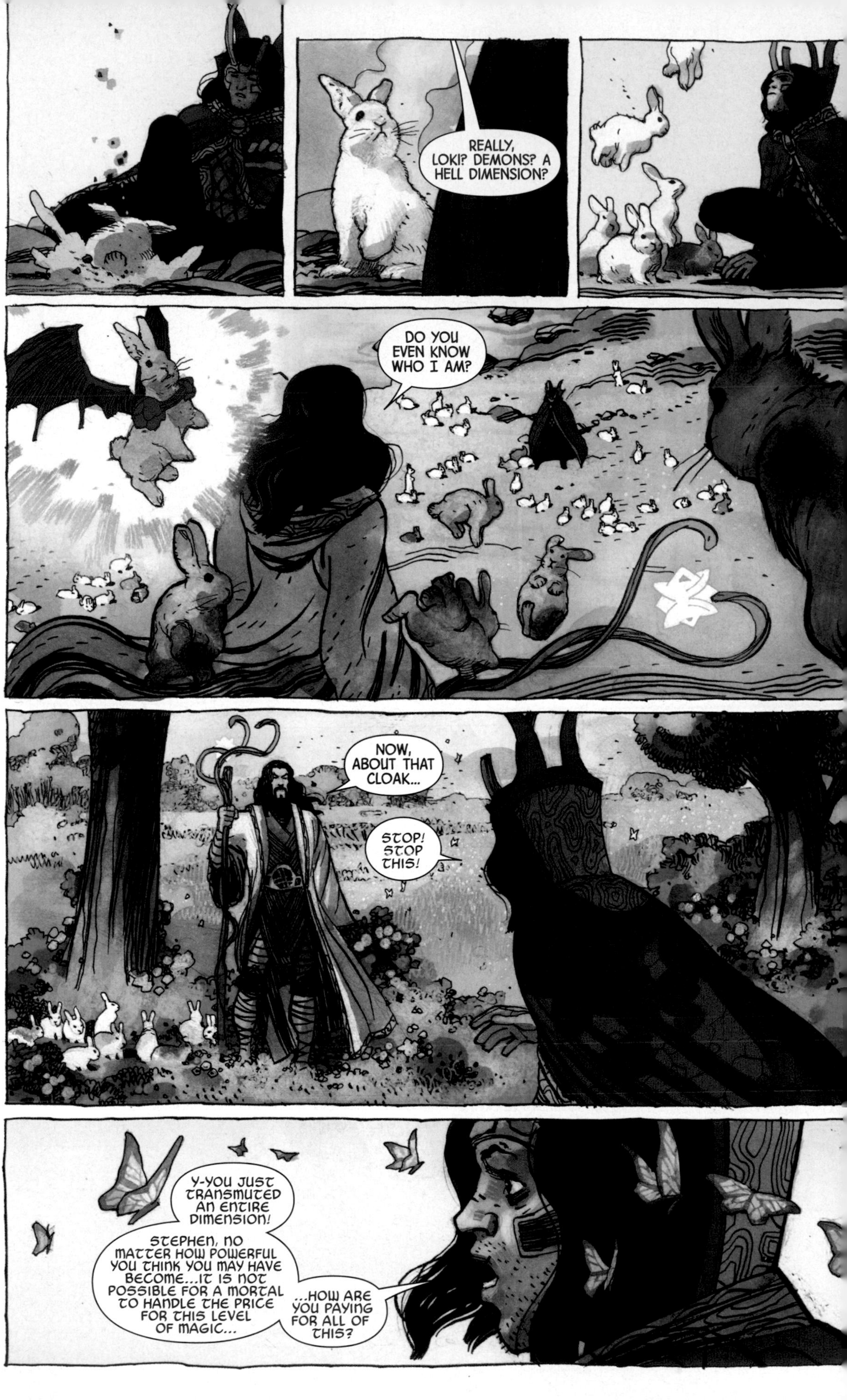
REALLY, LOKI? DEMONS? A HELL DIMENSION?
DO YOU EVEN KNOW WHO I AM?
NOW, ABOUT THAT CLOAK...
STOP! STOP THIS!
Y-YOU JUST TRANSMUTED AN ENTIRE DIMENSION!
STEPHEN, NO MATTER HOW POWERFUL YOU THINK YOU MAY HAVE BECOME...IT IS NOT POSSIBLE FOR A MORTAL TO HANDLE THE PRICE FOR THIS LEVEL OF MAGIC...
...HOW ARE YOU PAYING FOR ALL OF THIS?

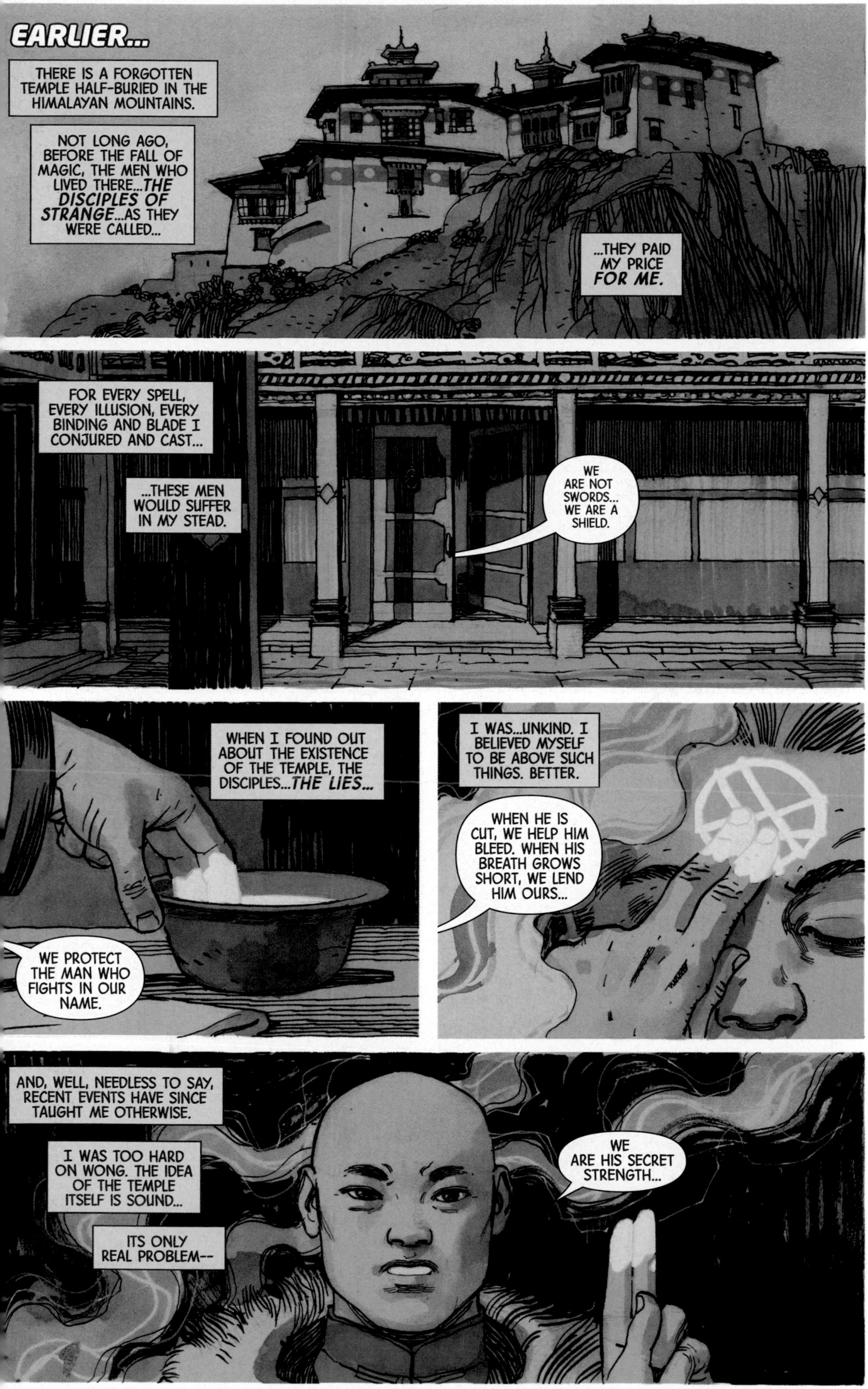
EARLIER...
THERE IS A FORGOTTEN TEMPLE HALF-BURIED IN THE HIMALAYAN MOUNTAINS.
NOT LONG AGO, BEFORE THE FALL OF MAGIC, THE MEN WHO LIVED THERE...THE DISCIPLES OF STRANGE...AS THEY WERE CALLED...
...THEY PAID MY PRICE FOR ME.
FOR EVERY SPELL, EVERY ILLUSION, EVERY BINDING AND BLADE I CONJURED AND CAST...
...THESE MEN WOULD SUFFER IN MY STEAD.
WE ARE NOT SWORDS... WE ARE A SHIELD.
WHEN I FOUND OUT ABOUT THE EXISTENCE OF THE TEMPLE, THE DISCIPLES...THE LIES...
WE PROTECT THE MAN WHO FIGHTS IN OUR NAME.
I WAS...UNKIND. I BELIEVED MYSELF TO BE ABOVE SUCH THINGS. BETTER.
WHEN HE IS CUT, WE HELP HIM BLEED. WHEN HIS BREATH GROWS SHORT, WE LEND HIM OURS...
AND, WELL, NEEDLESS TO SAY, RECENT EVENTS HAVE SINCE TAUGHT ME OTHERWISE.
I WAS TOO HARD ON WONG. THE IDEA OF THE TEMPLE ITSELF IS SOUND...
ITS ONLY REAL PROBLEM--
WE ARE HIS SECRET STRENGTH...

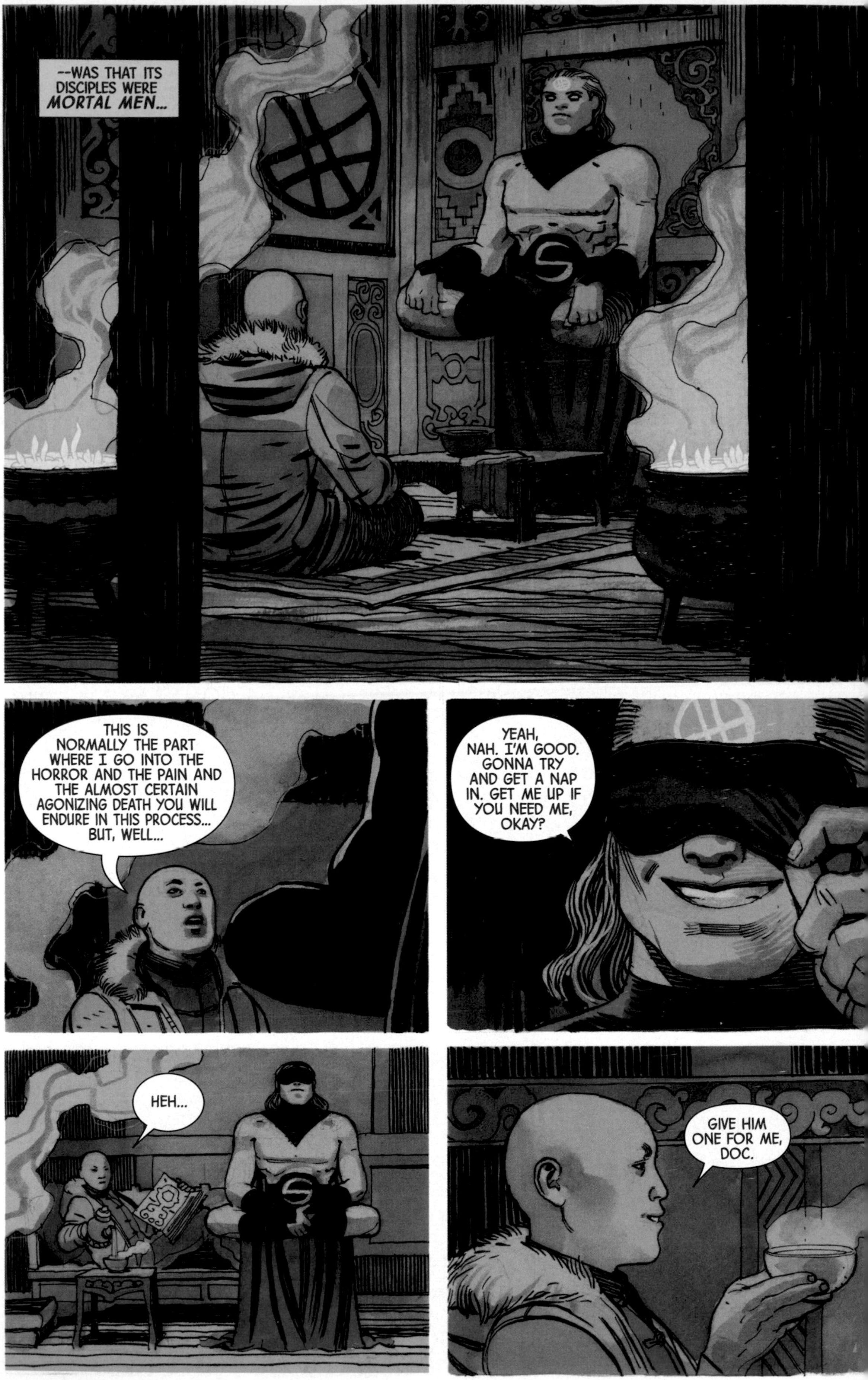
--WAS THAT ITS DISCIPLES WERE *MORTAL MEN*...
THIS IS NORMALLY THE PART WHERE I GO INTO THE HORROR AND THE PAIN AND THE ALMOST CERTAIN AGONIZING DEATH YOU WILL ENDURE IN THIS PROCESS... BUT, WELL...
YEAH, NAH. I'M GOOD. GONNA TRY AND GET A NAP IN. GET ME UP IF YOU NEED ME, OKAY?
HEH...
GIVE HIM ONE FOR ME, DOC.

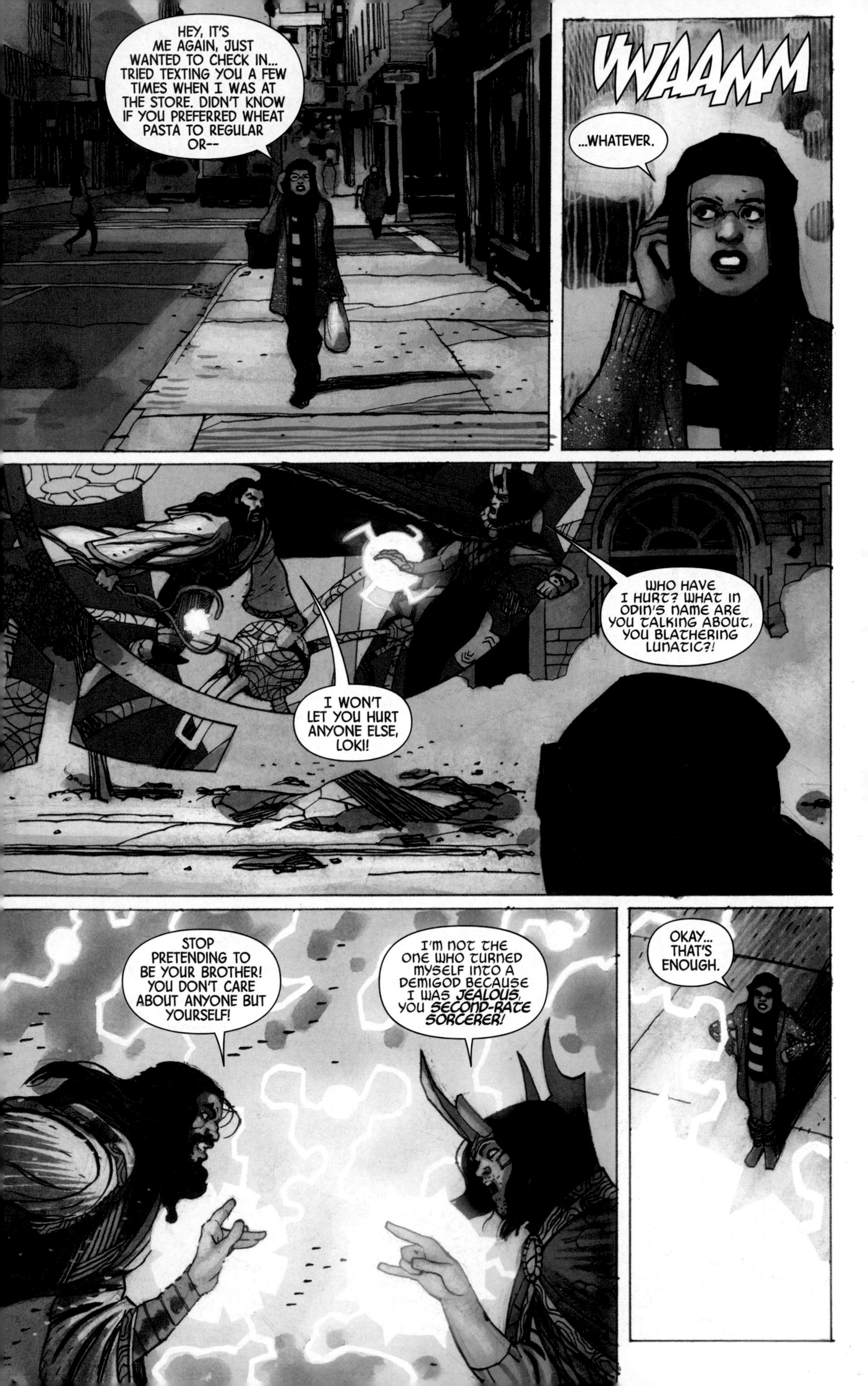
HEY, IT'S ME AGAIN, JUST WANTED TO CHECK IN... TRIED TEXTING YOU A FEW TIMES WHEN I WAS AT THE STORE. DIDN'T KNOW IF YOU PREFERRED WHEAT PASTA TO REGULAR OR--
WAAMM
...WHATEVER.
I WON'T LET YOU HURT ANYONE ELSE, LOKI!
WHO HAVE I HURT? WHAT IN ODIN'S NAME ARE YOU TALKING ABOUT, YOU BLATHERING LUNATIC?!
STOP PRETENDING TO BE YOUR BROTHER! YOU DON'T CARE ABOUT ANYONE BUT YOURSELF!
I'M NOT THE ONE WHO TURNED MYSELF INTO A DEMIGOD BECAUSE I WAS JEALOUS, YOU SECOND-RATE SORCERER!
OKAY... THAT'S ENOUGH.

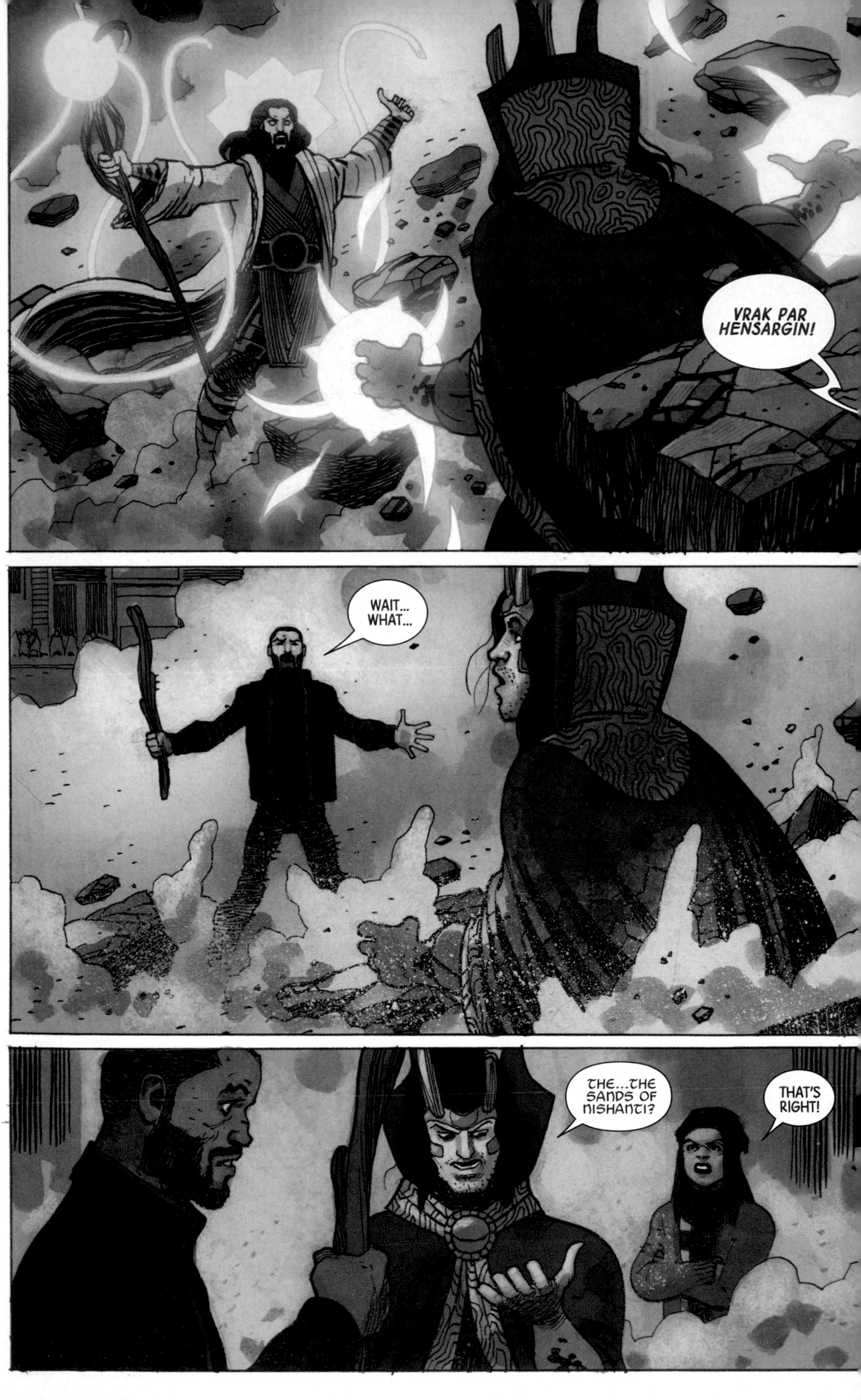
VRAK PAR HENSARGIN!
WAIT... WHAT...
THE...THE SANDS OF NISHANTI?
THAT'S RIGHT!

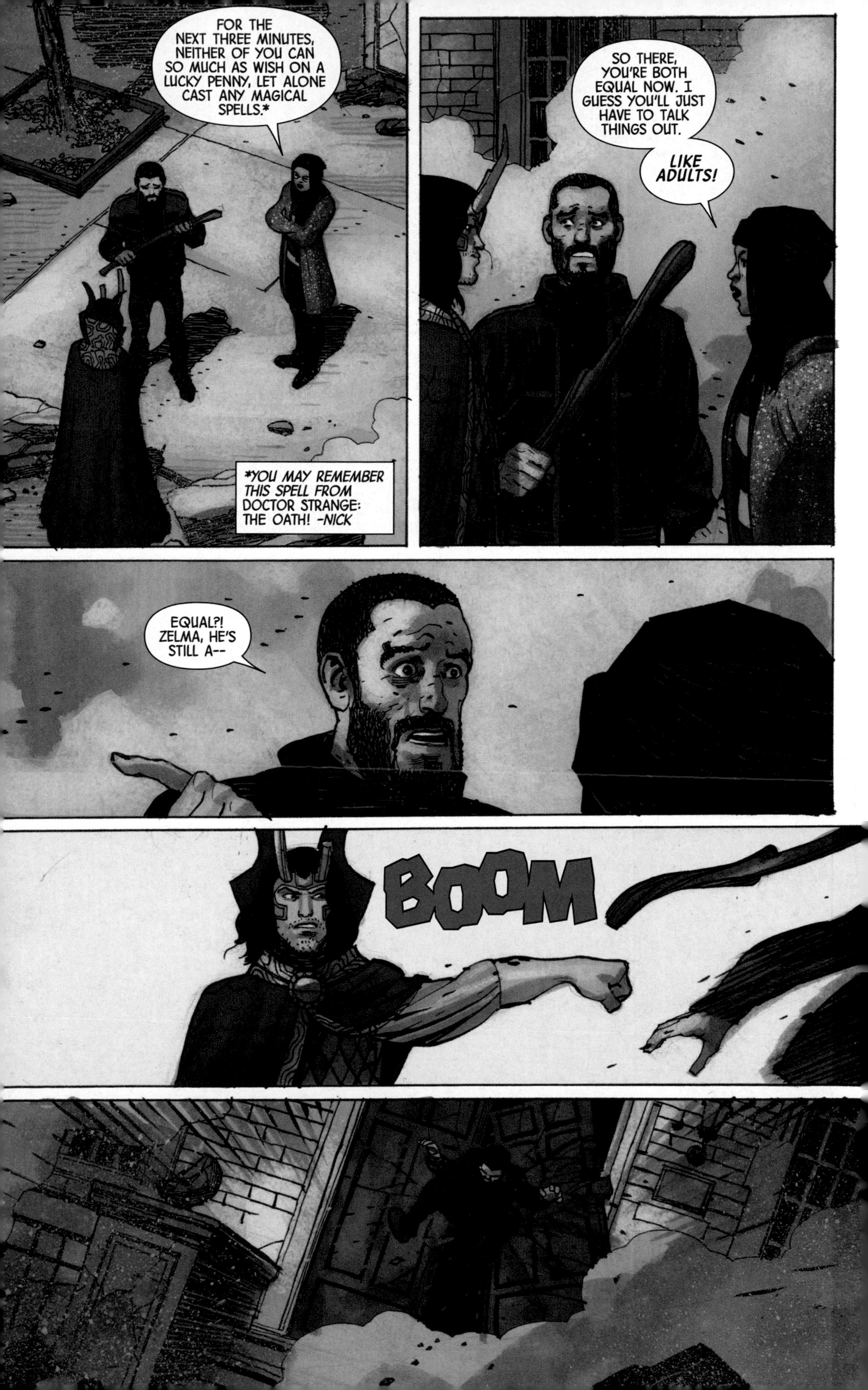

FOR THE NEXT THREE MINUTES, NEITHER OF YOU CAN SO MUCH AS WISH ON A LUCKY PENNY, LET ALONE CAST ANY MAGICAL SPELLS.*
*YOU MAY REMEMBER THIS SPELL FROM DOCTOR STRANGE: THE OATH! -NICK
SO THERE, YOU'RE BOTH EQUAL NOW. I GUESS YOU'LL JUST HAVE TO TALK THINGS OUT.
LIKE ADULTS!
EQUAL?! ZELMA, HE'S STILL A--
BOOM

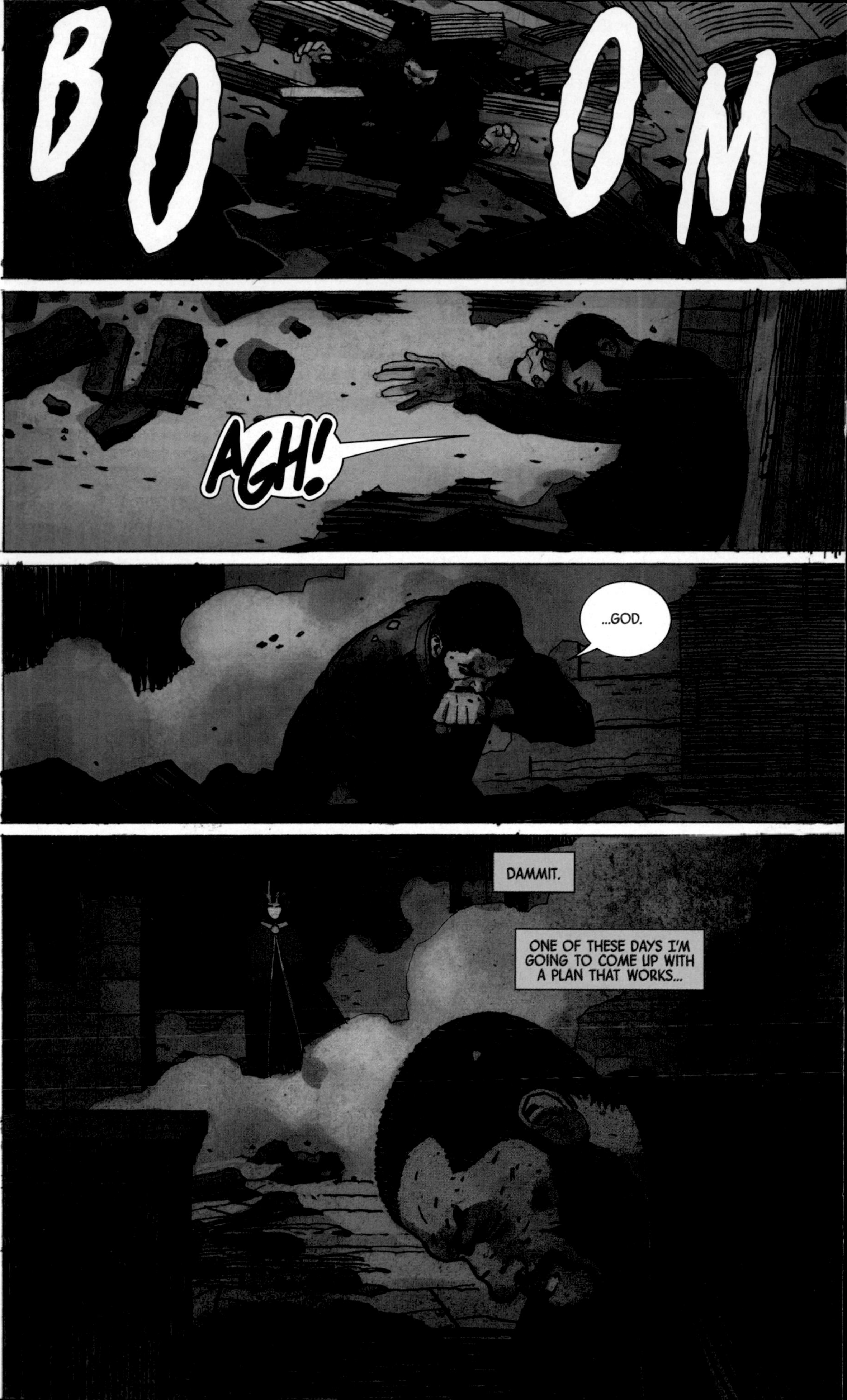
BOOM
AGH!
...GOD.
DAMMIT.
ONE OF THESE DAYS I'M GOING TO COME UP WITH A PLAN THAT WORKS...

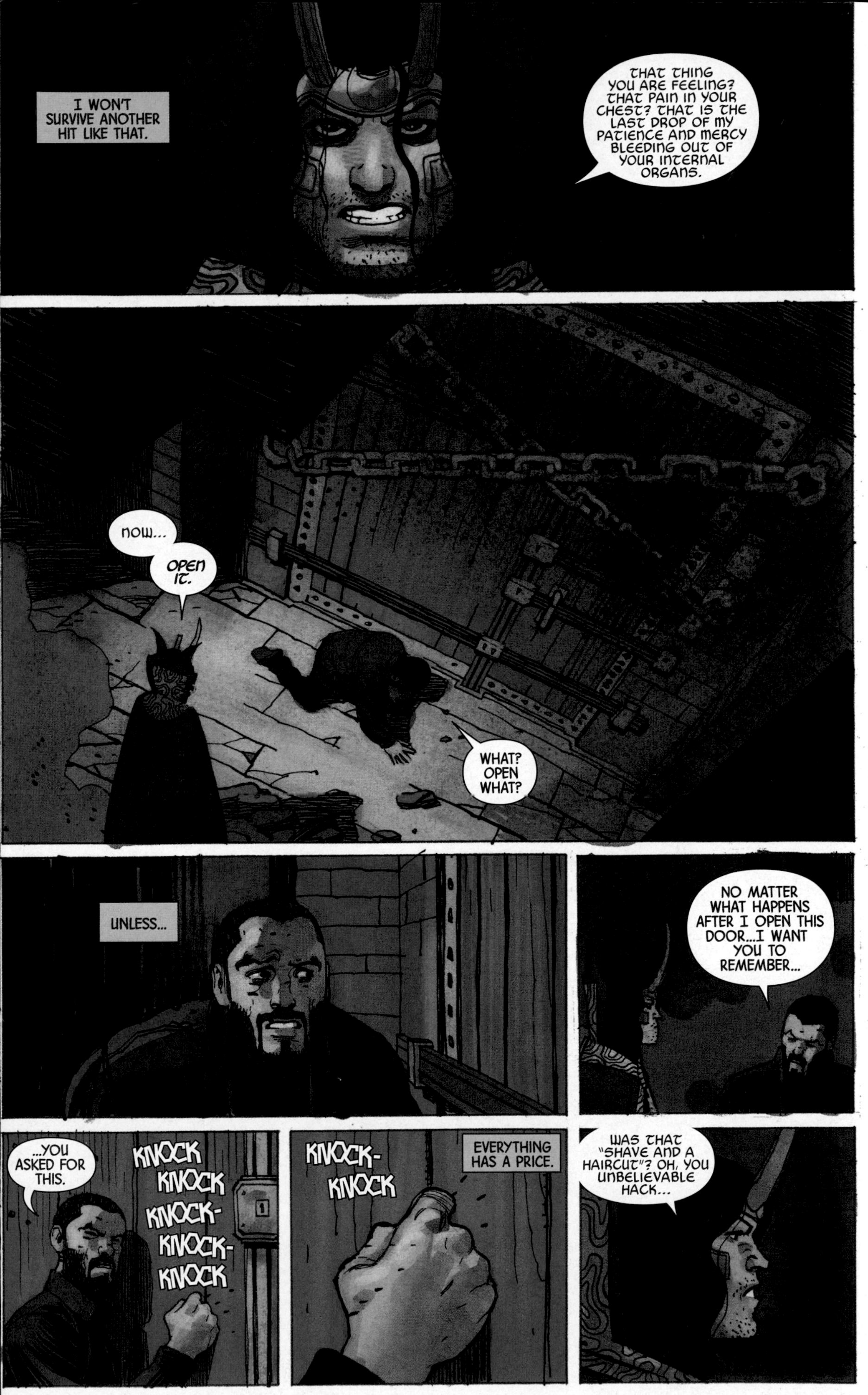
I WON'T SURVIVE ANOTHER HIT LIKE THAT.
THAT THING YOU ARE FEELING? THAT PAIN IN YOUR CHEST? THAT IS THE LAST DROP OF MY PATIENCE AND MERCY BLEEDING OUT OF YOUR INTERNAL ORGANS.
NOW...
OPEN IT.
WHAT? OPEN WHAT?
UNLESS...
NO MATTER WHAT HAPPENS AFTER I OPEN THIS DOOR...I WANT YOU TO REMEMBER...
...YOU ASKED FOR THIS.
KNOCK KNOCK KNOCK-KNOCK-KNOCK
KNOCK-KNOCK
EVERYTHING HAS A PRICE.
WAS THAT "SHAVE AND A HAIRCUT"? OH, YOU UNBELIEVABLE HACK...

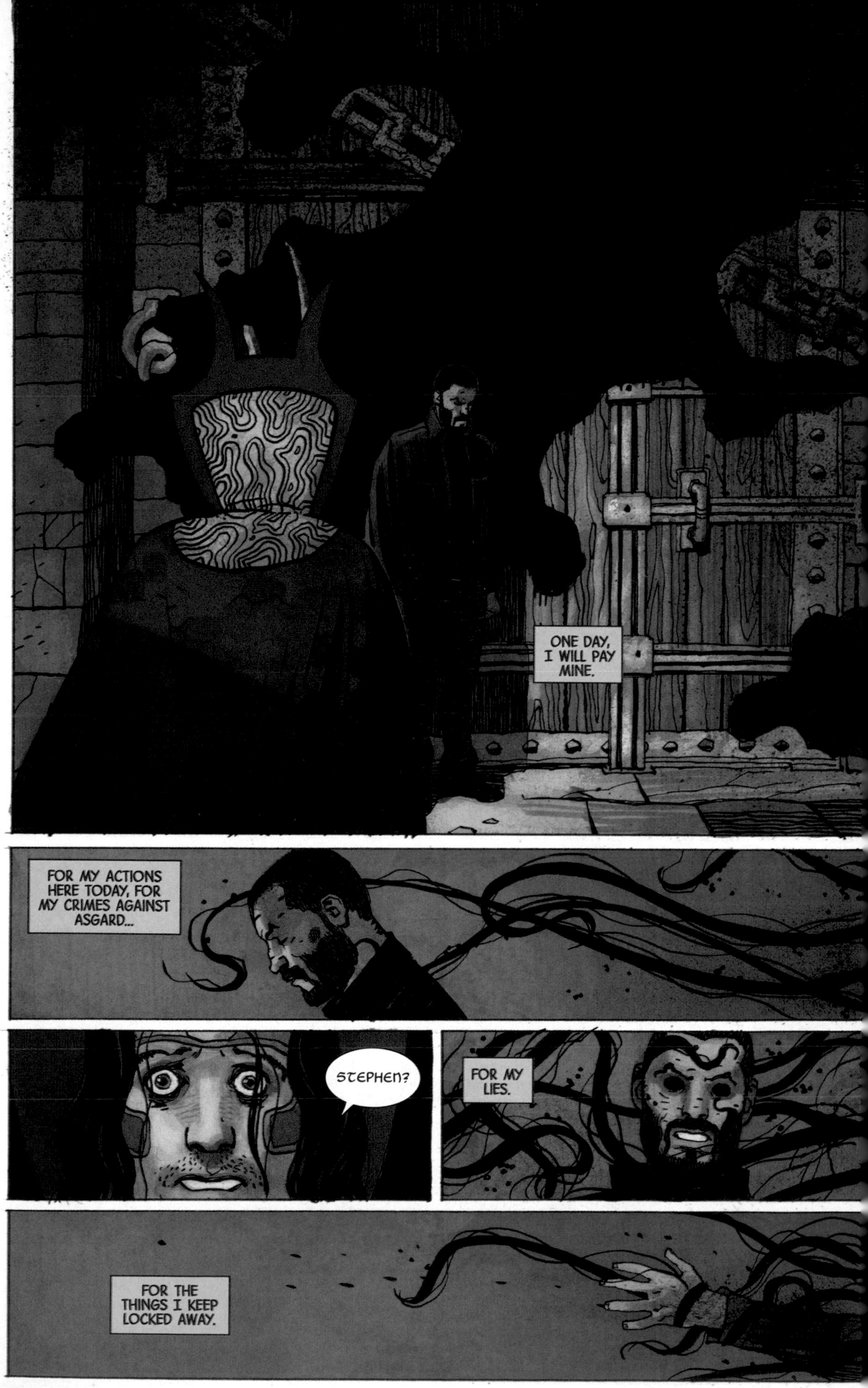
ONE DAY, I WILL PAY MINE.
FOR MY ACTIONS HERE TODAY, FOR MY CRIMES AGAINST ASGARD...
STEPHEN?
FOR MY LIES.
FOR THE THINGS I KEEP LOCKED AWAY.

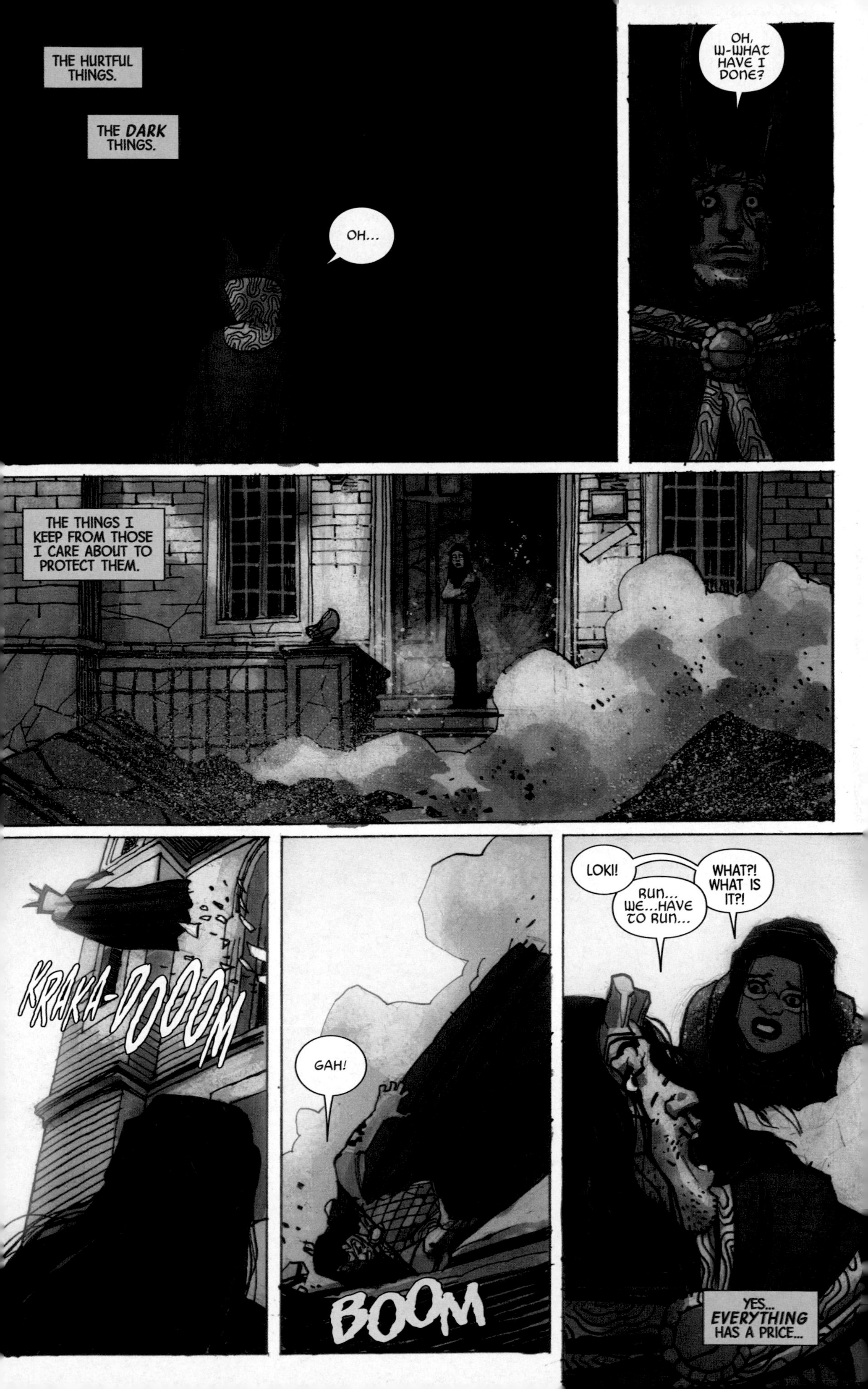
THE HURTFUL THINGS.
THE DARK THINGS.
OH...
OH, W-WHAT HAVE I DONE?
THE THINGS I KEEP FROM THOSE I CARE ABOUT TO PROTECT THEM.
KRAKA-DOOOM
GAH!
BOOM
LOKI!
WHAT?! WHAT IS IT?!
RUN... WE...HAVE TO RUN...
YES... EVERYTHING HAS A PRICE...

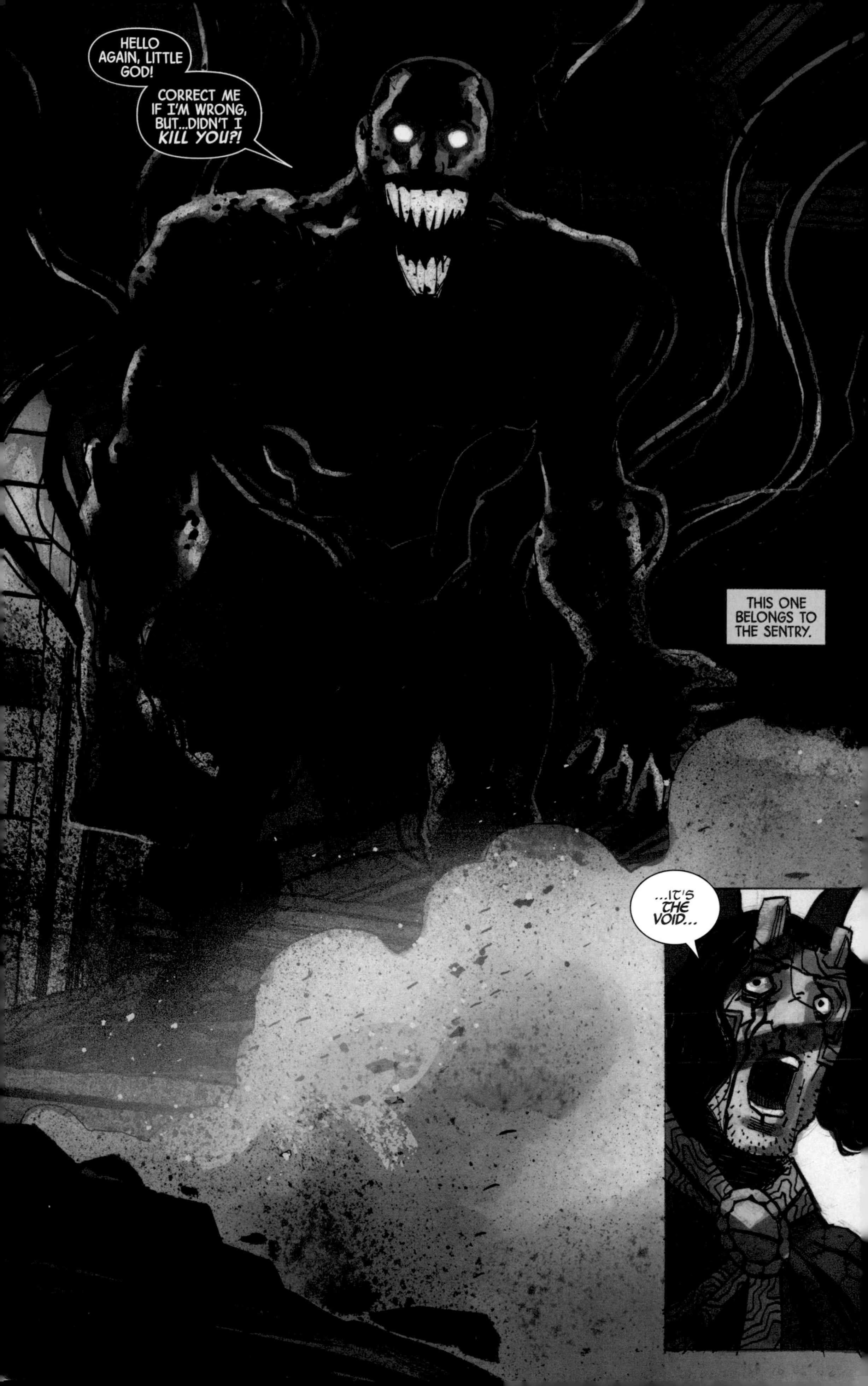
HELLO AGAIN, LITTLE GOD!
CORRECT ME IF I'M WRONG, BUT...DIDN'T I KILL YOU?!
THIS ONE BELONGS TO THE SENTRY.
...IT'S THE VOID...

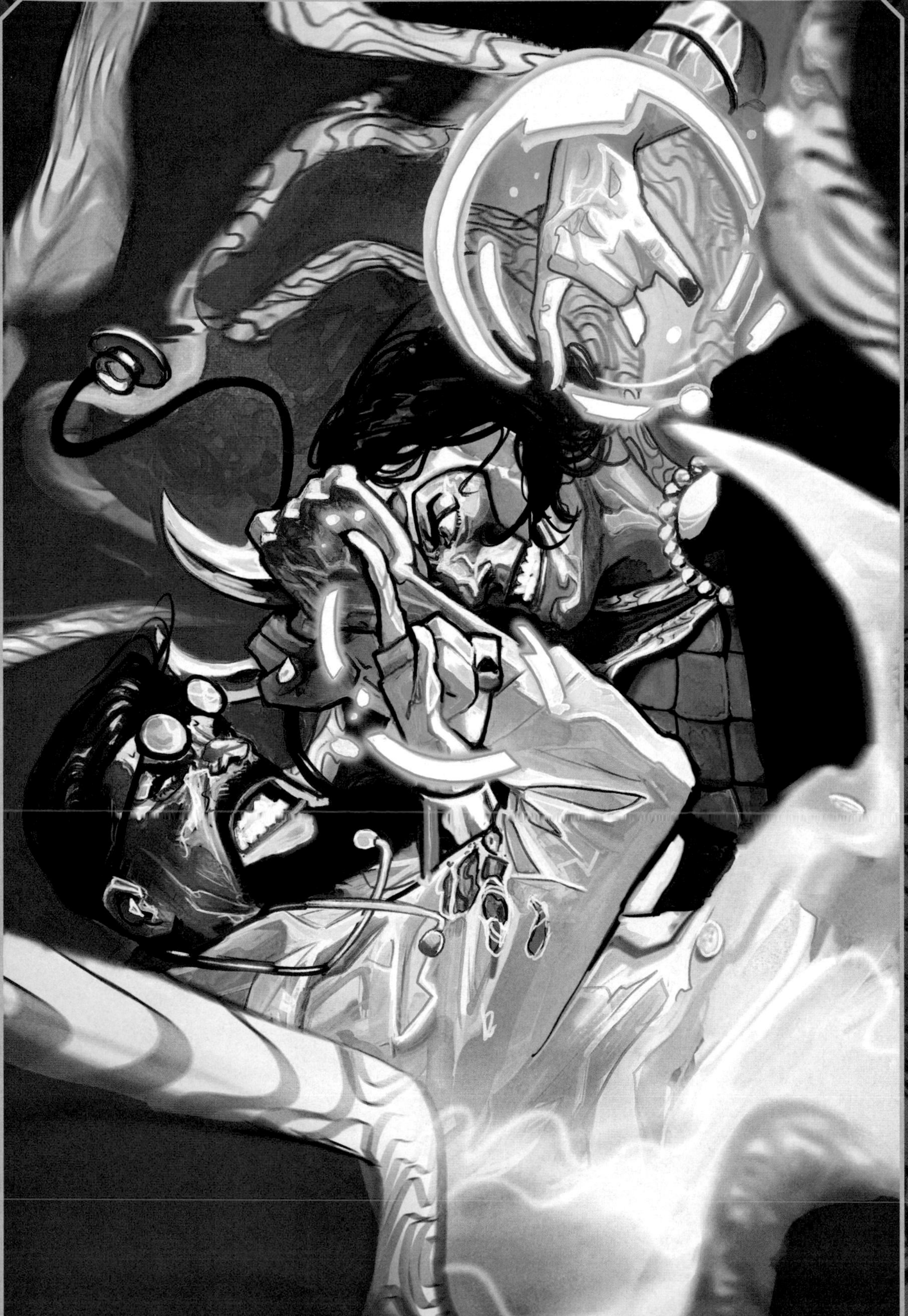

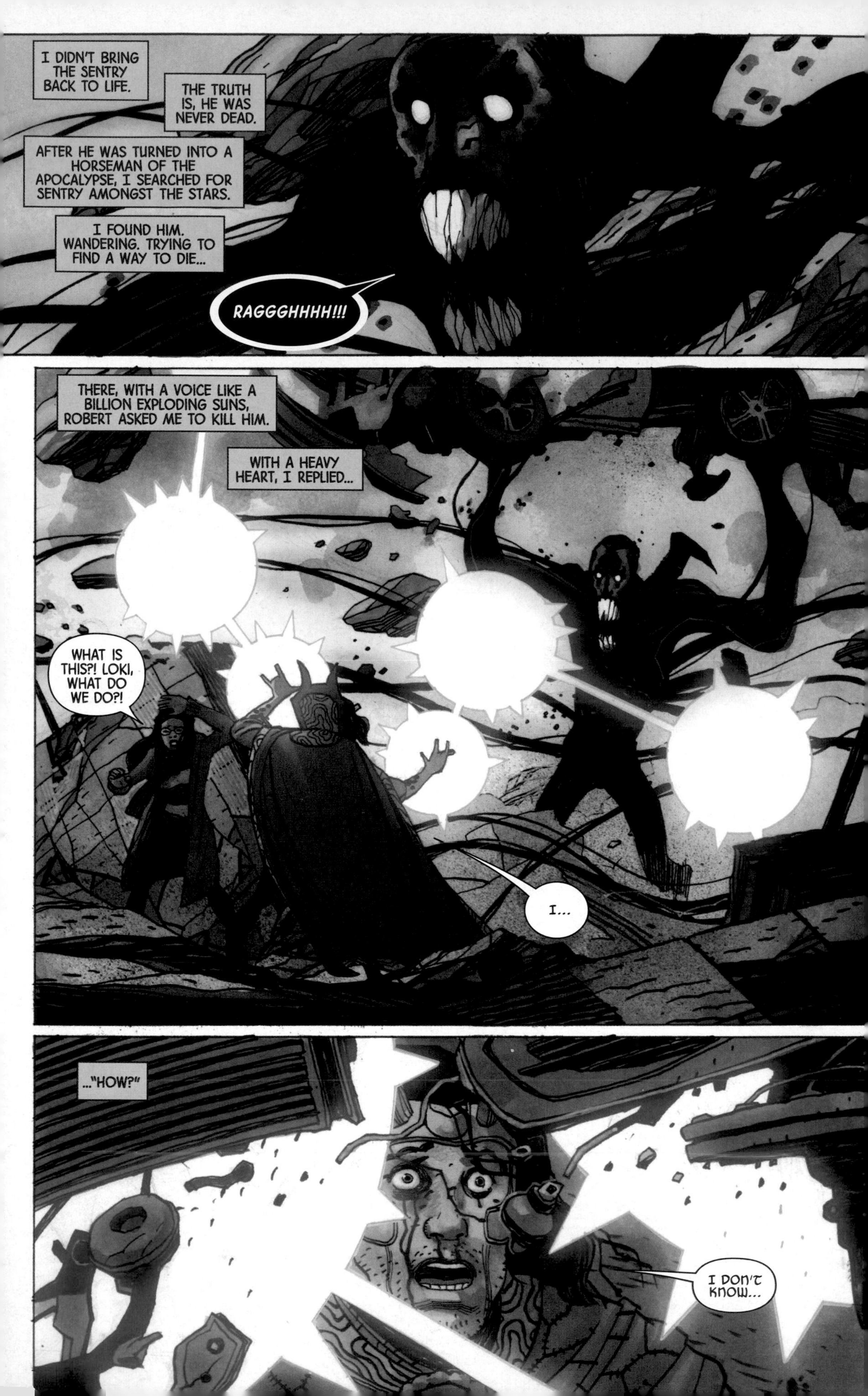
I DIDN'T BRING THE SENTRY BACK TO LIFE.
THE TRUTH IS, HE WAS NEVER DEAD.
AFTER HE WAS TURNED INTO A HORSEMAN OF THE APOCALYPSE, I SEARCHED FOR SENTRY AMONGST THE STARS.
I FOUND HIM. WANDERING. TRYING TO FIND A WAY TO DIE...
RAGGGHHHH!!!
THERE, WITH A VOICE LIKE A BILLION EXPLODING SUNS, ROBERT ASKED ME TO KILL HIM.
WITH A HEAVY HEART, I REPLIED...
WHAT IS THIS?! LOKI, WHAT DO WE DO?!
I...
..."HOW?"
I DON'T KNOW...

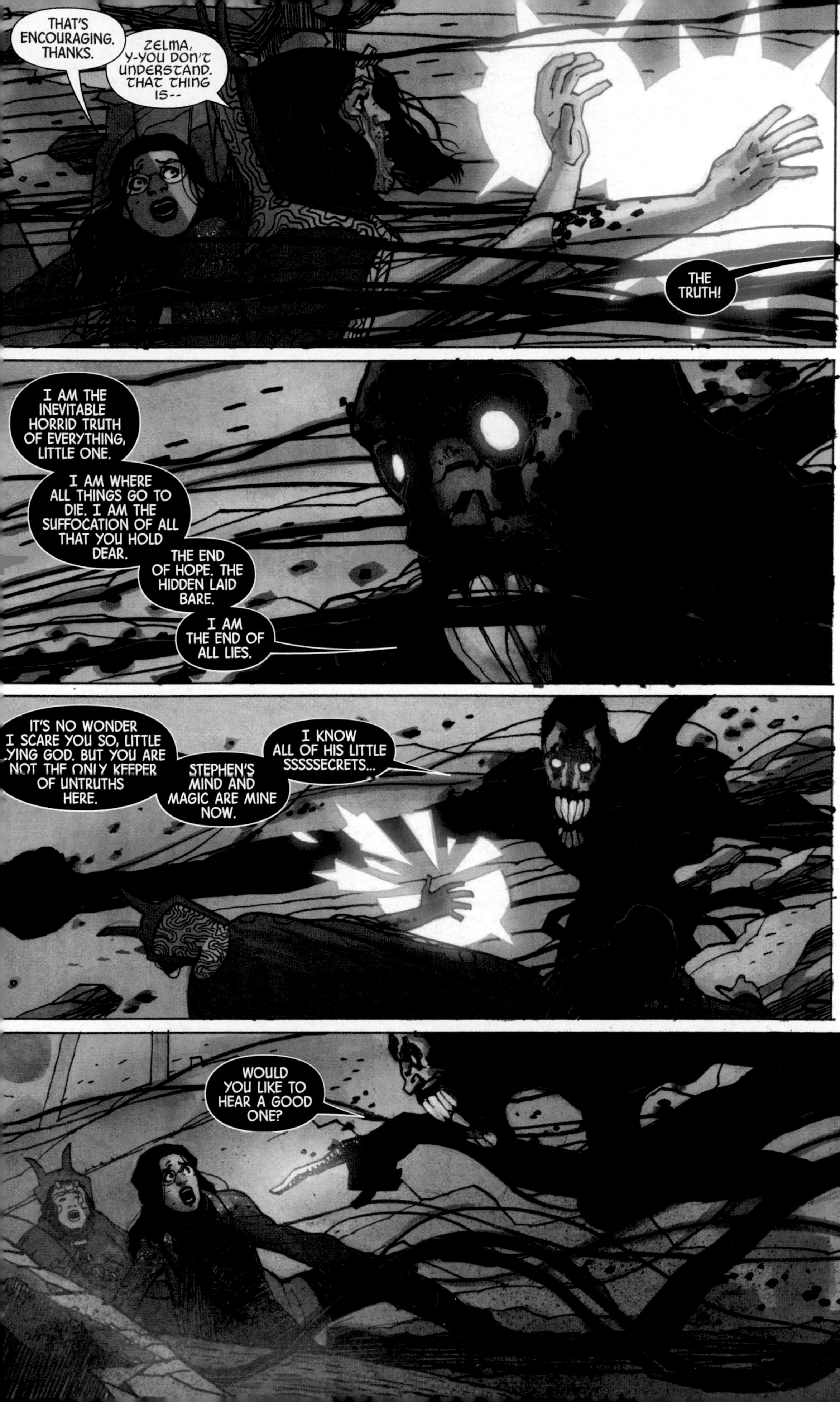
THAT'S ENCOURAGING. THANKS.
ZELMA, Y-YOU DON'T UNDERSTAND. THAT THING IS--
THE TRUTH!
I AM THE INEVITABLE HORRID TRUTH OF EVERYTHING, LITTLE ONE.
I AM WHERE ALL THINGS GO TO DIE. I AM THE SUFFOCATION OF ALL THAT YOU HOLD DEAR.
THE END OF HOPE. THE HIDDEN LAID BARE.
I AM THE END OF ALL LIES.
IT'S NO WONDER I SCARE YOU SO, LITTLE LYING GOD. BUT YOU ARE NOT THE ONLY KEEPER OF UNTRUTHS HERE.
STEPHEN'S MIND AND MAGIC ARE MINE NOW.
I KNOW ALL OF HIS LITTLE SSSSSECRETS...
WOULD YOU LIKE TO HEAR A GOOD ONE?

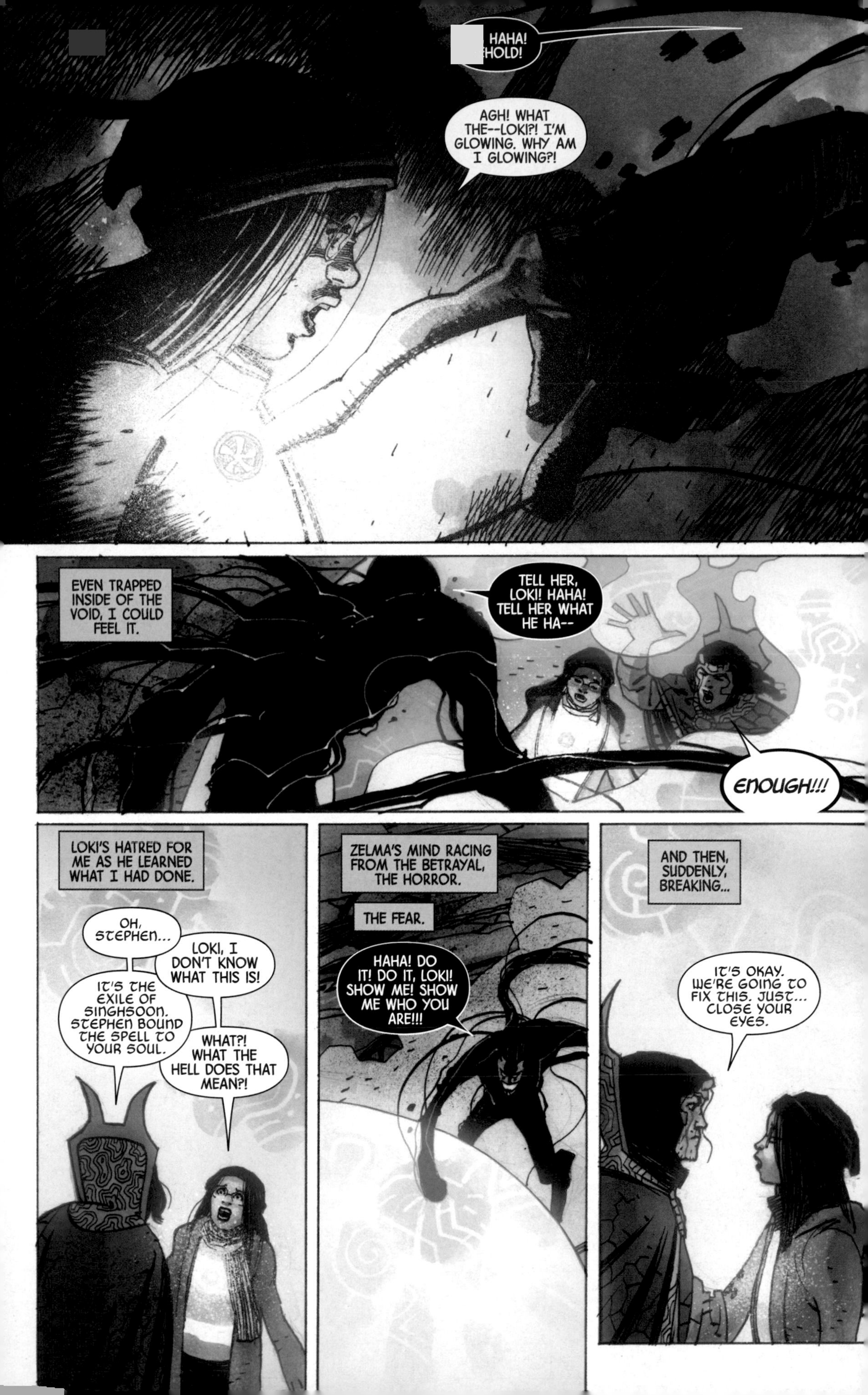
HAHA!
AGH! WHAT THE--LOKI?! I'M GLOWING. WHY AM I GLOWING?!
EVEN TRAPPED INSIDE OF THE VOID, I COULD FEEL IT.
TELL HER, LOKI! HAHA! TELL HER WHAT HE HA--
ENOUGH!!!
LOKI'S HATRED FOR ME AS HE LEARNED WHAT I HAD DONE.
OH, STEPHEN...
LOKI, I DON'T KNOW WHAT THIS IS!
IT'S THE EXILE OF SINGHSOON. STEPHEN BOUND THE SPELL TO YOUR SOUL.
WHAT?! WHAT THE HELL DOES THAT MEAN?!
ZELMA'S MIND RACING FROM THE BETRAYAL, THE HORROR.
THE FEAR.
HAHA! DO IT! DO IT, LOKI! SHOW ME! SHOW ME WHO YOU ARE!!!
AND THEN, SUDDENLY, BREAKING...
IT'S OKAY. WE'RE GOING TO FIX THIS. JUST... CLOSE YOUR EYES.

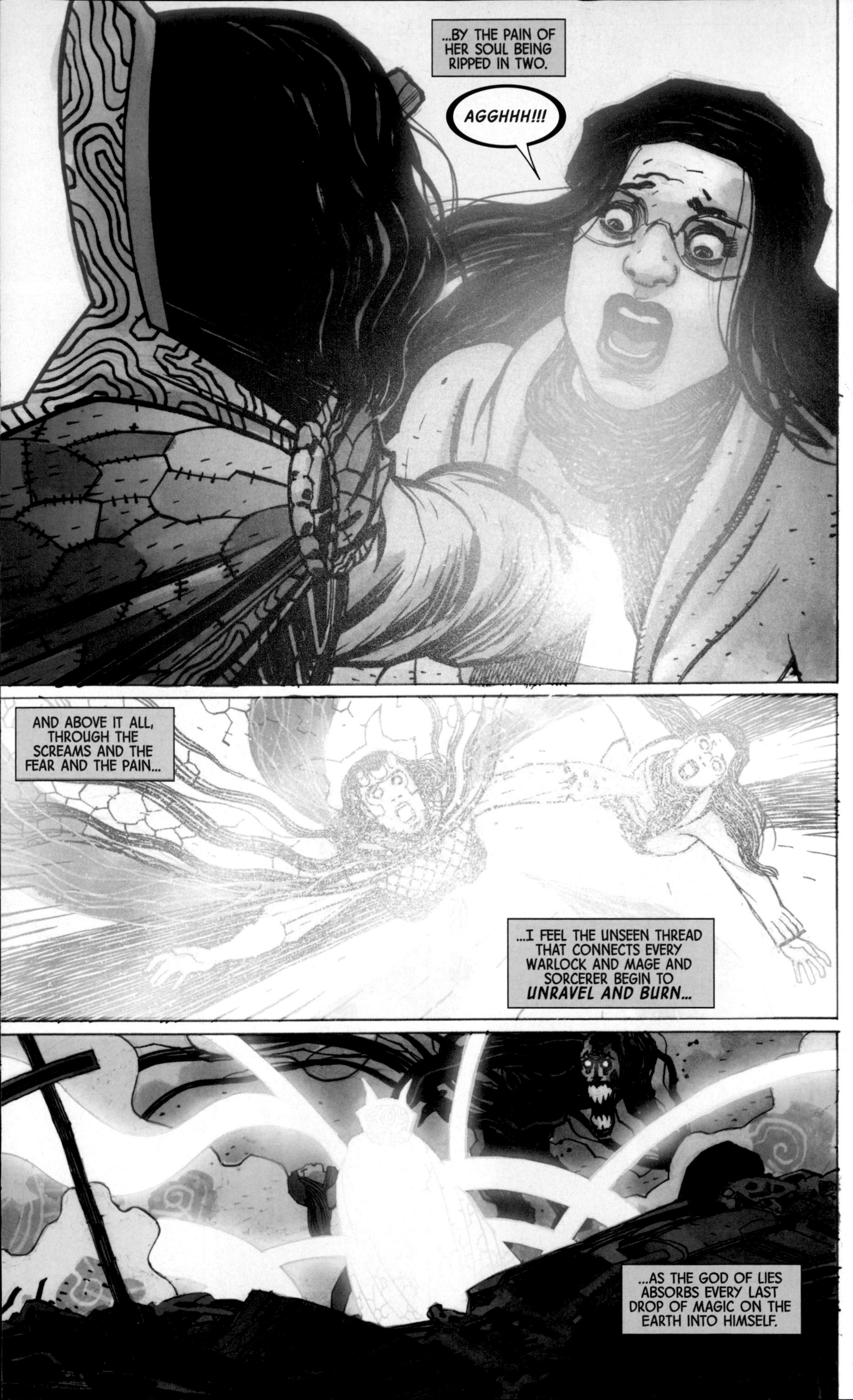
...BY THE PAIN OF HER SOUL BEING RIPPED IN TWO.
AGGHHH!!!
AND ABOVE IT ALL, THROUGH THE SCREAMS AND THE FEAR AND THE PAIN...
...I FEEL THE UNSEEN THREAD THAT CONNECTS EVERY WARLOCK AND MAGE AND SORCERER BEGIN TO UNRAVEL AND BURN...
...AS THE GOD OF LIES ABSORBS EVERY LAST DROP OF MAGIC ON THE EARTH INTO HIMSELF.

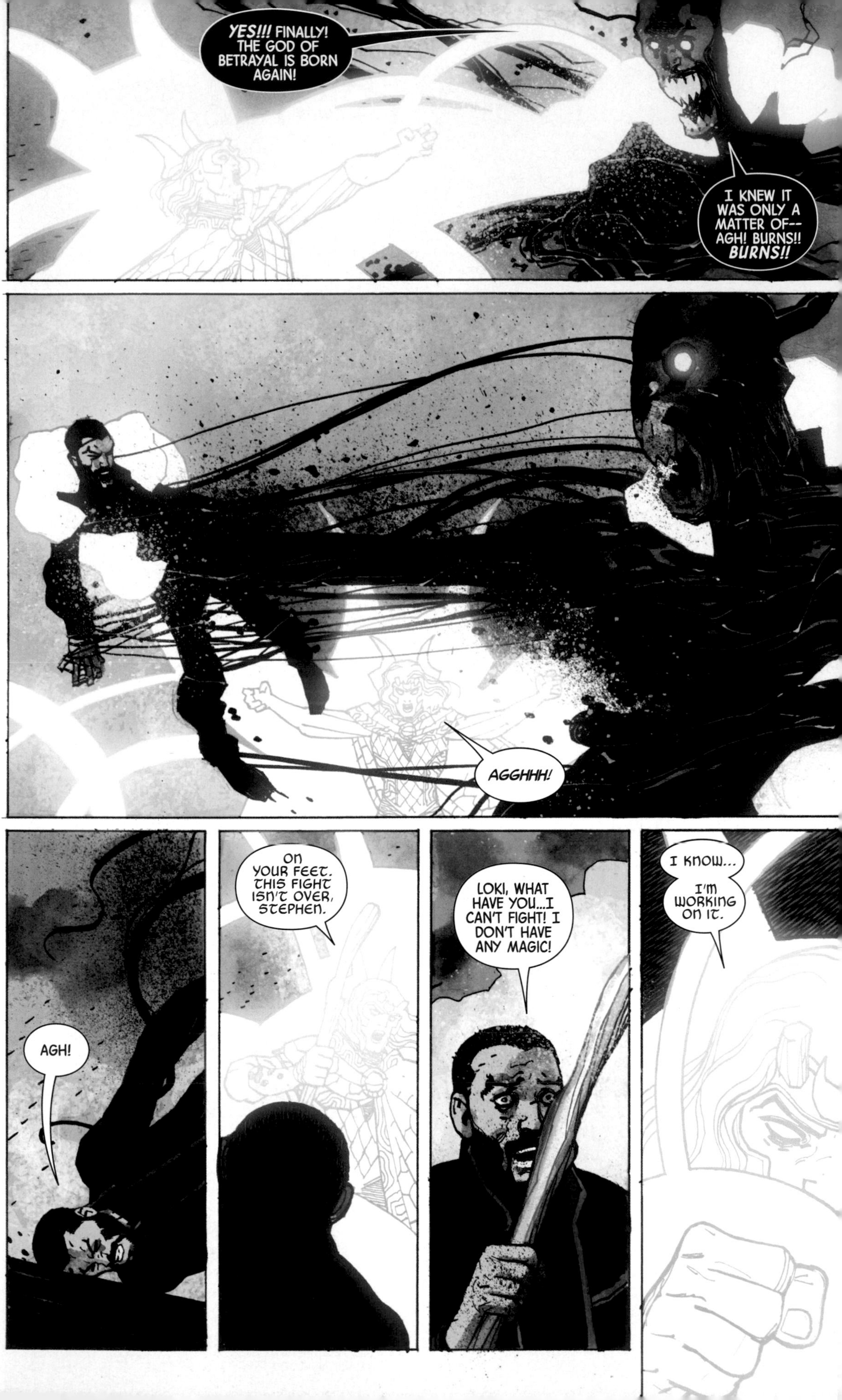
YES!!! FINALLY! THE GOD OF BETRAYAL IS BORN AGAIN!
I KNEW IT WAS ONLY A MATTER OF-- AGH! BURNS!! BURNS!!
AGGHHH!
AGH!
ON YOUR FEET. THIS FIGHT ISN'T OVER, STEPHEN.
LOKI, WHAT HAVE YOU...I CAN'T FIGHT! I DON'T HAVE ANY MAGIC!
I KNOW...
I'M WORKING ON IT.

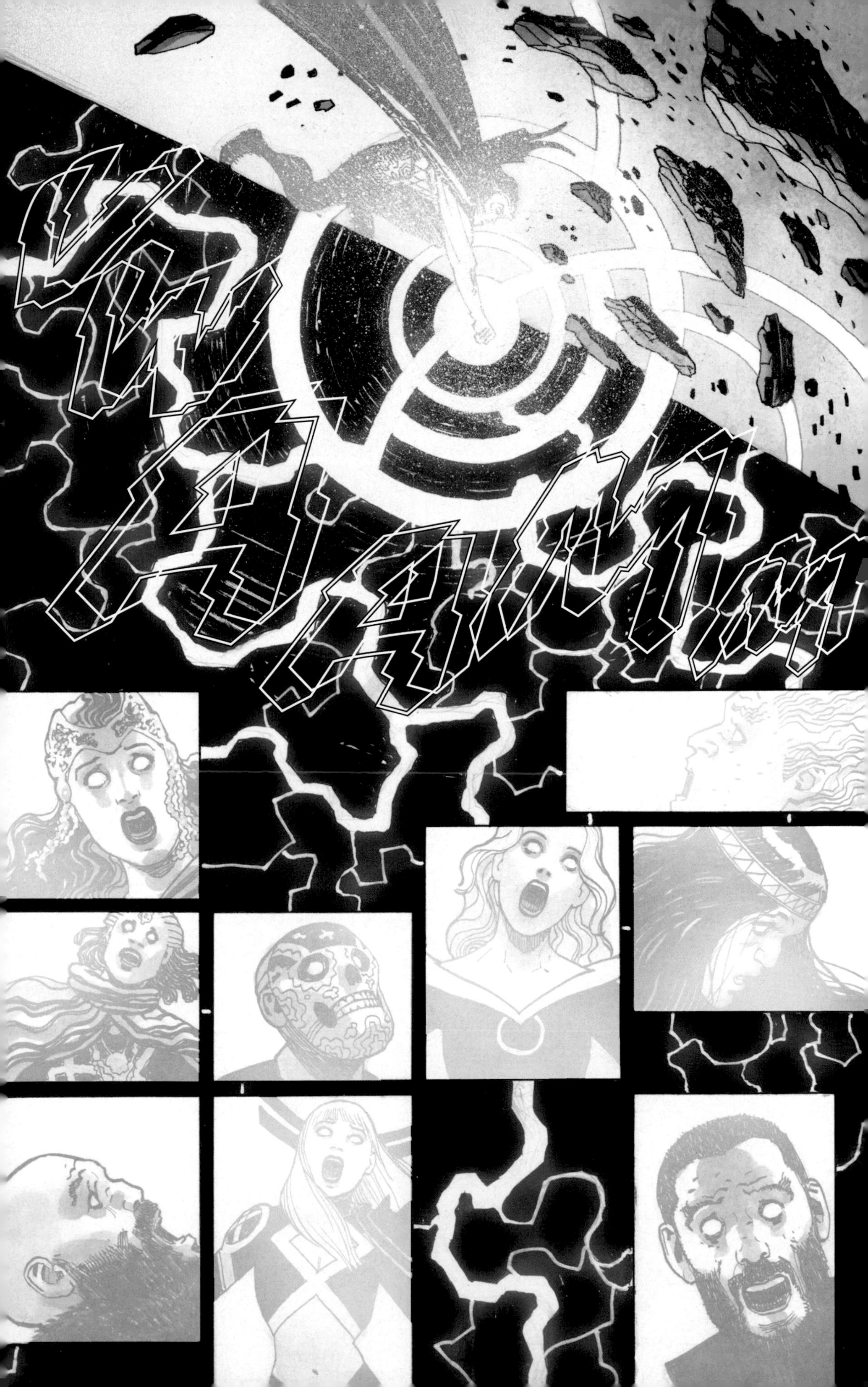

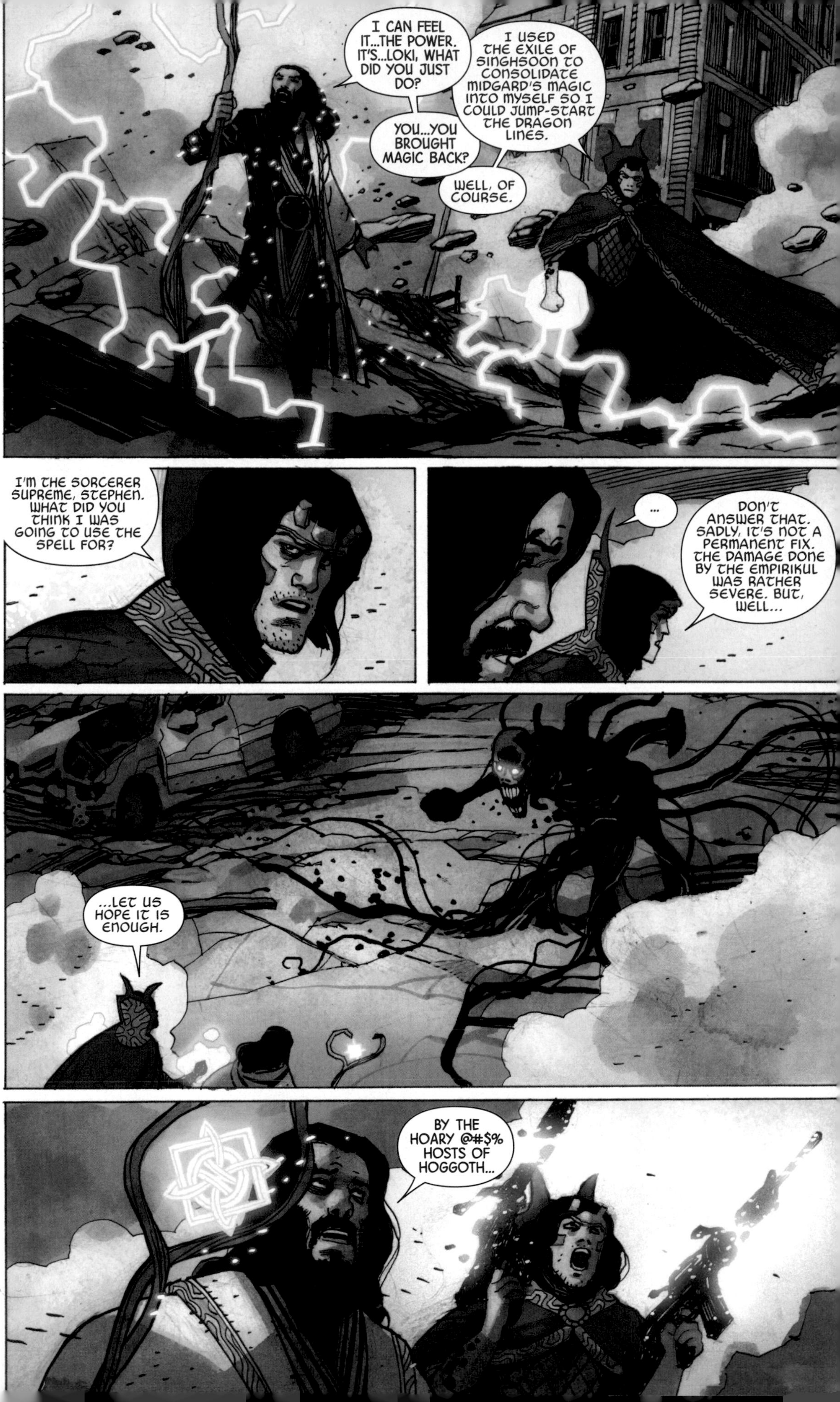
I CAN FEEL IT...THE POWER. IT'S...LOKI, WHAT DID YOU JUST DO?
I USED THE EXILE OF SINGHSOON TO CONSOLIDATE MIDGARD'S MAGIC INTO MYSELF SO I COULD JUMP-START THE DRAGON LINES.
YOU...YOU BROUGHT MAGIC BACK?
WELL, OF COURSE.
I'M THE SORCERER SUPREME, STEPHEN. WHAT DID YOU THINK I WAS GOING TO USE THE SPELL FOR?
...
DON'T ANSWER THAT. SADLY, IT'S NOT A PERMANENT FIX. THE DAMAGE DONE BY THE EMPIRIKUL WAS RATHER SEVERE. BUT, WELL...
...LET US HOPE IT IS ENOUGH.
BY THE HOARY @#$% HOSTS OF HOGGOTH...

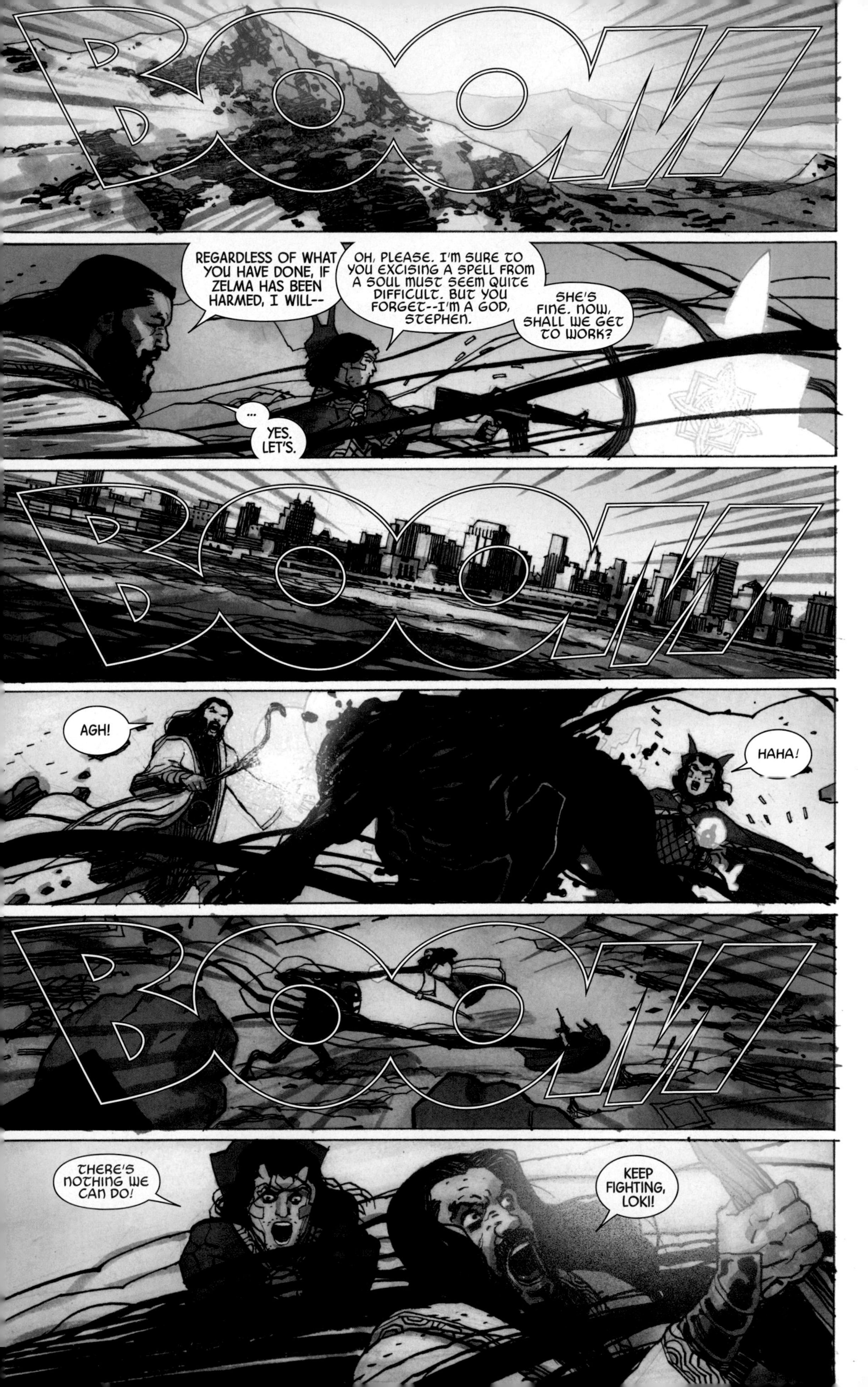
BOOM
REGARDLESS OF WHAT YOU HAVE DONE, IF ZELMA HAS BEEN HARMED, I WILL--
OH, PLEASE. I'M SURE TO YOU EXCISING A SPELL FROM A SOUL MUST SEEM QUITE DIFFICULT. BUT YOU FORGET--I'M A GOD, STEPHEN.
SHE'S FINE. NOW, SHALL WE GET TO WORK?
... YES. LET'S.
BOOM
AGH!
HAHA!
BOOM
THERE'S NOTHING WE CAN DO!
KEEP FIGHTING, LOKI!

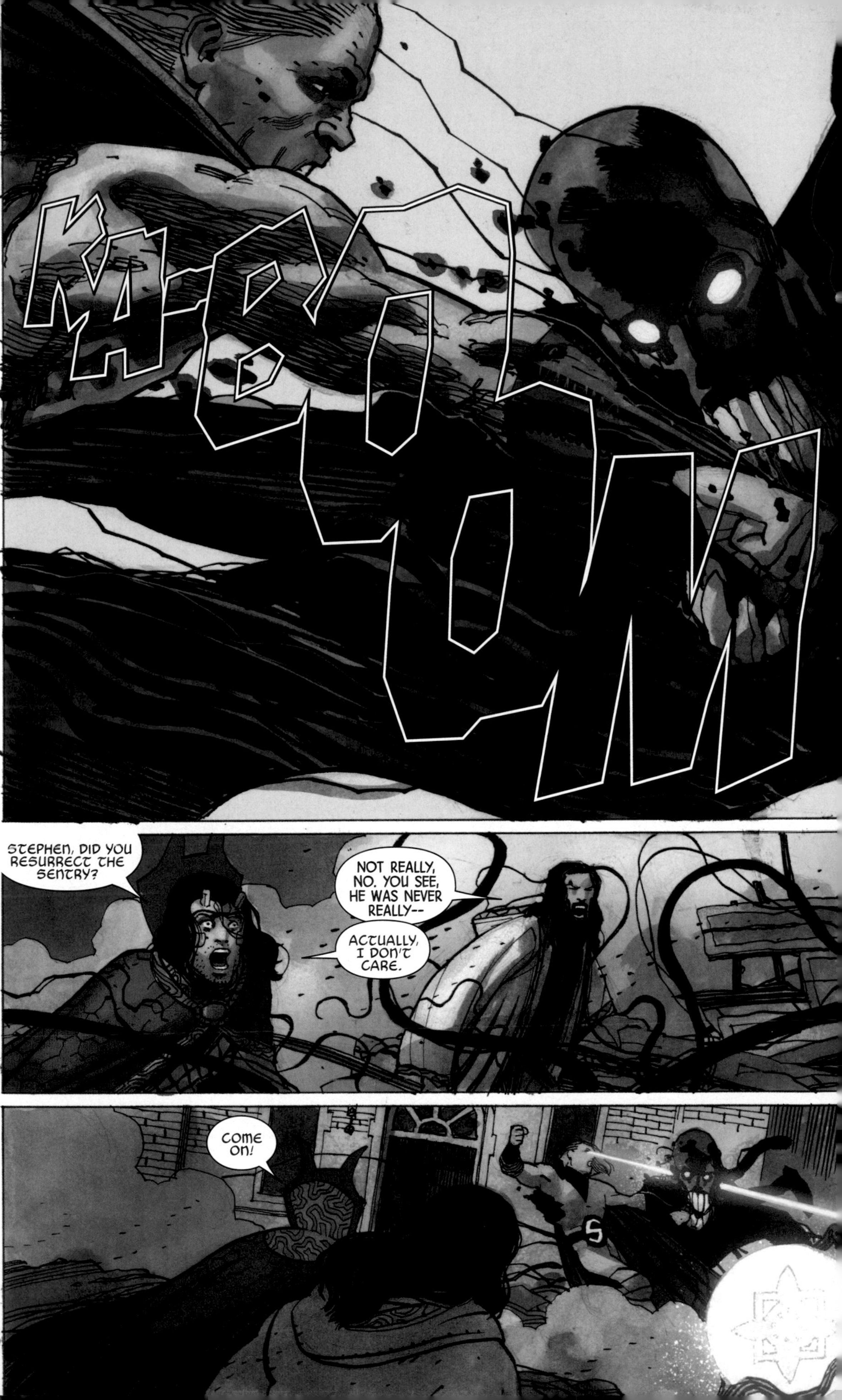
KA-BOOM
STEPHEN, DID YOU RESURRECT THE SENTRY?
NOT REALLY, NO. YOU SEE, HE WAS NEVER REALLY--
ACTUALLY, I DON'T CARE.
COME ON!

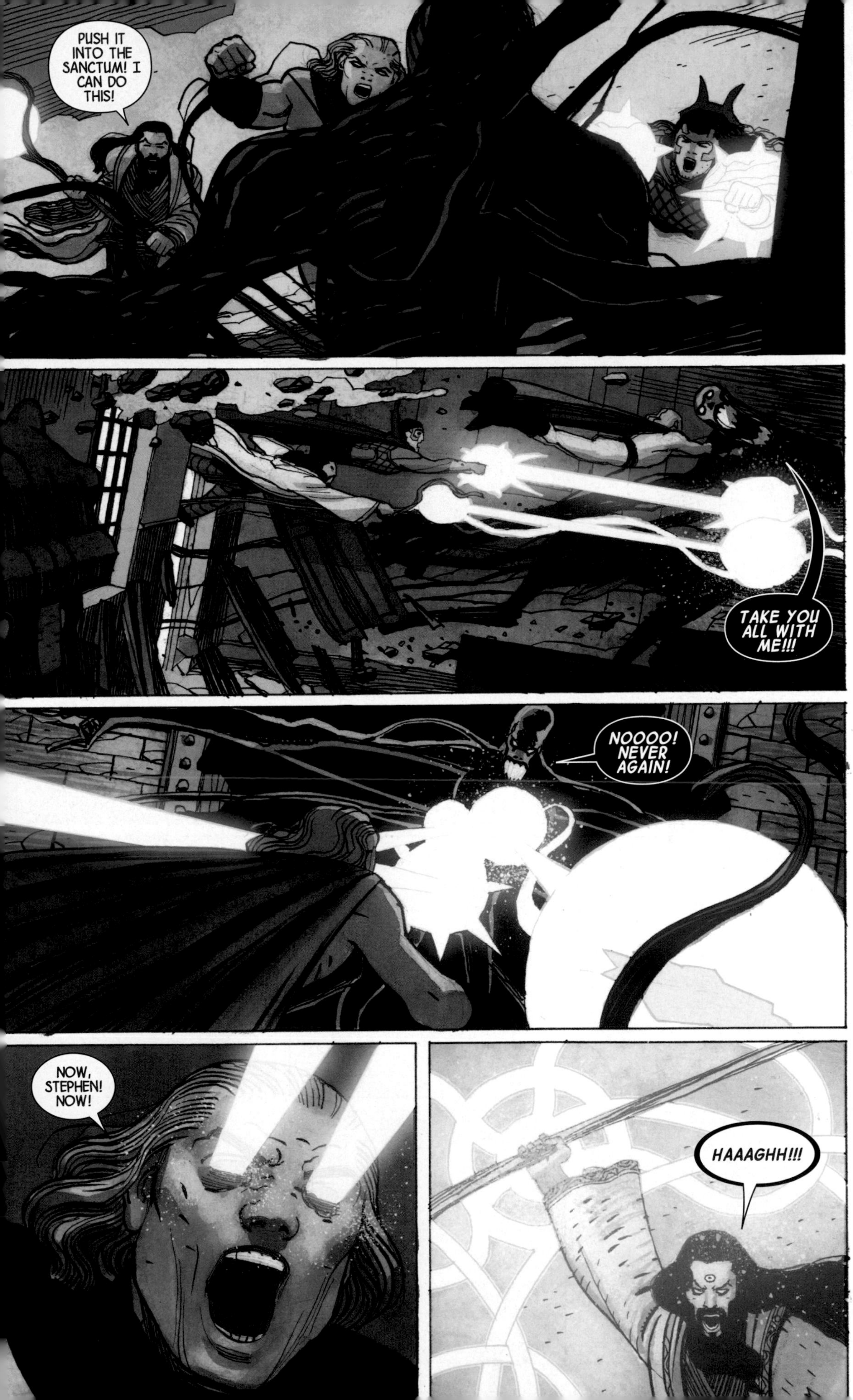
PUSH IT INTO THE SANCTUM! I CAN DO THIS!
TAKE YOU ALL WITH ME!!!
NOOOO! NEVER AGAIN!
NOW, STEPHEN! NOW!
HAAAGHH!!!

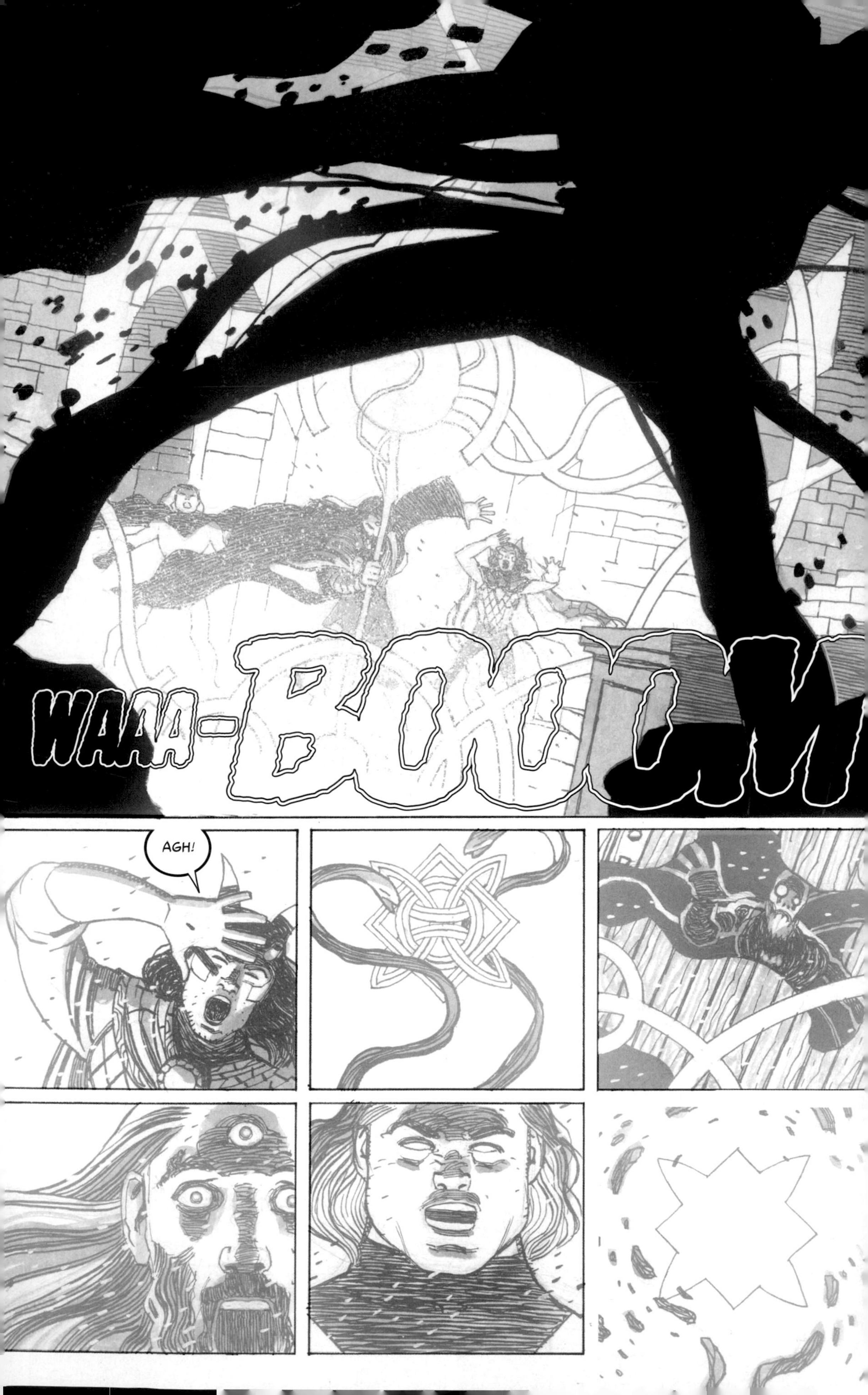
WAAA-BOOOM
AGH!

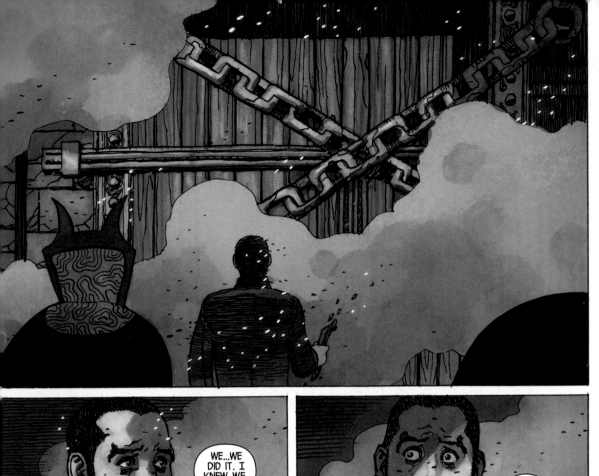

WE...WE DID IT. I KNEW WE COULD--

WAIT!

I TOLD YOU!

STEPHEN!!!

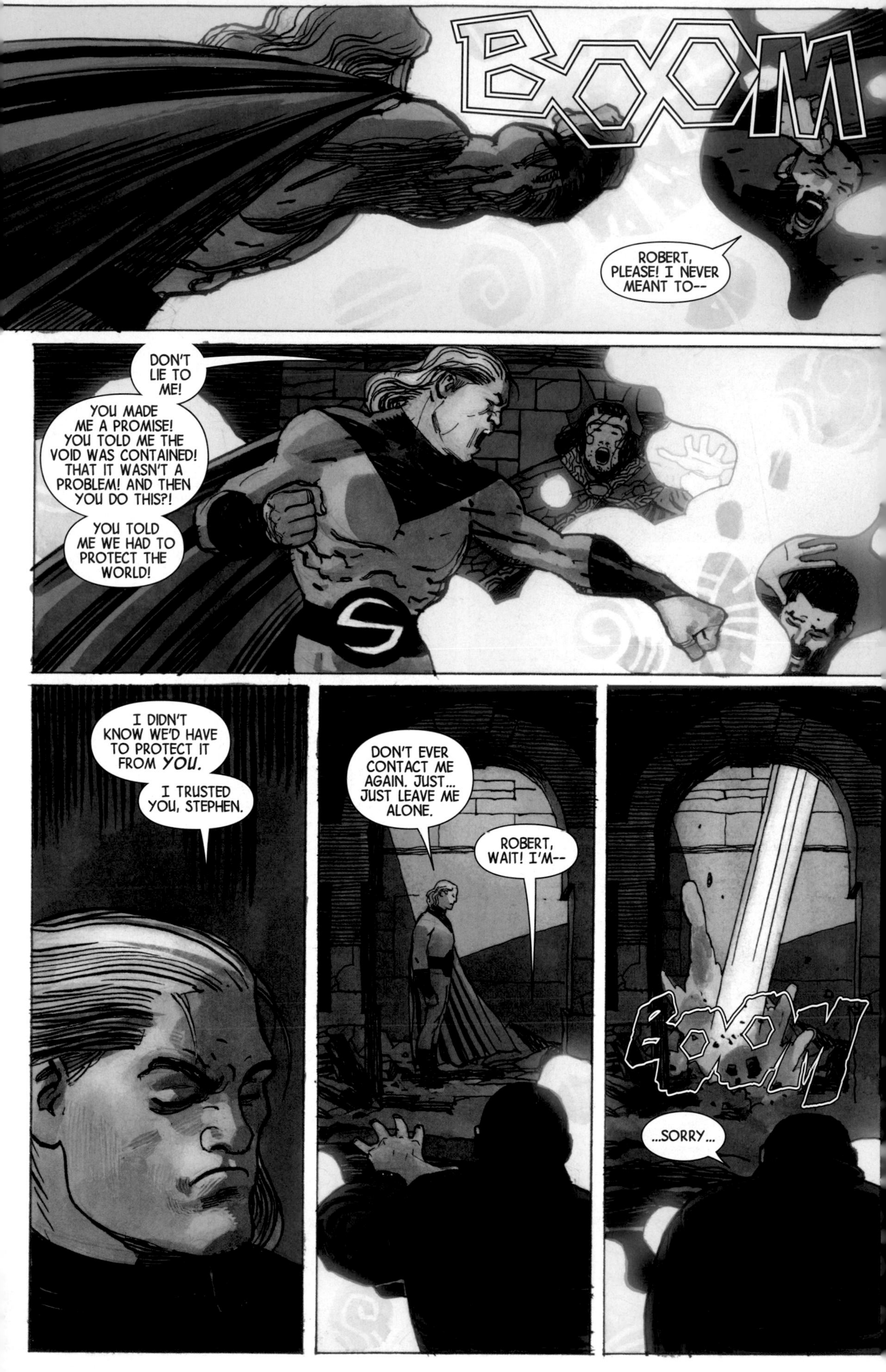
BOOM
ROBERT, PLEASE! I NEVER MEANT TO--
DON'T LIE TO ME!
YOU MADE ME A PROMISE! YOU TOLD ME THE VOID WAS CONTAINED! THAT IT WASN'T A PROBLEM! AND THEN YOU DO THIS?!
YOU TOLD ME WE HAD TO PROTECT THE WORLD!
I DIDN'T KNOW WE'D HAVE TO PROTECT IT FROM *YOU.*
I TRUSTED YOU, STEPHEN.
DON'T EVER CONTACT ME AGAIN. JUST... JUST LEAVE ME ALONE.
ROBERT, WAIT! I'M--
BOOM
...SORRY...

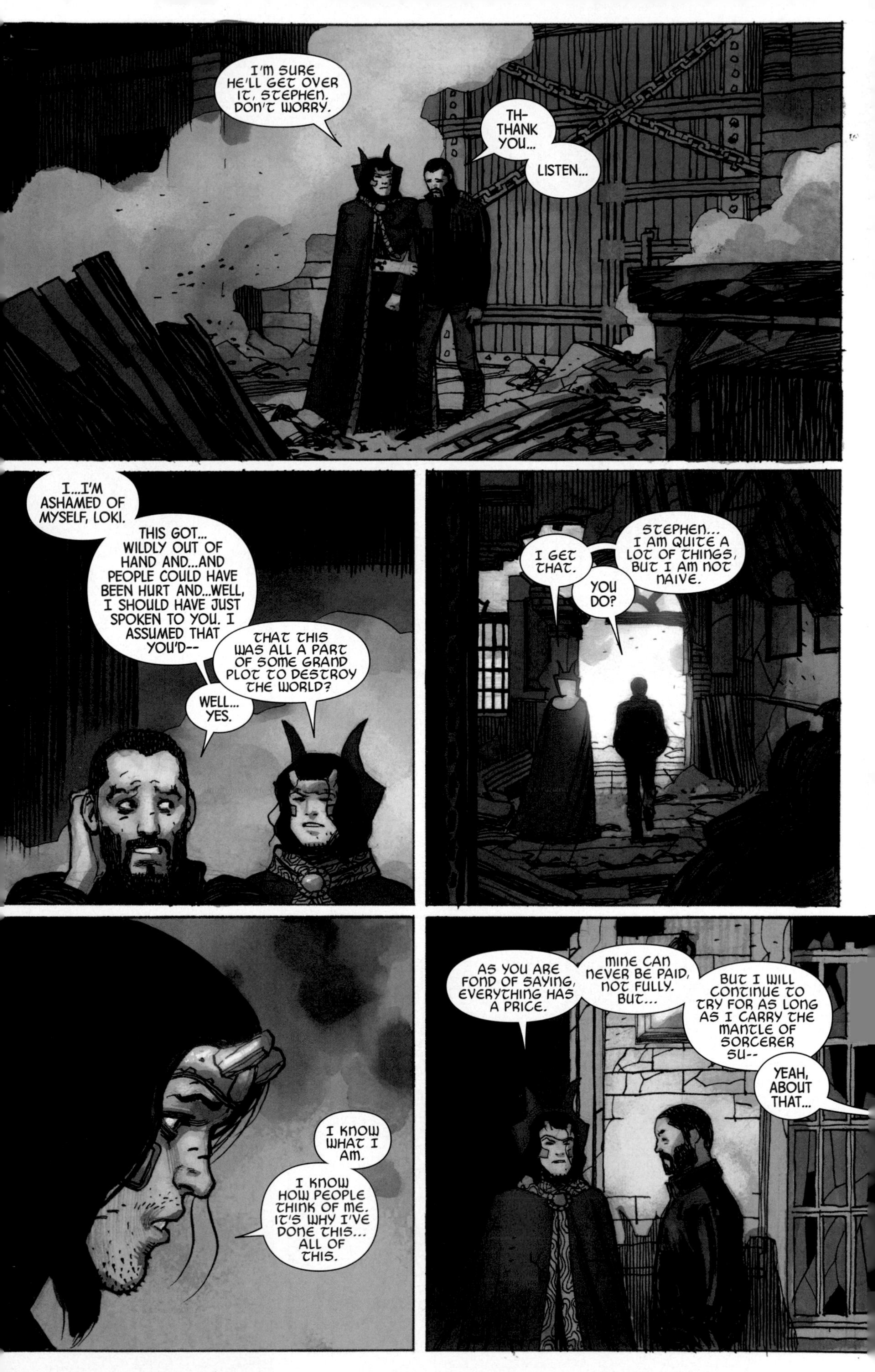
I'M SURE HE'LL GET OVER IT, STEPHEN. DON'T WORRY.
TH-THANK YOU...
LISTEN...
I...I'M ASHAMED OF MYSELF, LOKI.
THIS GOT... WILDLY OUT OF HAND AND...AND PEOPLE COULD HAVE BEEN HURT AND...WELL, I SHOULD HAVE JUST SPOKEN TO YOU. I ASSUMED THAT YOU'D--
THAT THIS WAS ALL A PART OF SOME GRAND PLOT TO DESTROY THE WORLD?
WELL... YES.
I GET THAT.
YOU DO?
STEPHEN... I AM QUITE A LOT OF THINGS, BUT I AM NOT NAIVE.
I KNOW WHAT I AM.
I KNOW HOW PEOPLE THINK OF ME. IT'S WHY I'VE DONE THIS... ALL OF THIS.
AS YOU ARE FOND OF SAYING, EVERYTHING HAS A PRICE.
MINE CAN NEVER BE PAID, NOT FULLY. BUT...
BUT I WILL CONTINUE TO TRY FOR AS LONG AS I CARRY THE MANTLE OF SORCERER SU--
YEAH, ABOUT THAT...

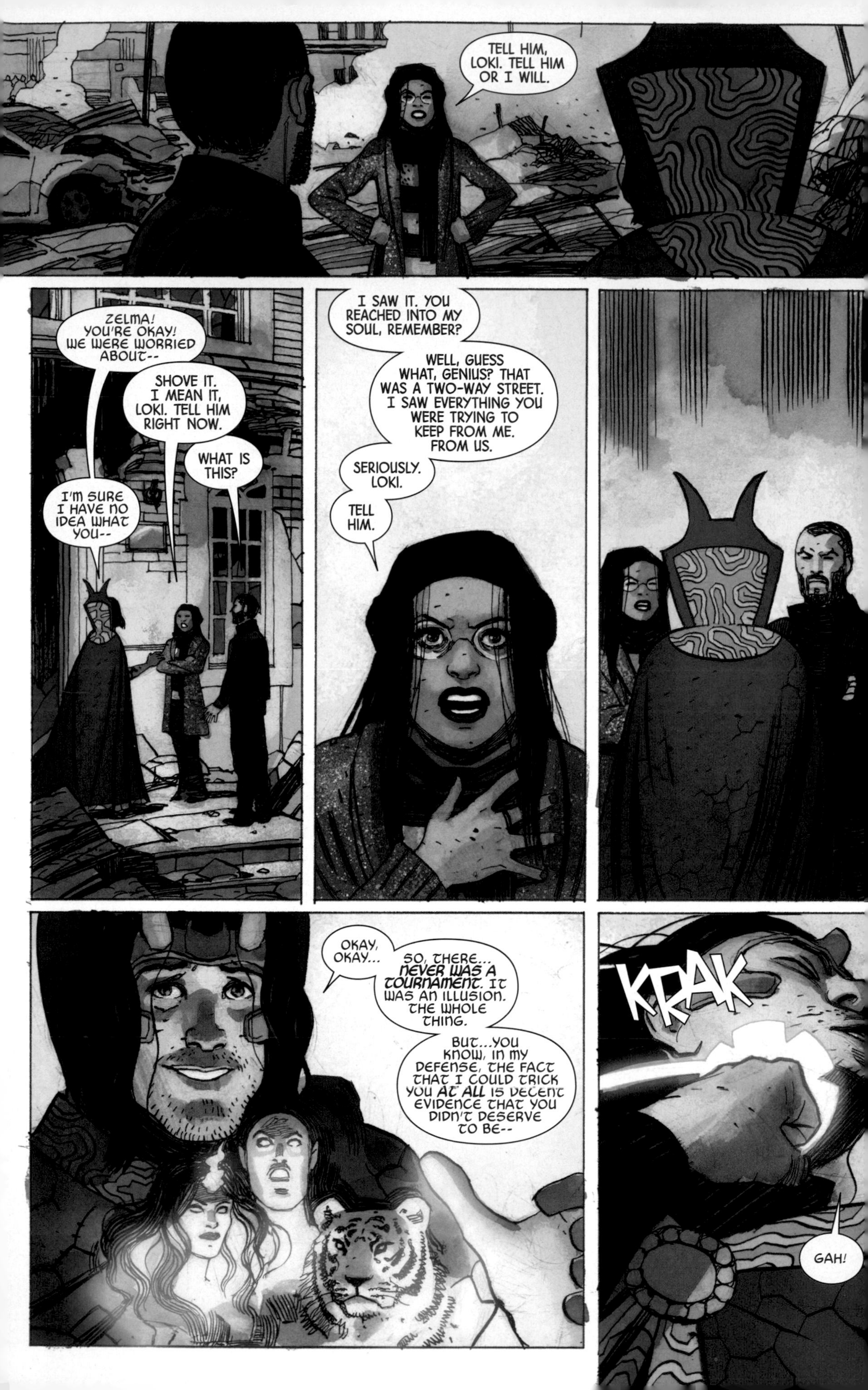
TELL HIM, LOKI. TELL HIM OR I WILL.
ZELMA! YOU'RE OKAY! WE WERE WORRIED ABOUT--
SHOVE IT. I MEAN IT, LOKI. TELL HIM RIGHT NOW.
WHAT IS THIS?
I'M SURE I HAVE NO IDEA WHAT YOU--
I SAW IT. YOU REACHED INTO MY SOUL, REMEMBER?
WELL, GUESS WHAT, GENIUS? THAT WAS A TWO-WAY STREET. I SAW EVERYTHING YOU WERE TRYING TO KEEP FROM ME. FROM US.
SERIOUSLY. LOKI.
TELL HIM.
OKAY, OKAY...
SO, THERE... NEVER WAS A TOURNAMENT. IT WAS AN ILLUSION. THE WHOLE THING.
BUT...YOU KNOW, IN MY DEFENSE, THE FACT THAT I COULD TRICK YOU AT ALL IS DECENT EVIDENCE THAT YOU DIDN'T DESERVE TO BE--
KRAK
GAH!

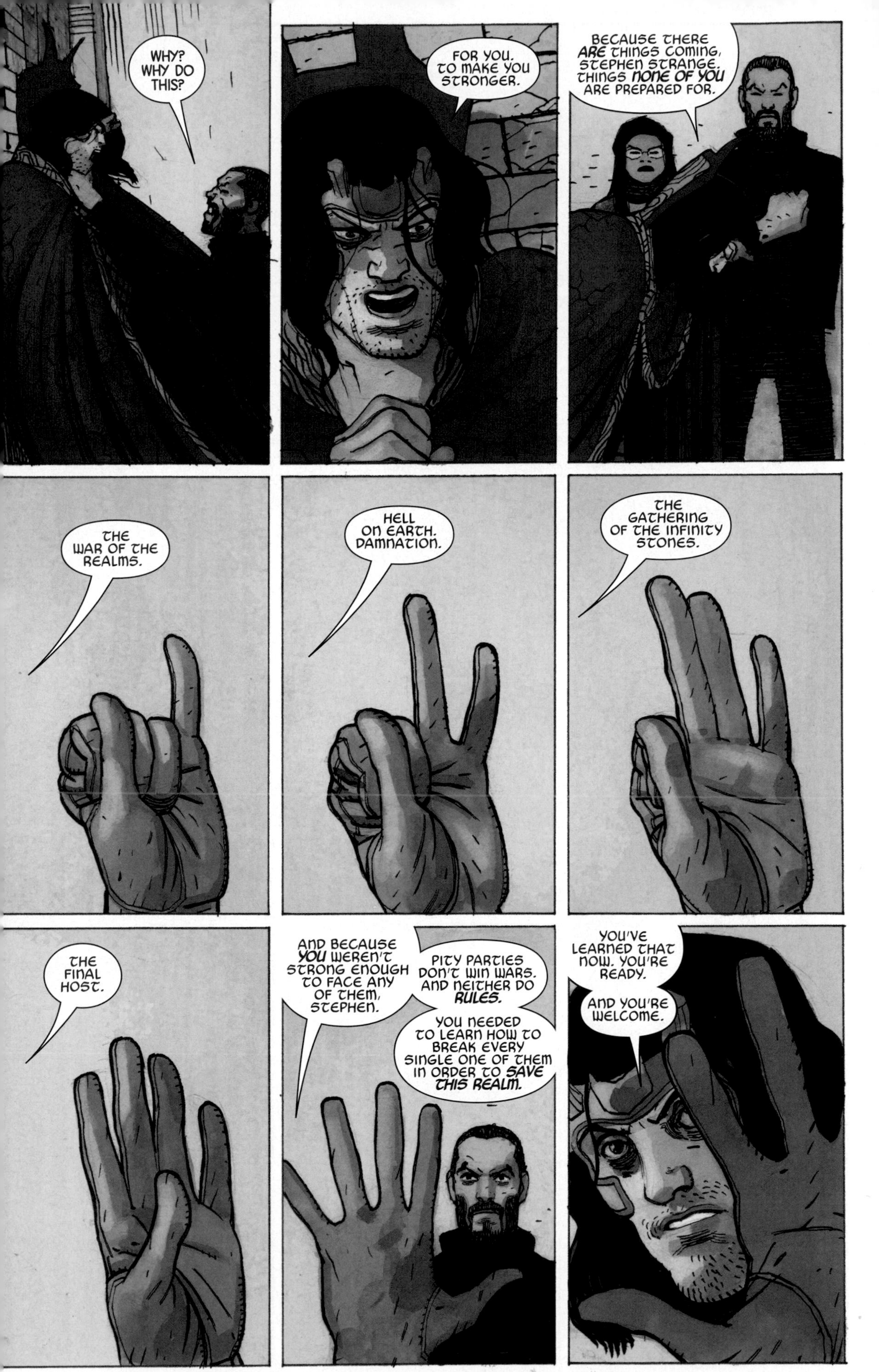
WHY? WHY DO THIS?
FOR YOU. TO MAKE YOU STRONGER.
BECAUSE THERE ARE THINGS COMING, STEPHEN STRANGE. THINGS NONE OF YOU ARE PREPARED FOR.
THE WAR OF THE REALMS.
HELL ON EARTH. DAMNATION.
THE GATHERING OF THE INFINITY STONES.
THE FINAL HOST.
AND BECAUSE YOU WEREN'T STRONG ENOUGH TO FACE ANY OF THEM, STEPHEN.
PITY PARTIES DON'T WIN WARS. AND NEITHER DO RULES.
YOU NEEDED TO LEARN HOW TO BREAK EVERY SINGLE ONE OF THEM IN ORDER TO SAVE THIS REALM.
YOU'VE LEARNED THAT NOW. YOU'RE READY.
AND YOU'RE WELCOME.

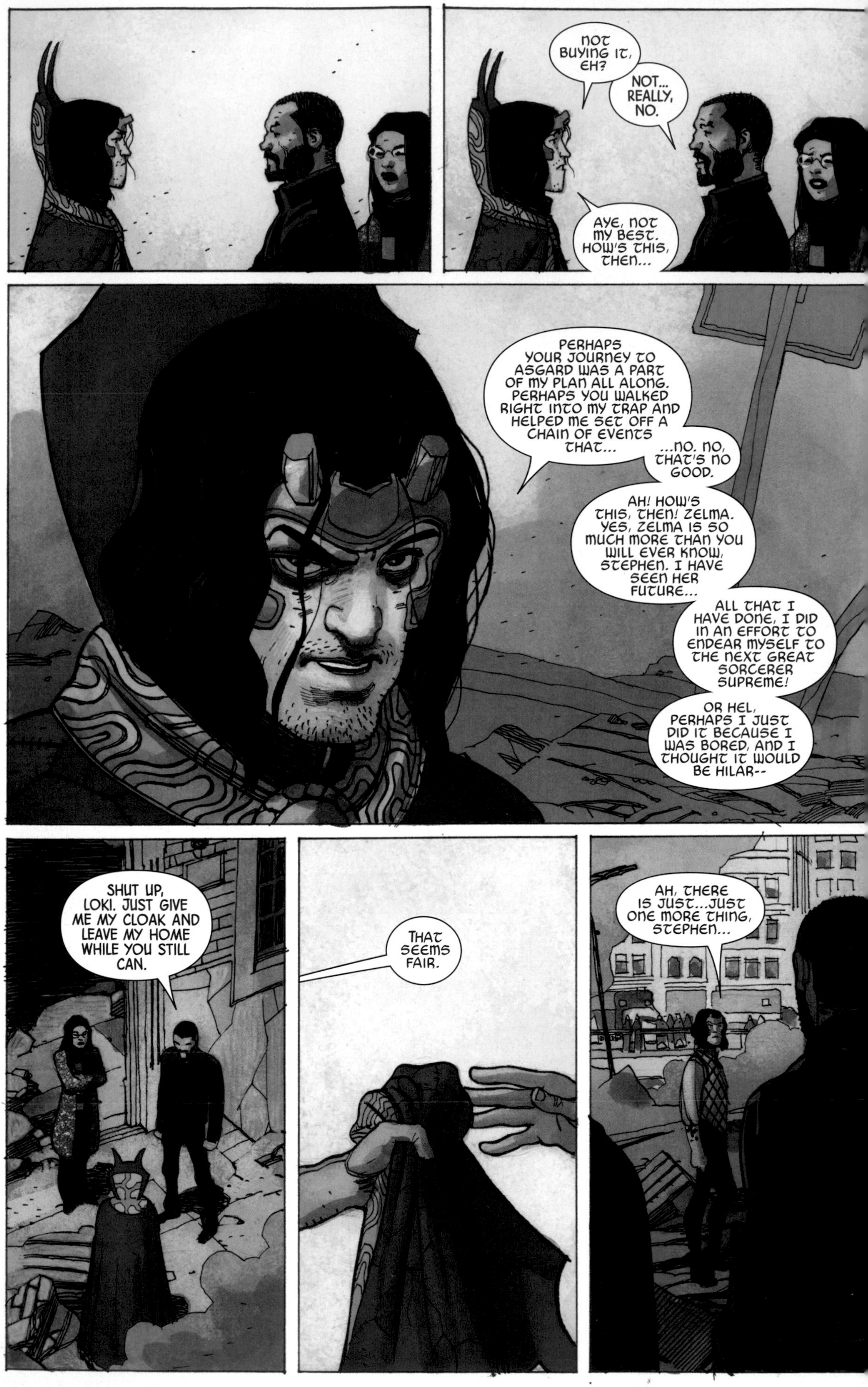

NOT BUYING IT, EH?
NOT... REALLY, NO.
AYE, NOT MY BEST. HOW'S THIS, THEN...
PERHAPS YOUR JOURNEY TO ASGARD WAS A PART OF MY PLAN ALL ALONG. PERHAPS YOU WALKED RIGHT INTO MY TRAP AND HELPED ME SET OFF A CHAIN OF EVENTS THAT...
...NO. NO, THAT'S NO GOOD.
AH! HOW'S THIS, THEN! ZELMA. YES, ZELMA IS SO MUCH MORE THAN YOU WILL EVER KNOW, STEPHEN. I HAVE SEEN HER FUTURE...
ALL THAT I HAVE DONE, I DID IN AN EFFORT TO ENDEAR MYSELF TO THE NEXT GREAT SORCERER SUPREME!
OR HEL, PERHAPS I JUST DID IT BECAUSE I WAS BORED, AND I THOUGHT IT WOULD BE HILAR--
SHUT UP, LOKI. JUST GIVE ME MY CLOAK AND LEAVE MY HOME WHILE YOU STILL CAN.
THAT SEEMS FAIR.
AH, THERE IS JUST...JUST ONE MORE THING, STEPHEN...

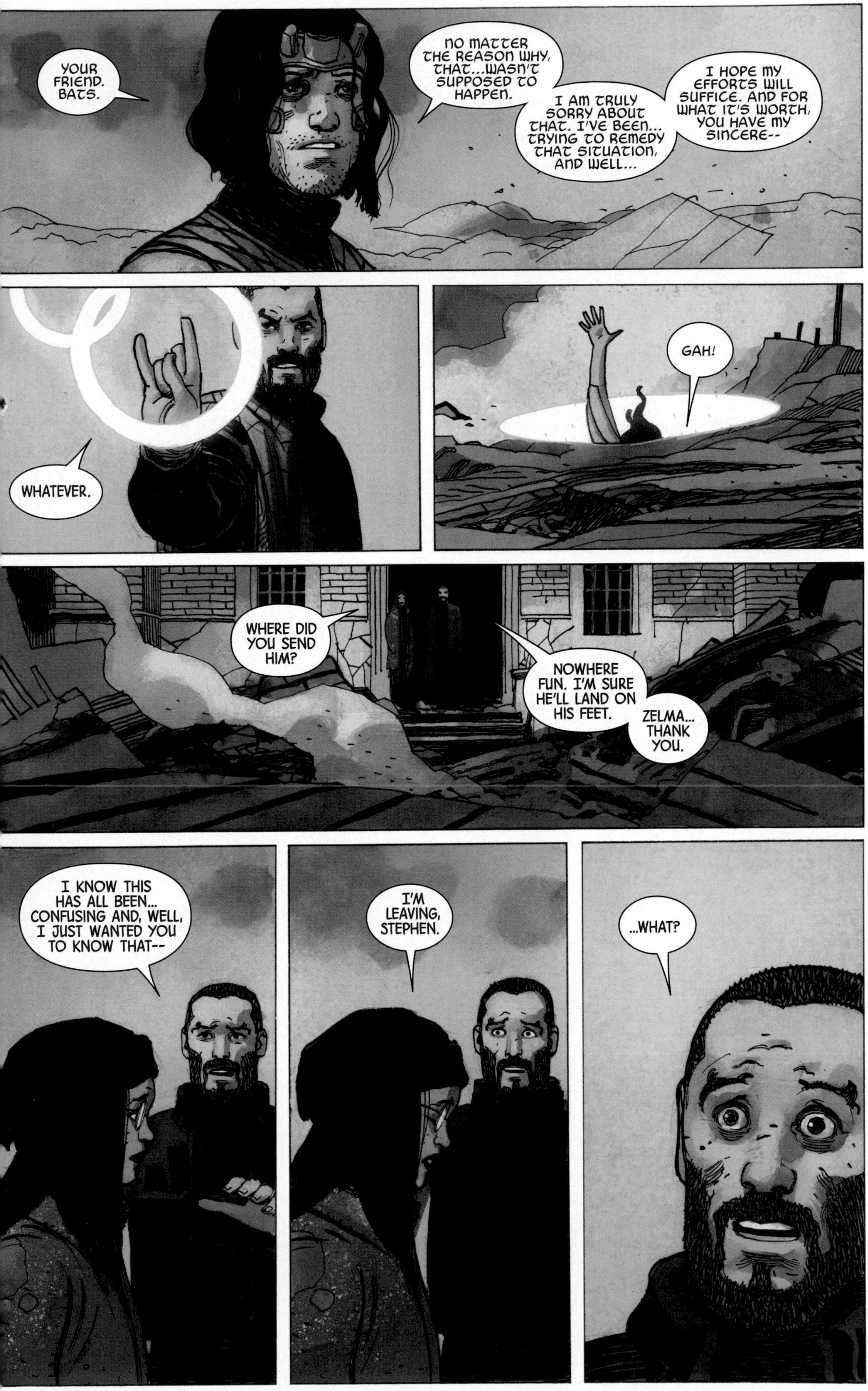
YOUR FRIEND. BATS.
NO MATTER THE REASON WHY, THAT...WASN'T SUPPOSED TO HAPPEN.
I AM TRULY SORRY ABOUT THAT. I'VE BEEN... TRYING TO REMEDY THAT SITUATION, AND WELL...
I HOPE MY EFFORTS WILL SUFFICE. AND FOR WHAT IT'S WORTH, YOU HAVE MY SINCERE--
WHATEVER.
GAH!
WHERE DID YOU SEND HIM?
NOWHERE FUN. I'M SURE HE'LL LAND ON HIS FEET.
ZELMA... THANK YOU.
I KNOW THIS HAS ALL BEEN... CONFUSING AND, WELL, I JUST WANTED YOU TO KNOW THAT--
I'M LEAVING, STEPHEN.
...WHAT?

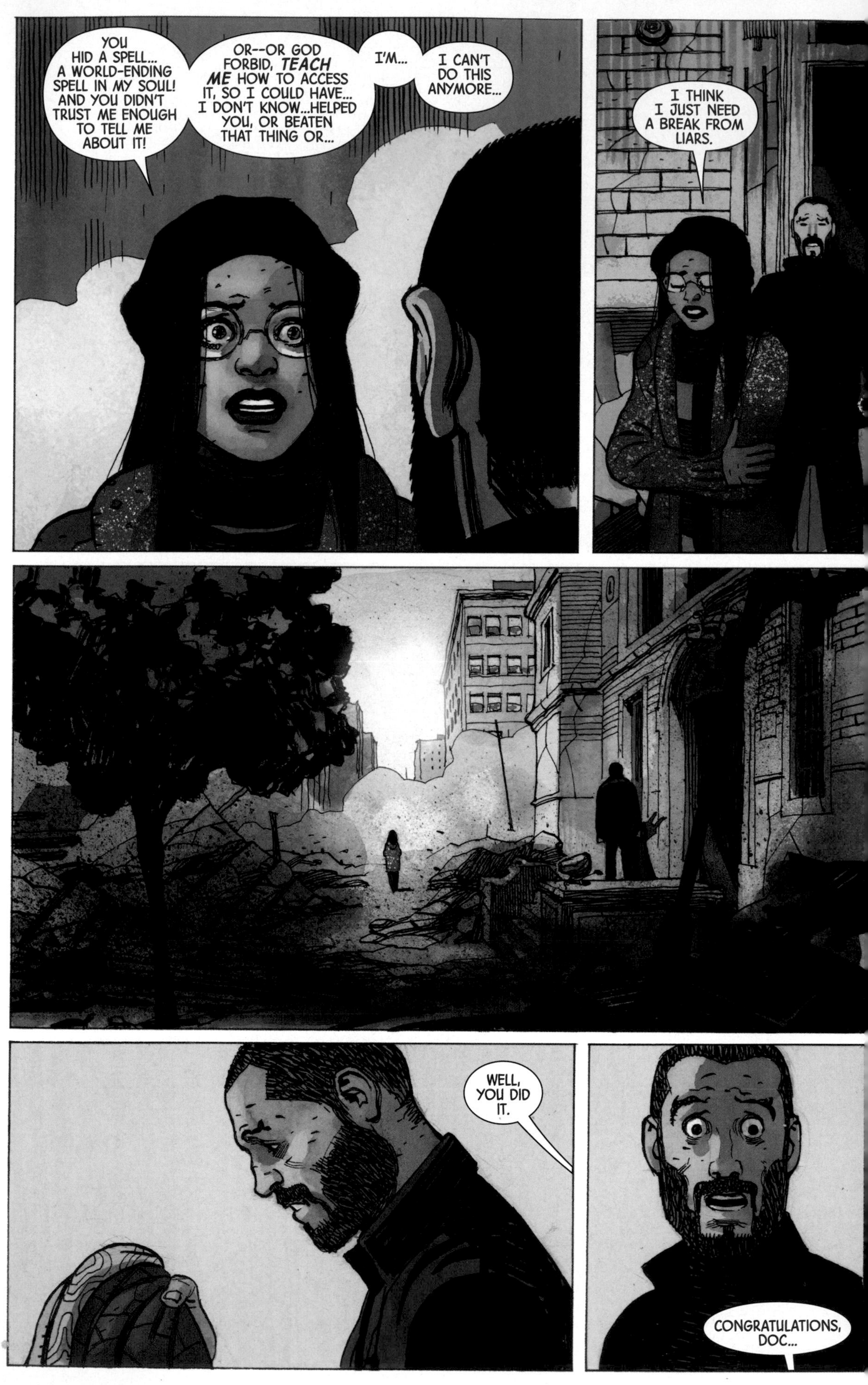
YOU HID A SPELL... A WORLD-ENDING SPELL IN MY SOUL! AND YOU DIDN'T TRUST ME ENOUGH TO TELL ME ABOUT IT!
OR--OR GOD FORBID, TEACH ME HOW TO ACCESS IT, SO I COULD HAVE... I DON'T KNOW...HELPED YOU, OR BEATEN THAT THING OR...
I'M...
I CAN'T DO THIS ANYMORE...
I THINK I JUST NEED A BREAK FROM LIARS.
WELL, YOU DID IT.
CONGRATULATIONS, DOC...

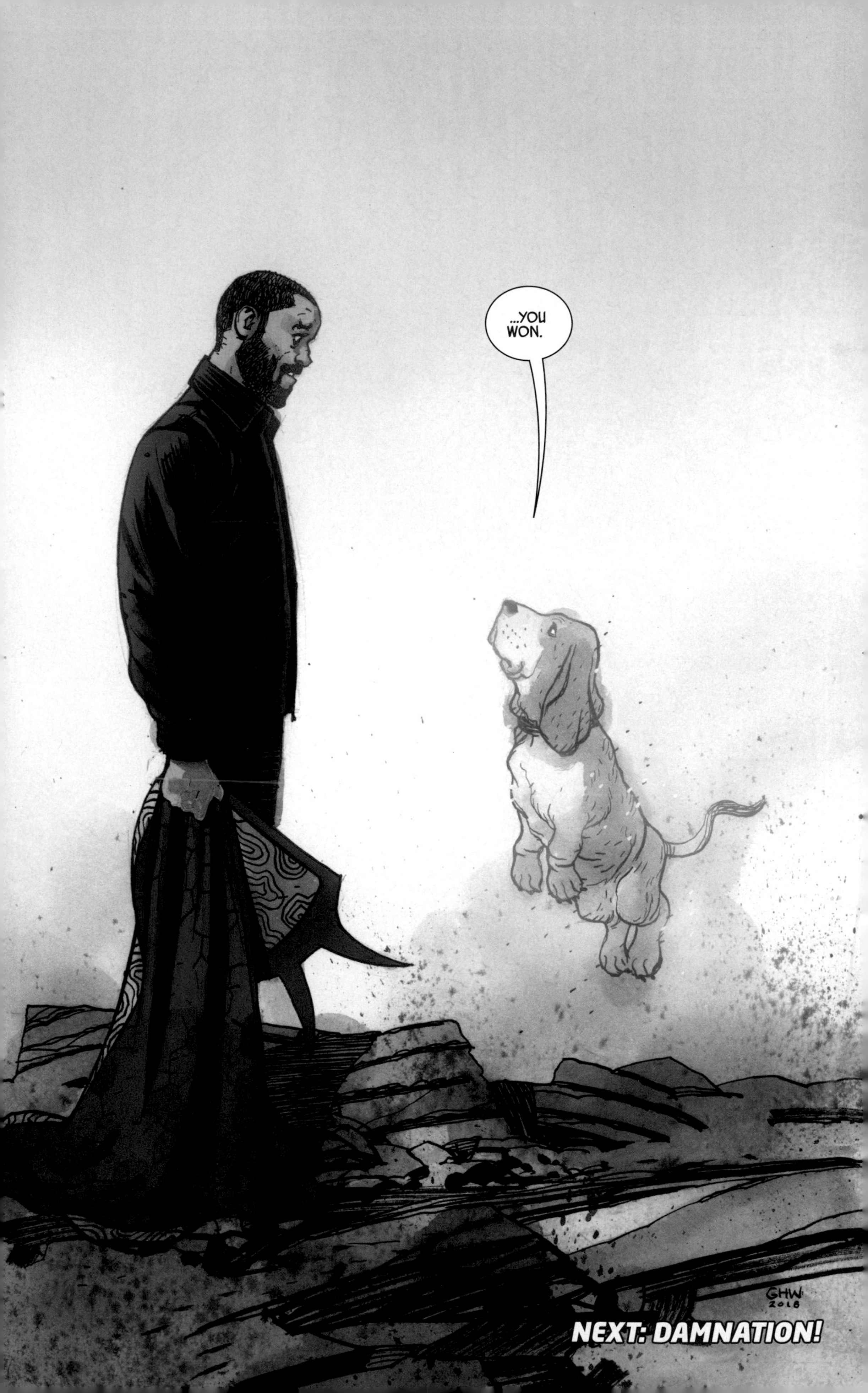
...YOU WON.
GHW 2018
NEXT: DAMNATION!

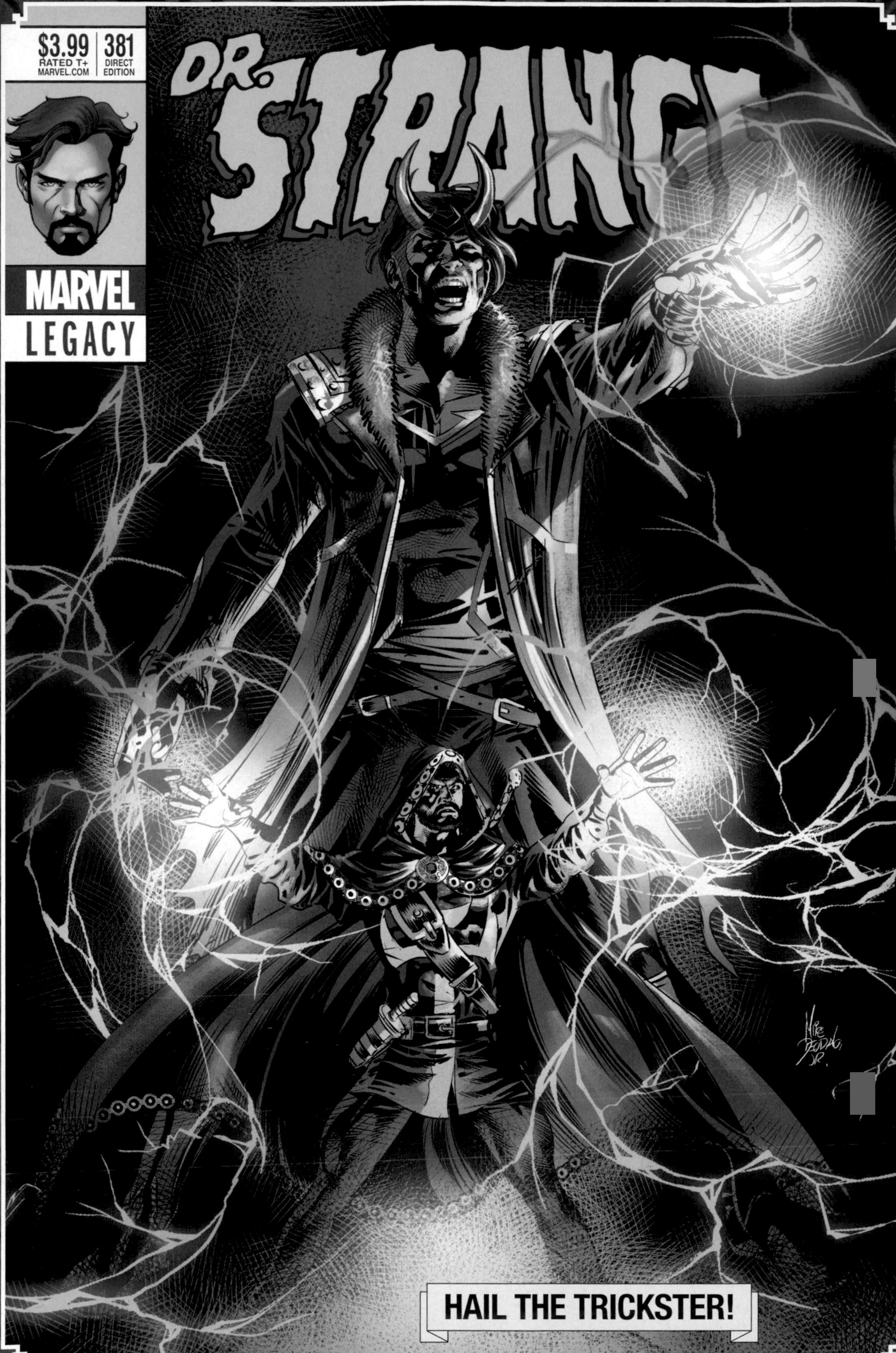
$3.99
RATED T+
MARVEL.COM
381
DIRECT EDITION
DR.
MARVEL
LEGACY
HAIL THE TRICKSTER!

MIKE DEODATO JR. & RAIN BEREDO
381 HOMAGE VARIANT

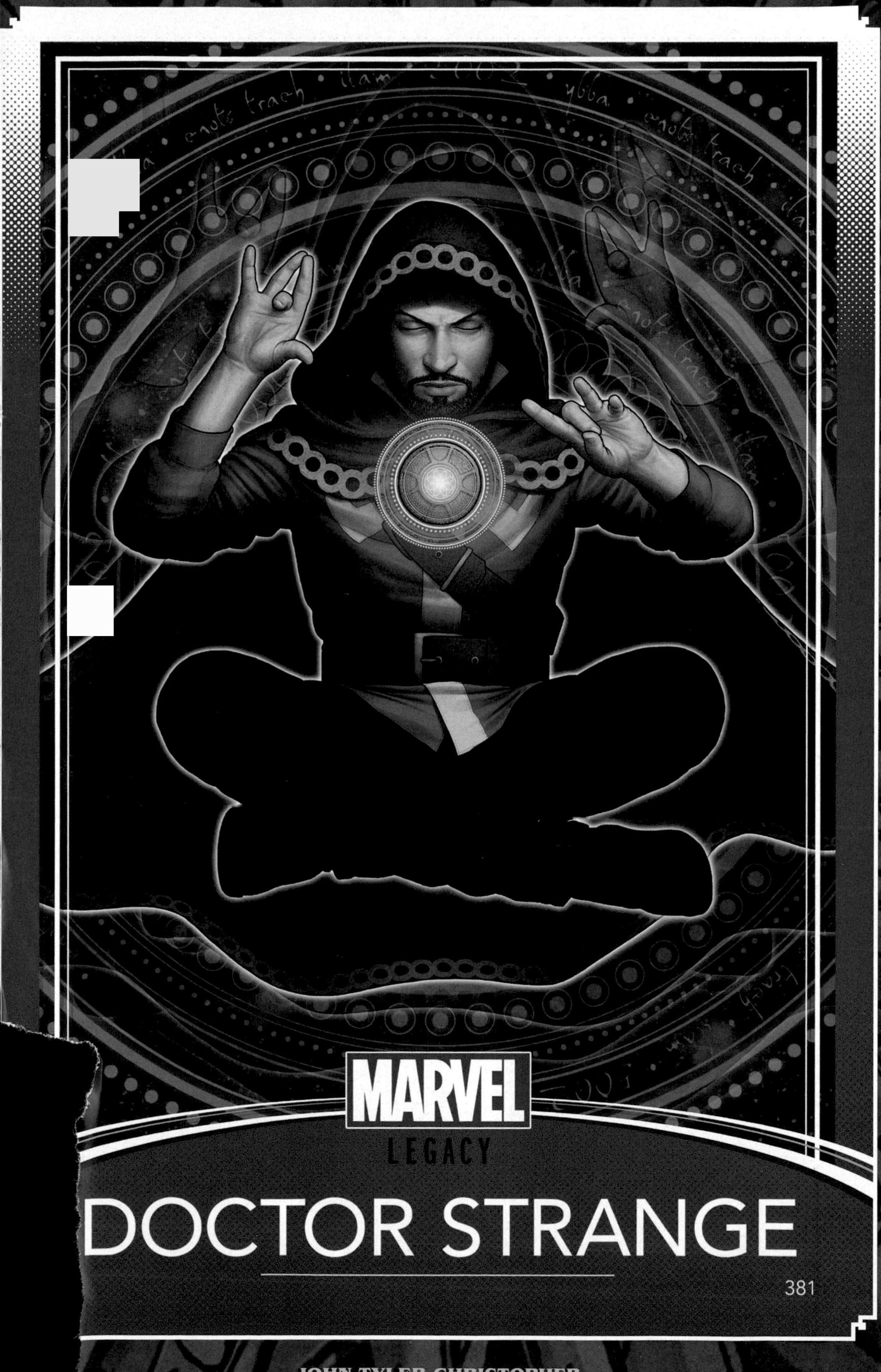
MARVEL
LEGACY
DOCTOR STRANGE
381

JOHN TYLER CHRISTOPHER
381 TRADING CARD VARIANT

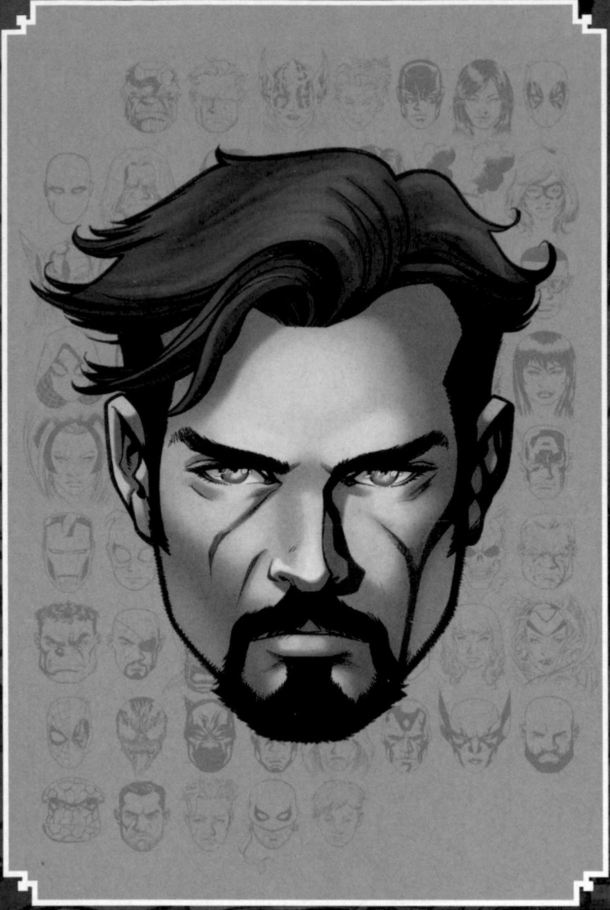

MIKE McKONE & RACHELLE ROSENBERG
381 LEGACY HEADSHOT VARIANT

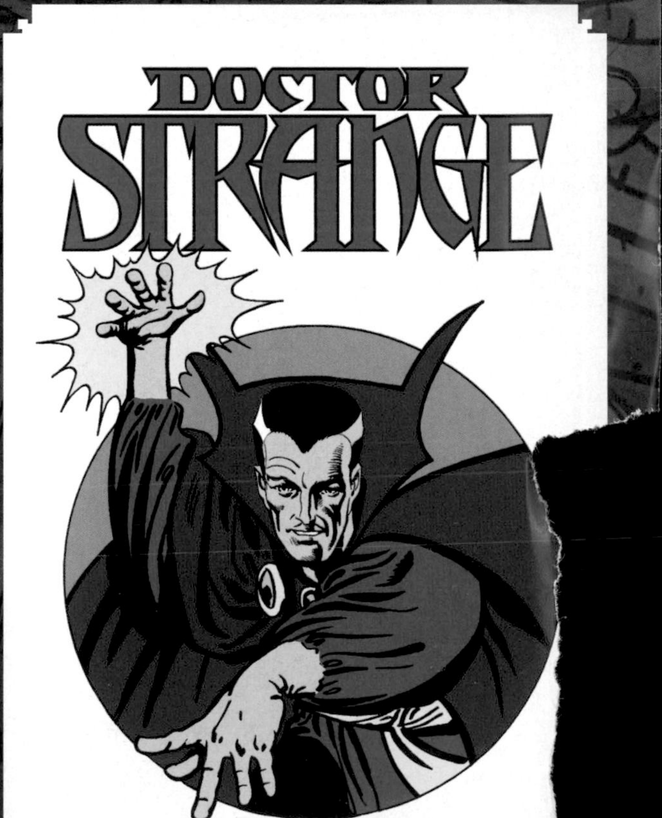
DOCTOR
STRANGE

STEVE DITKO
381 T-SHIRT VARIANT